Seaforth
WORLD NAVAL REVIEW
2010

Seaforth

WORLDNAVALREVIEW

2010

Editor
CONRAD WATERS

Frontispiece: One of a series of images taken of *Freedom* (LCS-1) during initial sea trials on Lake Michigan during August 2008 – see Chapter 3.3 for more images. The trials period commenced on 28th July 2008 and was highly successful – when surveyed by the USN's Board of Inspection and Survey (INSURV) only a very small number of material deficiencies remained outstanding. *(Lockheed Martin via USN)*

The editor welcomes correspondence and suggestions from readers. Please contact via Seaforth at info@seaforthpublishing.com. All correspondence should be marked FAO: Conrad Waters.

Copyright © Seaforth Publishing 2009
Plans © John Jordan and Ian Sturton 2009

First published in Great Britain in 2009 by
Seaforth Publishing
An imprint of Pen & Sword Books Ltd.
47 Church Street, Barnsley
S Yorkshire S70 2AS

www.seaforthpublishing.com
Email info@seaforthpublishing.com

British Library Cataloguing in Publication Data
A CIP data record for this book is available from the British Library

ISBN 978-1-84832-051-2

Typeset and designed by Stephen Dent
Printed and bound in China through Printworks International Ltd.

CONTENTS

1 OVERVIEW

INTRODUCTION

'The sinews of war are infinite money' wrote the renowned Roman statesman and orator Marcus Tullius Cicero during the first century BC. These words still hold good somewhat over 2,000 years later when reviewing the current state of the world's navies. Whilst the continued global economic dominance of the United States has ensured the ongoing mainte-nance of the *Pax Americana* across the world's oceans, the focus of international commercial activity and trade has been shifting steadily eastwards to the rapidly developing countries of the Asia-Pacific region. Although the full extent of the shift in the military balance will take longer to become apparent, it is already clear that the major Asian nations have formed a clear view of the advantages inherent in achieving 'blue water' maritime influence. At the moment, this awareness is largely made evident by the acquisition of the most up-to-date naval technology available from manufacturers in Europe, Russia or the US, albeit for installation in ships built increasingly in regional facilities. However, indigenous capabilities are expanding on the back of the rapid expansion of local industry. It is therefore not impossible to envisage a time when Mumbai, Ulsan and Shanghai come to rival the likes of Glasgow, Kiel or Newport News as the originators of the most potent warship designs.

The extent to which the balance of military spending has shifted in the period since the end of the Cold War is demonstrated by the information collated by the independent and widely respected Stockholm International Peace Research Institute (SIPRI). Key figures are highlighted in Table 1.0.1.[1] Overall global defence expenditure – at around US$1,200bn – has changed little in real terms in the period since the end of the Cold War. Within this figure, expenditure in Western and Central Europe has been broadly flat at just under US$300bn, whilst outlays in North America have increased from US$525bn to nearly US$600bn. However, spending by the Asian-Pacific nations has virtually doubled to US$200bn, thereby compensating for the collapse in the defence budgets of the former Soviet powers. Although it is important to view this information in some sort of context – the data suggests that the military spending of all the nations of Asia and Oceania combined remains little more than a third the amount committed by the United States – the general trend is clear. It is also worth noting that the SIPRI figures are based on market rather than 'real world' purchasing power parity exchange rates. In effect, the indicated level of spending in the higher-cost countries of the devel-oped world buys less advantage than the headline figures suggest.

The way that changed spending patterns have impacted the maritime balance of power can also be considered through an examination of force numbers. Although pure numerical comparisons are always subject to considerable hazard – for example, how meaningful is it to compare a state-of-the-art Type 45 destroyer with its 1950s Type 41 *Leopard* class predecessors still serving in Bangladesh's fleet – the data in Table 1.0.2 does provide scope for a number of observations.

Table 1.0.1: REGIONAL MILITARY EXPENDITURES 1988-2007

REGION	EXPENDITURE 1988	EXPENDITURE 1997	EXPENDITURE 2007	CHANGE 1998–2007
North America	US$499.0bn	US$347.0bn	US$562.0bn	12.6%
Latin America	US$26.0bn	US$29.0bn	US$36.0bn	39.5%
Western Europe	US$279.0bn	US$244.0bn	US$261.0bn	(6.5%)
Eastern & Central Europe	US$234.0bn	US$39.0bn	US$59.0bn	(74.9%)
Africa & Middle East	US$53.0bn	US$55.0bn	US$96.0bn	79.1%
Asia Pacific	US$102.0bn	US$130.0bn	US$200.0bn	96.1%
Total	US$1,195.0bn	US$844.0bn	US$1,214.0bn	1.6%

Information from the Stockholm International Peace Research Institute (SIPRI)

Reference: http://www.sipri.org

All figures in US$bn at constant 2005 prices and exchange rates rounded to the nearest US$1bn.

Figures do not necessarily add to totals due to rounding.

- Although nearly all the major fleets have shrunk in size since the end of the Cold War, the relative strength of the major Asian maritime nations has increased during this time. This undoubtedly reflects the budgetary environment already discussed. There has also been a significant shift in the balance of these regional fleets away from coastal and patrol forces in favour of more complex and deployable fleet units.

- The decline in Russian naval power since the end of the communist era is readily apparent. Overall fleet size is less than a third of its peak total. Recent signs of a resumption of Russian global deployments coupled with hyperbole from the country's politicians about the restoration of its former maritime influence have lead to suggestions that this decline is being reversed. However, it is difficult to envisage a return to a situation even close to the previous *status quo* without a generation's worth of sustained effort that is probably beyond Russia's current economic potential. It should also be noted that nearly all the current naval units listed are ageing Soviet-era designs, with the run-down local shipbuilding industry seemingly unable to complete replacements in any quantity.

- Although the United States Navy (USN) has also experienced a significant reduction in size, it still remains the dominant blue water maritime power by a considerable margin. This is all the more so when the technological capabilities of its units are taken into account.

Asian navies have become more influential in world maritime affairs. Here China's new Type 052B destroyer *Guangzhou* and Pakistan's older Type 21 frigate *Badr* are seen during a Pakistan-hosted multinational exercise in the Indian Ocean in an image that also depicts ships from Bangladesh and the USN. (*US Navy*)

Pure numerical comparisons are always subject to considerable hazard. The Philippine Second World War vintage *Cannon* class patrol frigate *Rajah Humabon* (ex USS *Atherton*), above, and Oman's modern *Qahir* class *Qahir Al Amwaj* (below) are both light surface escorts of broadly similar size but their capabilities are not comparable. *(US Navy / Conrad Waters)*

■ Looking at the broader picture, there has been a general shift in fleet composition, largely in line with the changed global political environment. This is most evident in the significant decline in Cold War-orientated submarine forces, as well as in the flotillas of patrol escorts that were configured to counter them. In contrast, there has been considerable investment in major amphibious vessels as a result of the greater emphasis being placed on expeditionary warfare and the desirability of being able to intervene in the offshore waters of the littoral. Technological considerations have also seemingly played a part. For example, the decline in fast attack craft possibly reflects the vulnerability of this type to helicopter and other countermeasures revealed during the Second Gulf War.[2] Similarly, whilst the decline in mine countermeasures vessels might appear strange given increased interest in amphibious operations, this is partly explained by the development of modularised remote mine-hunting systems and airborne alternatives.

This first edition of the new *Seaforth World Naval Review* attempts to provide an up-to-date overview of what is – necessarily – an evolving situation. Its methodology is to look at the current naval scene from three principal perspectives.

FLEET REVIEWS

The initial area of focus is on specific navies. The four regional review sub-sections provide an overview of the current composition of the world's major fleets, major operational developments and the strategic objectives that are driving future force levels and associated procurement decisions. A common theme is the extent to which the desire to maintain – or even increase – warship numbers has to be set against other, often conflicting, objectives. These include – particularly in the more advanced navies of the Western nations – the need to balance pure technological proficiency against affordability if numerical targets are to be achieved. Another interesting trade-off – possibly most keenly felt by the developing maritime powers – is the extent to which the time and cost penalties associated with developing indigenous design and build facilities should be prioritised over more readily available 'off the shelf' acquisitions. Often the answers to these questions are not purely driven by military considerations, with commercial and political issues also playing a part.

To help put these challenges into perspective, the

main geographical reviews are supported by more detailed supplements discussing the procurement and construction programmes being implemented by four of the world's largest fleets. Scott Truver's review of the USN indicates the extent to which even the most generously-resourced fleets face problems in striking a match between cutting-edge capability and the deployment of an adequate number of ships.

This is resulting in some significant changes to acquisition priorities, as evidenced by the decision to curtail construction of the *Zumwalt* (DDG-1000) class destroyers at just three ships in favour of the tried and tested *Arleigh Burke* (DDG-51) design. The strains inherent in this search for cost-effectiveness become even more acute when budgets are more limited, as Richard Beedall's overview of current

British Royal Navy transformational shipbuilding projects makes clear. China's People's Liberation Army Navy (PLAN) appears to benefit from a more favourable financial backdrop and Dawei Xia's article describes some of the impressive new ships it is putting into service. The development of a substantial merchant shipbuilding sector has doubtless helped this process. In spite of a significant history of warship construction, the rival Indian Navy appears to be facing more of a struggle commissioning its more recent indigenous designs. However, as described by Mrityunjoy Mazumdar, there is a strong local willingness to develop the necessary infrastructure needed to support the requirements of an increasingly influential naval power.

SIGNIFICANT WARSHIPS

The current naval scene is next examined in the context of some of the more significant new warship designs that are now being put into service. The time taken to design, construct and commission major warships seems to be expanding as technological complexity increases. For example, preliminary studies into the replacement of Britain's *Invincible* class support carriers began in the early 1990s but it is likely to be 2015 before the first of the replacement *Queen Elizabeth* class enters service.[3] As a result, all but the most recently-built ships have their origins in the requirements of the Cold War and it is only now that a response to the asymmetric threats of early twenty-first century warfare is becoming apparent in warship design. A particularly good example of this new generation of warships is the USN's first littoral combat ship *Freedom* (LCS-1), which is described by

An artist's impression of the DDG-1000 class destroyer *Zumwalt*. The USN's decision to curtail construction of the design at just three units demonstrates that even the most generously-resourced fleets have to live within their means. *(Northrop Grumman)*

Table 1.0.2: MAJOR FLEET STRENGTHS 1989-2009

COUNTRY	USA		UK		FRANCE		ITALY		SPAIN		RUSSIA[1]		INDIA		CHINA[1]		JAPAN		S KOREA	
Year	1989	2009	1989	2009	1989	2009	1989	2009	1989	2009	1989	2009	1989	2009	1989	2009	1989	2009	1989	2009
Aircraft Carrier (CVN/CV)	15	11	–	–	2	1	–	–	–	–	4	1	–	–	–	–	–	–	–	–
Support Carrier (CVS/CVH)	–	–	3	3	1	1	1	2	1	1	2	–	2	1	–	–	–	1	–	–
Strategic Missile Sub (SSBN)	33	14	4	4	6	3	–	–	–	–	65	16	–	–	1	3	–	–	–	–
Attack Submarine (SSGN/SSN)	95	57	17	8	4	6	–	–	–	–	120	20	1	–	4	5	–	–	–	–
Patrol Submarine (SSK)	–	–	9	–	10	–	9	6	8	4	95	20	18	16	105	55	17	16	–	11
Battleships/Battlecruisers (BB/BC)	4	–	–	–	–	–	–	–	–	–	3	2	–	–	–	–	–	–	–	–
Fleet Escort (CGN/CG/ DDG/FFG)	207	107	46	24	18	18	17	16	9	10	100	35	17	20	15	45	43	43	7	19
Patrol Escort (DD/FFG/FSG/FS)	–	1	–	–	24	15	16	8	10	–	165	55	7	8	35	30	18	8	31	28
Missile Attack Craft (PGG/PTG)	6	–	–	–	–	–	7	–	12	–	175	50	6	12	200	65	5	6	11	1
Mine Countermeasures (MCMV)	22	14	37	16	19	16	18	12	12	6	225	45	22	10	50	20	34	29	11	9
Major Amp (LHD/LPD/LPH/LSD)	38	31	2	7	3	4	2	3	–	2	3	1	–	1	–	1	–	3	–	1

1 Figures for Russia and China are approximate.

The time taken to design, construct and commission major warships is lengthy. It will be over twenty years between preliminary design studies into the British Royal Navy's CVF and the commissioning of first of class *Queen Elizabeth*. *(BVT Surface Fleet)*

Scott Truver. Specifically designed to support operations offshore, *Freedom*'s ability to accept modularised weapons packages provides it with the flexibility needed to adapt to a wide range of potential threats in rapid order.

Another warship now being tagged as having world-leading littoral warfare capabilities is the United Kingdom's first Type 45 air-defence destroyer, *Daring*. Originally conceived as a response to the Royal Navy's weaknesses to aircraft and missile attack revealed during the 1982 Falklands Conflict, *Daring*'s cutting-edge Sea Viper missile system is capable of shielding friendly forces from hostile air operations during both coastal and blue water oper-

Below: Navies are adapting to asymmetrical threats. A good example of this trend is provided by the USN's first littoral combat ship *Freedom* (LCS-1), which can accept a range of modularised mission packages to combat anti-access in coastal waters. *(Lockheed Martin)*

ations. However, the planned total of twelve ships has been halved as a result of defence cutbacks and the remainder of the class are likely to spend much of their time as escorts for the two new *Queen Elizabeth* CVF aircraft carriers. Formal construction of the initial member of the class commenced during 2009. Prior to her completion, Europe's most modern carrier will be the Italian *Cavour*, which is the third significant warship subject to detailed review. Enrico Cernuschi and Vincent O'Hara describe the *Marina Militare*'s new flagship against the backdrop of pragmatism and flexibility that lie at the heart of Italy's naval doctrine.

TECHNOLOGICAL DEVELOPMENTS

The final section of this review looks at the naval scene from a technological perspective. As Italy's significant investment in *Cavour* demonstrates, the ability to deploy maritime air power remains a necessity for the world's leading navies and increasing numbers of fleets are attempting to join the carrier 'club'. David Hobbs' examination of the state of both fixed-wing and rotary aviation is therefore an essential element of any consideration of the current naval balance, providing an up-to-date assessment of the latest developments. However, aircraft form just one component of the wide range of weapons systems on which maritime supremacy ultimately depends. Norman Friedman's authoritative overview of current developments in this extremely broad area examines how the improved situational awareness provided by enhanced and more closely networked sensors might be able to provide at least partial compensation for the overall reduction in fleet sizes that has been the inevitable result of cost growth. Technology continues to develop at a rapid rate, with increased use of unmanned sensors particularly relevant in improving the clarity of the overall 'picture'.

SUMMARY

In overview, therefore, this first edition of the *Seaforth World Naval Review* arrives at a time when the post-Cold War maritime environment seems to becoming a little clearer. Navies are steadily evolving away from the structures and equipment that were designed to operate in an environment of massive superpower confrontation in favour of more flexible forces better suited to combating the spectrum of threats inherent in the new world order. The importance of adaptability to the leading naval powers cannot be overstated. For example, units involved in counter-

Sensors continue to evolve to provide an improved situational picture. Thales' innovative Integrated Mast, which is currently being installed in each of the four Dutch *Holland* class offshore patrol vessels, is one way of improving their efficiency and reliability. *(Thales)*

terrorist or anti-piracy operations in the Indian Ocean might suddenly be called upon to intervene in a regional confrontation involving possible opponents equipped with the most potent technology.

In general terms, the traditional 'Western' maritime powers – lead by the USN – have responded well to this challenge. Appropriate fleet adjustments are being implemented in spite of inevitable false steps. The US is also working hard to strengthen existing and build new alliances to bolster its influence, of which increased co-operation with India is just one example. The necessity for this improved structure of alliances is, however, partly being driven by a lack of resources to counter all potential threats that America's longstanding European allies no longer have the ability or willingness fully to make good. The increasing influence of the Asian nations in world maritime affairs is evident here, as elsewhere.

ACKNOWLEDGEMENTS

The production of such a wide-ranging examination as the *Seaforth World Naval Review* inevitably involves the co-operation of a large number of people and it is appropriate to acknowledge some of the

more significant contributions here. Primary thanks must go to publishing editor Rob Gardiner for supporting this attempt to produce an affordable but comprehensive summary of modern naval developments. The guidance provided by John Jordan and Stephen Dent, with whom I have had a long association through the annual *Warship*, has been of significant value. I have also been helped by a superb group of initial contributors, all of whom have worked hard to give substance to a somewhat vague initial concept. A lot of companies have assisted with information and photographs, with Catherine Thurogood and Charles Thompson of BVT, Ute Arriens of HDW, Esther Benito Lope of Navantia and Frank van de Wiel of Thales Nederland going beyond the call of duty in this regard. In addition, BVT's Ross McClure gave up much of his valuable time to provide me a tour of the Type 45 destroyer *Dauntless*. I need also to acknowledge my bank colleague Paolo Alfieri for penetrating the labyrinthine public relations department of Italy's *Marina Militare* to secure some excellent images of *Cavour*. Finally, I would like to thank my family for their patience during the long hours that it has taken to produce this book, particularly that of my wife Susan for undertaking initial proof-reading, as well as the help of my son Alexander and parents Anthony and Mary for assisting me with many early-morning photographic assignments over the years.

Conrad Waters, Editor
30 June 2009

Notes

1. A detailed overview of trends in global military expenditure can be found in the various annual editions of the Stockholm International Peace Research Institute's *SIPRI Yearbook* (Oxford, OUP).

2. For a good description of the vulnerability of fast attack craft during the Second Gulf War, see Norman Friedman, *Navies in the Nuclear Age* (London, Conway Maritime Press, 1993), Chapter 5, pp 105–7.

3. Although now somewhat outdated, an excellent description of the principles of surface warship design is contained in P J Gates' *Surface Warships: An Introduction to Design Principles* (London, Brassey's Defence Publishers, 1987).

4. Unless otherwise indicated, every effort has been made to update information and tables to 30 June 2009.

2.1 WORLD FLEET REVIEWS

THE AMERICAS Regional Review

The naval environment in the Americas is inevitably dominated by events in the United States. In spite of a broadly favourable financial backdrop during the Republican Presidency of George W Bush, the United States Navy (USN) has been subject to an ongoing struggle to maintain a technologically advanced and numerous fleet. To some extent, these two requirements have been in conflict. The high costs involved in developing and then deploying the latest equipment – however necessary this might be – have left insufficient funding to strengthen overall fleet numbers.[1] For example, the USN's latest estimates suggest that it will require average spending considerably in excess of US$20bn p.a. to meet its long-range shipbuilding plan, whilst actually expenditure is likely to be little more than half this level. The problem has been made worse by poor execution of shipbuilding strategy. Significant cost growth and schedule delays have become persistent features of recent shipbuilding programmes.[2] As such, it has proved impossible for the USN to make material progress towards its stated intention of rebuilding the fleet from a current force of just over 280 vessels to a medium-term average of 313 ships.

Part of the solution is likely to revolve around the implementation of more effective shipbuilding practices. There is some evidence of embryonic progress in this area, for example the decision to concentrate the construction of all three remaining *Zumwalt* (DDG-1000) class destroyers in one shipyard. It also seems that President Barack Obama's new administration is willing to sacrifice some quality to benefit quantity. For example, relatively cost-effective programmes such as the Littoral Combat Ship (LCS) have been given priority at the expense of high-end surface combatants, such as *Zumwalt*. At the same time, there have been some signs that the 313-ship target will be abandoned, perhaps as a result of the overall examination of defence posture that is currently taking place as part of the 2010 Quadrennial Defense Review (QDR).

If the USN's overall numbers are limited further, it is likely that additional emphasis will be placed on the key collaborative tenets of the navy's current maritime doctrine, 'A Cooperative Strategy for 21st Century Seapower'. First released on 17 October 2007 at an international seapower symposium held at Newport, Rhode Island, the strategy is regarded as the brainchild of the current Chairman of the Joint Chiefs of Staff, Admiral Mike Mullen. Adding the maintenance of Maritime Security and the provision of Humanitarian Assistance & Disaster Response to the USN's traditional core capabilities of Forward Presence, Deterrence, Sea Control and Power Projection, the strategy essentially gives much greater priority to the USN's role in conflict prevention than hitherto. Whilst the USN – and its counterparts in the US Marine Corps and US Coast Guard – will retain a full range of combat capabilities to fight and win wars, the maintenance of maritime security through co-operative engagement is considered the most effective way of serving US national interests in an age of asymmetric threats. The practical effects of the strategy can already be seen in the increased emphasis being placed on regional alliances with countries such as Australia, India and Japan, as well as collaborative self-help ventures along the lines of the Africa Partnership Station.

Author: Conrad Waters

A lawyer by training but a banker by profession, Conrad Waters was educated at Liverpool University prior to being called to the bar at Gray's Inn in 1989. His interest in maritime affairs was first stimulated by a long-family history of officers in merchant navy service and he has been writing articles on historical and current naval affairs for the last twenty years. This has included six years producing the 'World Navies in Review' chapter of the influential annual *Warship*. When not combating the aftermath of the global credit crunch in his role as Head of Credit Analysis at the European arm of one of the world's largest banks, Conrad lives with wife Susan and children Emma, Alexander and Imogen in Haslemere, Surrey.

Opposite: The Canadian frigate *Vancouver* is pictured alongside the US carrier *John C Stennis* (CVN-74) in this 2002 image. Current USN strategy is placing increased emphasis on international co-operation at a time when its own force levels are under strain. *(US Navy)*

Table 2.1.1: FLEET STRENGTHS IN THE AMERICAS – LARGER NAVIES (MID-2009)

COUNTRY	ARGENTINA	BRAZIL	CANADA	CHILE	ECUADOR	PERU	USA	VENEZUELA
Aircraft Carrier (CVN/CV)	–	1	–	–	–	–	11	–
Strategic Missile Submarine (SSBN)	–	–	–	–	–	–	14	–
Attack Submarine (SSN/SSGN)	–	–	–	–	–	–	57	–
Patrol Submarine (SSK)	3	5	4	4	2	6	–	2
Fleet Escort (CG/DDG/FFG)	4	9	15	8	2	9	107	6
Patrol Escort/Corvette (FFG/FSG/FS)	9	5	–	–	6	–	1	–
Missile Armed Attack Craft (PGG/PTG)	2	–	–	7	3	6	–	6
Mine Countermeasures Vessel (MCMV)	–	6	12	–	–	–	14	–
Major Amphibious Units (LHD/LPD/LPH/LSD)	–	2	–	–	–	–	31	–

To some extent, this change in strategic direction will only have a limited impact on the rest of the Americas, most of which has already long been entwined in a close diplomatic relationship with the United States. However, it would appear that the growing realisation of the limitations of USN maritime power might result in a more conciliatory approach being taken where regional disputes do exist, for example the question as to whether the North-West Passage should be considered as Canadian internal waters. This issue is certainly influencing Canadian defence policy, as evidenced by plans that will see the creation of a new naval base in the heart of the Canadian Arctic at Nanisivik and the acquisition of up to eight ice-strengthened Arctic patrol vessels over the next few years. In general terms, the broader Arctic is seeing a greater degree of militarisation, in part due to the greater emphasis being attached to the region's significant natural resources. Similar considerations are also having an impact in Latin America, where Brazil is embarking on a substantial programme of naval expansion as part of plans to afford more protection to offshore oil fields. Mineral wealth has been helping other Latin American countries, notably Chile, finance much-needed naval modernisation. However, it will be interesting to see whether a generally more positive regional funding environment survives the aftermath of the current global 'credit crunch'.

Table 2.1.1 provides a summary of larger regional fleet strengths as at mid-2009.

MAJOR NORTH AMERICAN NAVIES – CANADA

Although overshadowed by the much larger forces of its southern neighbour, the relatively small Canadian navy is a balanced and effective fleet. Key components are four *Victoria* (ex-*Upholder*) class patrol submarines and fifteen fleet escorts of the *Iroquois* and *Halifax* classes. These principal units are listed in more detail in Table 2.1.2. Roughly evenly divided between Atlantic and Pacific flotillas, the fleet has been particularly active in support of US-led anti-terrorism missions under the overall umbrella of Operation 'Enduring Freedom', involving significant deployments to the Persian Gulf and Indian Ocean. This has also included related anti-piracy missions.

The most significant recent acquisition has been the somewhat problematic transfer of the second-hand *Upholder* class submarines from the United Kingdom under a C$750m (US$650m) deal agreed in 1998. The initial refurbishment of the four boats, which had been laid up in reserve for some time, was more difficult and took longer than first expected. In addition, the final submarine to be transferred, *Chicoutimi* (ex-*Upholder*) had the misfortune to suffer a fatal electrical fire on 5 October 2004 after being swamped by a high wave whilst running on the surface in opened-up condition during her delivery voyage. A decision was subsequently taken to defer repair work until the other submarines had completed planned upgrades and this is now scheduled to begin in 2010. These other class members have also only seen limited operational use in Canadian service, although the signing of an in-service support contract during 2008 with a consortium headed by the UK's Babcock International promises better things. The current plan appears to involve rotating the boats through a programme of extended docking periods, with the ultimate aim being to keep one submarine operational on both the Atlantic and Pacific coasts. The class shares many technological features with Britain's current generation of nuclear-powered attack submarines and has the potential to provide Canada with a powerful underwater capability should full operational status be established.

Surface programmes are currently focused on the mid-life modernisation of the *Halifax* class frigates and construction of three Joint Support Ships (JSS) in replacement of current replenishment vessels. The former project is well advanced. It involves provision of new command and control (C^2) and electronic warfare systems – as well upgrades to radar, communications and missiles – in addition to structural and mechanical refurbishment. Shipyards in Halifax, Nova Scotia and Victoria, British Colombia have received contracts totalling C$900m to carry out the necessary maintenance and repairs, whilst a team headed by Lockheed Martin Canada was awarded combat systems integration and ongoing support work in agreements valued at C$2bn in November 2008. Modernisation work is currently scheduled to start by 2010, with the final refit concluded in 2017. In the longer term, both the *Halifax* and *Iroquois* classes are likely to be replaced with a single class of major surface combatant.

Progress with the JSS project has been less good. Originally conceived in 2004 by the then Liberal Party administration, the programme has been

Seen here arriving at Canada's west coast, the damaged Canadian submarine *Chicoutimi* will soon commence refit and repair under the Victoria In-Service Support Contract. *(Canadian Forces)*

Table 2.1.2: CANADIAN NAVY: PRINCIPAL UNITS AS AT MID-2009

TYPE	CLASS	NUMBER	TONNAGE	DIMENSIONS	PROPULSION	CREW	DATE
Principal Surface Escorts							
Destroyer – DDG	IROQUOIS	3	5,100 tons	130m x 15m x 5m	COGOG, 29 knots	280	1972
Frigate – FFG	HALIFAX	12	4,800 tons	134m x 16m x 5m	CODOG, 29 knots	225	1992
Submarines							
Submarine – SSK	VICTORIA (UPHOLDER)	4	2,500 tons	70m x 8m x 6m	Diesel-electric, 20+ knots	50	1990

supported by the current Canadian Conservative government and forms a key part of their 'Canada First' defence strategy. Whilst detailed information is sparse, the new ships are intended to improve the country's potential for expeditionary warfare by combining replenishment, sealift and logistical support capabilities in a c.28,000-ton, 200m hull. Delivery was originally to be in the 2012 to 2016 timeframe. Unfortunately, negotiations with the two shortlisted contractors were terminated on 22 August 2008 when it emerged that they were not able to meet the budget for the required specification. There have been reports that Canada is now considering collaboration with the Royal Netherlands Navy, who

are planning a similar vessel in replacement for the elderly replenishment ship *Zuiderkruis*. However, achievement of significant savings might involve construction in a foreign yard, which would run contrary to the requirements of the government's 'Buy Canada' policy.

MAJOR NORTH AMERICAN NAVIES – UNITED STATES NAVY

Although subject to numerous challenges, the USN remains the world's most potent 'blue water' fleet by a substantial margin. Table 2.1.3 summarises principal units, whilst Chapter 2.1A provides a much more detailed review of the major warship

classes and current fleet renewal programmes.

As mentioned in the Introduction to this chapter, the USN is currently awaiting the outcome of the 2010 Quadrennial Defense Review. This will determine whether the target of a 313-ship navy is to be retained. Pending this decision, the navy has elected not to update its annual long-range construction plan that sets out how targeted fleet numbers will be achieved. As a result, the most up to date information is contained in the February 2008, FY2009 plan, which has already been rendered obsolete by decisions such as the termination of the DDG-1000 class at three vessels in favour of construction of a modernised variant of the DDG-51 *Arleigh Burke*

Table 2.1.3: UNITED STATES NAVY: PRINCIPAL UNITS AS AT MID-2009

TYPE	CLASS	NUMBER	TONNAGE	DIMENSIONS	PROPULSION	CREW	DATE
Aircraft Carriers							
Aircraft Carrier – CVN	NIMITZ (CVN-68)	10	101,000 tons	340m x 41/78m x 12m	Nuclear, 30+ knots	5,700	1975
Aircraft Carrier – CVN	ENTERPRISE (CVN-65)	1	93,000 tons	342m x 41/76m x 12m	Nuclear, 30+ knots	5,900	1961
Principal Surface Escorts							
Cruiser – CG	TICONDEROGA (CG-47)	22	9,900 tons	173m x 17m x 10m	COGAG, 30+ knots	365	1983
Destroyer – DDG	ARLEIGH BURKE (DDG-51) – Flight IIA	27	9,200 tons	155m x 20m x 10m	COGAG, 30 knots	380	2000
Destroyer – DDG	ARLEIGH BURKE (DDG-51) – Flights I/II	28	8,800 tons	154m x 20m x 10m	COGAG, 30+ knots	340	1991
Frigate – FFG	OLIVER HAZARD PERRY (FFG-7)	30	4,100 tons	143m x 14m x 8m	COGAG, 30 knots	215	1977
Littoral Combat Ship – FSG	FREEDOM (LCS-1)	1	3,100 tons	115m x 17m x 4m	CODAG, 45+ knots	<50[1]	2008
Submarines							
Submarine – SSBN	OHIO (SSBN-726)	14	18,800 tons	171m x 13m x 12m	Nuclear, 20+ knots	155	1981
Submarine – SSGN	OHIO (SSGN-726)	4	18,800 tons	171m x 13m x 12m	Nuclear, 20+ knots	160	1981
Submarine – SSN	VIRGINIA (SSN-774)	5	8,000 tons	115m x 10m x 9m	Nuclear, 25+ knots	135	2004
Submarine – SSN	SEAWOLF (SSN-21)	3[2]	9,000 tons	108m x 12m x 11m	Nuclear, 25+ knots	140	1997
Submarine SSN	LOS ANGELES (SSN-688)	45	7,000 tons	110m x 10m x 9m	Nuclear, 25+ knots	145	1976
Major Amphibious Units							
Amph. Assault Ship – LHD	WASP (LHD-1)	8[3]	41,000 tons	253m x 32/42m x 9m	Steam, 20+ knots	1,100	1989
Amph Assault Ship – LHD	TARAWA (LHA-1)	2	40,000 tons	250m x 32/38m x 8m	Steam, 24 knots	975	1976
Landing Platform Dock – LPD	SAN ANTONIO (LPD-17)	4	25,000 tons	209m x 32m x 7m	Diesel, 22+ knots	360	2005
Landing Platform Dock – LPD	AUSTIN (LPD-4)	5	17,000 tons	171m x 25m x 7m	Steam, 21 knots	420	1965
Landing Ship Dock – LSD	WHIDBEY ISLAND (LSD-41)	12[4]	16,000 tons	186m x 26m x 6m	Diesel, 20 knots	420	1985

Notes:

1 Plus mission-related crew   **2** Third of class, SSN-23 is longer and heavier   **3** LHD-8 has many differences   **4** Includes four LSD-49 HARPERS FERRY variants

Three views of the US *Arleigh Burke* Flight II class destroyer *Mitscher* (DDG-57) departing Portsmouth, UK on 12 November 2008. Construction of a modified version of the class is planned as an alternative to more DDG-1000 type destroyers. *(Conrad Waters)*

class.[3] For the sake of reference, however, Table 2.1.4 compares the current fleet as of June 2009 with that planned for FY2020 under the February 2008 planning assumptions.

Whilst there is, therefore, considerable long-term uncertainty, the navy continues to be reinforced in the short term by large numbers of extremely potent warships. The carrier force has moved to all-nuclear propulsion with the delivery of *George H W Bush* (CVN-77) in replacement for *Kitty Hawk* (CV-63), which was formally retired on 12 May 2009 after forty-eight years of service. Meanwhile, surface force numbers have stabilised after an ongoing period of decline with the serial commissioning of later members of the Flight IIA *Burke* variant. A similar result is being seen in the submarine flotillas as a result of the steady build-up of *Virginia* (SSN-774) class numbers. The latter design is one of the major successes of post-Cold War USN shipbuilding programmes and production looks set to be stepped up to two boats p.a. from FY2011 now that design changes have reduced unit costs to a long-targeted US$2bn. The construction programme for the *San Antonio* (LPD-17) class of amphibious transport dock has been much less successful. Delayed delivery,

massive cost overruns and slipshod fabrication – there were several thousand defects on the lead ship – all combined to make the project an example of the worst of US shipbuilding. However, quality on the latest ships is considerably improved and increasing numbers are entering service. Fourth of class – *Green Bay* (LPD-20) – commissioned on 24 January 2009 and *New York* (LPD-21) is also scheduled to join the fleet before year-end.

Operationally, the USN continues to be extremely busy, with the Indian Ocean a particular focal point of attention. Increased involvement in anti-piracy activities – most notably through the initiation of Combined Task Force 151 off the Horn of Africa – has been an additional burden over and above the ongoing anti-terrorism mission and increased emphasis on multinational naval co-operation that

have been the key themes of recent years. This new assignment has had its successes, not least the rescue of US merchant navy captain Richard Phillips by Special Forces deployed on the destroyer *Bainbridge* (DDG-96) in an April 2009 incident that left three of the pirates dead. Phillips had been seized after a botched attempt to hijack the American-flagged *Maersk Alabama*, in what was reportedly the first pirate attack on a US vessel since the nineteenth century. The Pacific Ocean and adjacent seas are also major areas of USN activity. Defensive deployments in response to North Korean nuclear and long-range missile tests have supplemented a longer-term transfer of forces from the Atlantic to the Pacific to counterbalance China's growing influence. Whilst current US policy towards China seems keen to place emphasis on collaboration rather than confrontation, the potential for conflict remains. The latter country is particularly sensitive about US surveillance activities in its economic zone, as demonstrated by harassment of the Military Sealift Command vessel *Impeccable* (T-AGOS-23) by Chinese vessels whilst engaged in this activity during March 2009. More recently, the destroyer *John S McCain* (DDG-56) saw her towed array damaged by a collision with a Chinese submarine in international waters off the Philippines, suggesting the People's Liberation Army Navy (PLAN) is also engaged in its own surveillance operations.

Although receiving much less publicity than the USN, the US Coast Guard forms a core part of US maritime capabilities and has an increasingly important homeland security role in the current age of asymmetrical threats. Operating under the Department of Homeland Security during peacetime, it would most likely fall under the control of the Navy Department in time of war. Faced with the problem of block obsolescence of its main seagoing and airborne assets, it embarked on an ambitious modernisation programme in 2002 with the signing of a long-term agreement with the Integrated Coast Guard Systems consortium of Lockheed Martin and Northrop Grumman as part of a project known as

Table 2.1.4: PLANNED USN FLEET DEVELOPMENT TO 2020

SHIP TYPE	AIRCRAFT CARRIER	BALLISTIC MISSILE SUB	OTHER SUBMARINE	MAJOR SURFACE SHIP	FRIGATE	LCS	AMPHIBIOUS SHIP	SUPPORT SHIP
Mid 2009	11	14	57	77	30	1	33	60
Plan – FY 2020	11	14	52	88	–	55	31	62

Note: 2009 Amphibious Ships include two command ships.

Bainbridge (DDG-96) off the coast of Somalia. She was involved in the successful rescue of US merchant navy captain Richard Phillips from Somali pirates in April 2009. *(US Navy)*

The US Coast Guard forms an important component of overall US maritime capabilities and extensive modernisation is underway. This is the first national security cutter *Bertholf* (WMSL-750) on trials. *(Northrop Grumman)*

'Deepwater'. Unfortunately, the unprecedented delegation of project management decisions to the private sector that Deepwater instigated did not work well in practice. The emergence of structural problems in both new-build and modernised vessels was just one of a series of problems that resulted in management of the project being brought under the control of an 'in-house' Acquisitions Directorate when the initial contract period ended in 2007.

The Acquisitions Directorate continues to work to deliver the main capabilities envisaged by Deepwater. Three new classes of ocean-going national security cutter (eight vessels), offshore patrol cutter (twenty-five vessels) and inshore fast response cutter (fifty-eight vessels) form a major part of this investment programme. The lead ship of the first class – *Bertholf* (WMSL-750) – was commissioned on 4 August 2008 prior to final acceptance in May 2009. Two other members of the class are under construction, with *Waesche* (WMSL-751) scheduled for delivery before the end of 2009. Displacing around 4,300 tons in full load condition and powered by CODAG propulsion providing a maximum sustained speed of 28 knots, *Bertholf* is armed with a 57mm main gun

and a close-in weapons system (CIWS) and can operate one helicopter and two unmanned aerial vehicles. As such, she can be considered as a powerfully-armed corvette-type vessel that will form a useful supplement to the USN's littoral combat ships in lower-threat environments.

OTHER NORTH AND CENTRAL AMERICAN NAVIES

South of the US border, **Mexico** fields a large but little-publicised navy that is largely focused on anti-narcotics and natural resource protection operations. The fleet can be roughly divided into a small core of front-line warships that have almost exclusively been obtained second-hand from the United States and a much larger flotilla of patrol vessels, many of which are of indigenous construction. The key components of the former force include four *Allende* (ex-*Knox*) class frigates acquired between 1997 and 2001, two older vessels of the *Bravo* (ex-*Bronstein*) class and two landing ship tanks of the former *Newport* type. There are also two former Israeli SAAR 4.5 fast attack craft. The more numerous patrol vessels include a series of Mexican-built offshore patrol vessels of the

Trinidad and Tobago is waiting delivery of three 90-metre helicopter-equipped offshore patrol vessels from the UK's BVT Surface Fleet. *(VT Group)*

Holzinger, *Sierra*, *Durango* and *Oaxaca* classes commissioned between 1991 and 2003. With a full load displacement of between 1,300 and 1,700 tons, these are relatively low-technology vessels equipped with a medium-calibre gun and helicopter flight deck but are eminently suitable for their purpose. The Mexican government has recently announced the resumption of construction of two suspended vessels of the latest *Oxaca* class as part of a budget increase that will fund the purchase of additional helicopters and fixed-wing patrol aircraft, as well as a considerable expansion of the navy's marines. Investment is also being made in a network of radars that will operate in conjunction with the offshore patrol vessels to improve surveillance of oilfields in the Gulf of Mexico.

The need to protect oil assets is also driving one of the other major naval acquisition projects in Central America; the **Trinidad and Tobago** Coast Guard's purchase of three helicopter-equipped offshore patrol vessels from the UK's BVT Surface Fleet. Ordered under a £150m (US$240m) contract announced in April 2007, the project's execution has encountered some technical difficulties that has seem work transferred from the group's Portsmouth yard to its facilities on the Clyde to minimise construction delays. The first vessel should commence sea trials by the end of 2009, with all three in service by 2011.

MAJOR SOUTH AMERICAN NAVIES – ARGENTINA

Once arguably the foremost navy within South America's ABC (Argentina – Brazil – Chile) club of

The former *Newport* class tank landing ship *Papaloapan*, now in service with Mexico's fleet. Mexico operates a small core of former USN vessels, supported by significant numbers of home-grown patrol ships for constabulary duties. *(US Navy)*

Table 2.1.5: ARGENTINEAN NAVY: PRINCIPAL UNITS AS AT MID-2009

TYPE	CLASS	NUMBER	TONNAGE	DIMENSIONS	PROPULSION	CREW	DATE
Principal Surface Escorts							
Destroyer – DDG	**ALMIRANTE BROWN** (MEKO 360)	4	3,600 tons	126m x 15m x 6m	COGOG, 30 knots	200	1983
Frigate – FFG	**ESPORA** (MEKO 140)	6	1,500 tons	91m x 1m x 4m	Diesel, 27 knots	95	1985
Corvette – FSG	**DRUMMOND** (A-69)	3	1,200 tons	80m x 10m x 5m	Diesel, 24 knots	95	1978
Submarines							
Submarine – SSK	**SANTA CRUZ** (TR 1700)	2	2,300 tons	66m x 7m x 7m	Diesel-electric, 25 knots	30	1984
Submarine – SSK	**SALTA** (Type 209)	1	1,200 tons	54m x 6m x 6m	Diesel-electric, 22 knots	30	1974

leading maritime powers, the *Armada Argentina* is now almost a shadow of its former self after almost two decades of under-funding following the Falklands War. Whilst reports suggest that some money has been found to commence refits of the TR1700 class submarine *San Juan* and the TNC45 fast attack craft *Indómita*, it appears that there is still no money for new construction. For example, plans for a new class of offshore patrol vessel based on the Fassmer OPV80 design used for Chile's 'Danubio IV' programme look set to be postponed due to budget cuts, albeit the project has been accorded sufficient importance that it will still probably go ahead in due course.

The core of the current surface fleet is composed of four MEKO 360 type destroyers of the *Almirante Brown* class delivered from Germany during 1983–4 and six smaller MEKO 140 type *Espora* frigates built locally between 1985 and 2004. These are supplemented by three older French-built A-69 type corvettes of the *Drummond* class. Underwater forces comprise two TR1700 *Santa Cruz* submarines and the sole remaining Type 209/1100 boat, *Salta*. Table 2.1.5 provides further details.

MAJOR SOUTH AMERICAN NAVIES – BRAZIL

Although the *Marinha do Brasil* has also experienced funding difficulties in recent years, the future environment looks significantly brighter as the country's politicians embark on a major uplift in defence spending to compensate for previous under-investment. As elsewhere, the need to protect valuable offshore resources is ensuring that maritime forces obtain a considerable proportion of the new money available.

Brazil's key medium-term objective is to recapitalise its underwater forces, including the realisation of long-held ambitions to deploy nuclear-powered attack submarines. France's DCNS has been selected as the strategic partner to develop this programme, which will see the construction of four conventionally-powered submarines of the *Scorpène* design and a prototype nuclear-powered boat under a €6.7bn (US$9.4bn) agreement announced on 23 December 2008. The programme will be carried out in alliance with Brazilian conglomerate Odebrecht and involves the construction of a new submarine base in Rio de Janeiro prior to delivery of the first vessel in 2015. Although most of the technology involved in the new vessels will be of French origin, the nuclear propulsion system of the attack submarine will be entirely of Brazilian design and manufacture.

Brazil has also turned to France for help with the design of its new generation of offshore patrol vessels, with CMN's Vigilante 400 CL54 design being used as the basis for local build of the 500-ton NAPA 500 class. Two ships of this type are now in the final stages of construction in Brazil and an agreement licensing four additional vessels was signed in September 2008. The priority placed on ensuring the effective policing of Brazil's extensive exclusive economic zone (EZZ) means that orders for further vessels of this type are likely, whilst plans for a larger patrol vessel type are also under consideration.

A summary of principal fleet units is set out in Table 2.1.6. These include the aircraft carrier *São Paulo* (ex-*Foch*), five variants of the Type 209 submarine design, nine frigates of the *Broadsword* and *Niterói* classes and five smaller corvettes. The latter include the long-awaited *Barroso*, a modification of

Table 2.1.6: BRAZILIAN NAVY: PRINCIPAL UNITS AS AT MID-2009

TYPE	CLASS	NUMBER	TONNAGE	DIMENSIONS	PROPULSION	CREW	DATE
Aircraft Carriers							
Aircraft Carrier – CV	**SÃO PAULO** (FOCH)	1	33,500 tons	265m x 32/51m x 9m	Steam, 30 knots	1,700	1963
Principal Surface Escorts							
Frigate – FFG	**GREENHALGH** (Type 22-Batch 1)	3	4,700 tons	131m x 15m x 6m	COGOG, 30 knots	270	1979
Frigate – FFG	**NITERÓI**	6	3,700 tons	129m x 14m x 6m	CODOG, 30 knots	220	1976
Corvette – FSG	**INHAÚMA**	4	2,100 tons	96m x 11m x 5m	CODOG, 27 knots	125	1989
Corvette – FSG	**BARROSO**	1	2,400 tons	103m x 11m x 6m	CODOG, 30 knots	145	2008
Submarines							
Submarine – SSK	**TIKUNA** (Type 209 – modified)	1	1,600 tons	62m x 6m x 6m	Diesel-electric, 22 knots	40	2005
Submarine – SSK	**TUPI** (Type 209)	4	1,500 tons	61m x 6m x 6m	Diesel-electric, 22+ knots	30	1989
Major Amphibious Units							
Landing Ship Dock – LSD	**CEARÁ** (LSD-28)	2	12,000 tons	156m x 26m x 6m	Steam, 21 knots	350	1956

Vessels from Argentina (*Almirante Brown*), Brazil (*Rademaker*) and Spain (*Santa Maria*) steam in formation during a US-sponsored UNITAS exercise. Brazil's allocation of a substantial budget for defence modernisation might feed through into new surface ships but Argentina's surface flotilla will continue to struggle with inadequate funding. *(US Navy)*

the previous *Inhaúma* class. She was finally delivered on 19 August 2008, nearly fourteen years after being laid down. Amphibious forces have also been bolstered by the transfer of surplus 'Knight' class logistic landing ships from the UK. The former *Sir Bedivere* was commissioned as *Almirante Saboia* on 21 May 2009, following her half-sister *Sir Galahad* (now *Garcia D'Avila*) into Brazilian naval service.

MAJOR SOUTH AMERICAN NAVIES – CHILE

Whilst not benefiting from quite the same level of investment as that earmarked by Brazil for military modernisation, Chile's armed forces have also been reasonably well resourced in recent years. This has partly been a result of the favourable economic impact of the world-wide boom in commodity prices on Chile's copper-dominated export industry, a trend which has now partly reversed. In the meantime, however, the eight-strong surface fleet has been entirely renewed with the acquisition of surplus frigates from the UK and the Netherlands. This process was completed with the arrival of the Type 23 frigate *Almirante Condell* (ex-*Marlborough*) in Valparaiso on 21 October 2008. Similarly, the submarine fleet has been bolstered by the purchase of two new Franco-Spanish *Scorpène* patrol submarines and the modernisation of the two existing Type 209/1300 *Thomson* class boats. Table 2.1.7 summarises current fleet strength.

In common with many other Latin American navies, Chile is placing much emphasis on developing more robust offshore patrol capabilities. The first of two initial Fassmer OPV80 type vessels, *Piloto Pardo*, was handed over to the *Armada de Chile* on 13 June 2008 following completion by local ship-builder ASMAR's Talcahuano yard. Displacing 1,725 tons in full load condition, she is powered by twin Wärtsilä 12V 26 diesels that produce a maximum speed of 20 knots and a range of 8,000 miles at 12 knots. A second member of the class will be completed before the end of 2009 and Chile is also promoting the design as a solution to other Latin American countries' offshore patrol needs.

MAJOR SOUTH AMERICAN NAVIES – PERU

Traditionally the operator of the region's fourth largest navy, Peru's naval forces rival those of Chile in overall size, if not in capability. The surface fleet is now focused on a homogeneous flotilla of eight

Table 2.1.7: CHILEAN NAVY: PRINCIPAL UNITS AS AT MID-2009

TYPE	CLASS	NUMBER	TONNAGE	DIMENSIONS	PROPULSION	CREW	DATE
Principal Surface Escorts							
Frigate – FFG	**ALMIRANTE WILLIAMS** (Type 22-Batch 2)	1	5,500 tons	148m x 14m x 7m	COGOG, 30+ knots	260	1988
Frigate – FFG	**ALMIRANTE COCHRANE** (Type 23)	3	4,200 tons	133m x 16m x 7m	CODLAG, 28 knots	185	1990
Frigate – FFG	**CAPITÁN PRAT** (L class)	2	3,800 tons	131m x 15m x 6m	COGOG, 30 knots	200	1986
Frigate – FFG	**ALMIRANTE RIVEROS** (M class)	2	3,300 tons	122m x 14m x 4m	CODOG, 30 knots	160	1992
Submarines							
Submarine – SSK	**O'HIGGINS** (Scorpène)	2	1,700 tons	66m x 6m x 6m	Diesel-electric, 22 knots	30	2005
Submarine – SSK	**THOMSON** (Type 209)	2	1,400 tons	60m x 6m x 6m	Diesel-electric, 22 knots	35	1984

Chile's Type 23 frigate *Almirante Cochrane* (the former Royal Navy *Norfolk*) pictured whilst still in UK waters during 2007. The acquisition of three surplus RN members of the class was successfully completed with the arrival of *Almirante Condell* (ex-*Marlborough*) in Valparaiso on 21 October 2008. *(Conrad Waters)*

Peru's surface fleet is now focused on a
homogeneous flotilla of eight *Lupo* class frigates.
This is the locally-built *Mariategui*. (US Navy)

Table 2.1.8: PERUVIAN NAVY: PRINCIPAL UNITS AS AT MID-2009

TYPE	CLASS	NUMBER	TONNAGE	DIMENSIONS	PROPULSION	CREW	DATE
Principal Surface Escorts							
Cruiser – CL	**ALMIRANTE GRAU** (DE RUYTER)	1	12,200 tons	187m x 17m x 7m	Steam, 32 knots	950	1953
Frigate – FFG	**CARVAJAL** (LUPO)	8	2,500 tons	112m x 12m x 4m	CODOG, 35 knots	185	1977
Submarines							
Submarine – SSK	**ANGAMOS** (Type 209)	6[1]	1,200 tons	54m x 6m x 6m	Diesel-electric, 22 knots	30	1980

Notes

1 Peru operates both T209/1100 and T209/1200 submarines. Details refer to the Type 209/1100 variant

Homogeneity also extends to Peru's underwater forces. This June 2009 photo shows Type 209 submarines *Pisagua*, *Chipana* and *Islay* in surface formation. *(US Navy)*

Italian-designed *Lupo* class frigates after transfer of four former *Marina Militare* vessels to join the original four *Carvajal* variants ordered during the 1970s. The Peruvian newspaper *La República* has reported that modernisation of the class's radar and fire control systems was recently authorised. Other significant surface units include six *Velarde* fast attack craft completed in France in the early 1980s, as well as the veteran cruiser *Almirante Grau* (the former Dutch *De Ruyter*). Laid down in 1939, she is the world's last conventionally-armed cruiser. Her near 1,000-strong crew must be a considerable drain on the fleet's overall resources. Having already passed several previously reported decommissioning dates, it is unlikely she will be retained much longer and the planned transfer of surplus *Newport* class tank landing ships from the US to bolster amphibious capabilities may herald her demise. The landing ships will be accompanied by six Sea King helicopters, greatly enhancing the navy's aviation arm.

The underwater force comprises six diesel-electric patrol submarines of HDW's Type 209/1100 and Type 209/1200 classes that were ordered in three separate batches for delivery between 1975 and 1983. Although therefore also somewhat elderly, many have been subject to local modernisation and they remain a potent – and homogeneous – force. There have also been reports that they are to be equipped with new German AEG SUT 264 heavy-weight torpedoes. Table 2.1.8 lists major units

OTHER SOUTH AMERICAN NAVIES

None of the other Latin American countries can field fleets to match those of the larger maritime powers, albeit **Venezuela** is investing significant sums in enhancing offshore patrol capabilities. A 2005 contract with Spain's Navantia envisages the construction of four oceanic and four offshore patrol vessels, the latter to be coast-guard operated. Construction of the latter 1,500-ton class is now well advanced and the first should be delivered by the end of 2009. All eight vessels will be in service by 2011. Venezuela has also been reported as discussing the purchase of as many as four new 'Kilo' class submarines from Russia as part of a developing alliance that is causing the US considerable concern in its own backyard. If the contract is confirmed, the

Above: Colombia's Type 209 submarines are being modernised under a contract signed with HDW. This is *Tayrona*, first commissioned in 1975. *(Thyssen Krupp Marine Systems)*

Left: The Fassmer OPV80 type vessel *Piloto Pardo*, which is now in service with Chile's fleet. Argentina and Colombia are also interested in the design. *(Armada de Chile)*

new submarines would probably replace Venezuela's two existing Type 209 class boats.

Colombia has also earmarked some funds for naval modernisation and a contract was announced with Thyssen Krupp Marine Systems' HDW unit for the local upgrade of the country's own Type 209 submarines in January. The country also envisages local construction of at least one Fassmer OPV80 patrol ship similar to Chile's *Piloto Pardo*.

Meanwhile, neighbouring **Ecuador** has turned to Chile's ASMAR for refurbishment of its pair of Type 209 submarines. It has also taken delivery of two former Chilean *Leander* class frigates to replace older variants of the class previously transferred from Britain.

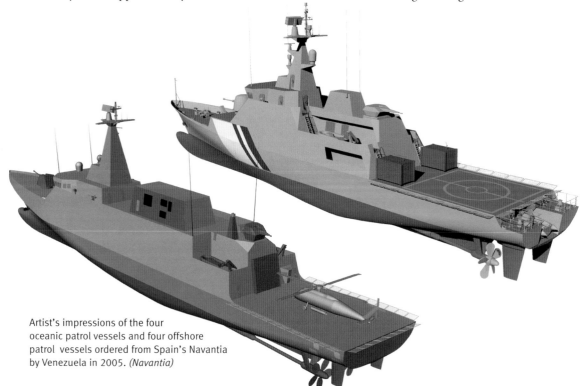

Artist's impressions of the four oceanic patrol vessels and four offshore patrol vessels ordered from Spain's Navantia by Venezuela in 2005. *(Navantia)*

Notes

1. Please see Chapter 4.1 for Norman Friedman's review of the overall factors impacting the current development of naval technology.

2. The US Government Accountability Office (GAO) has released a series of reports criticising the poor business planning inherent in a wide range of USN naval programmes. Common problems include decisions taken to push ahead with construction when designs have not reached sufficient maturity, poor cost estimation and lack of subsequent cost control. Please refer to Paul L Francis, *Defense Acquisitions: Realistic Business Cases Needed to Execute Navy Shipbuilding Programmes*, GAO-07-943T (Washington, DC, US GAO, 2007) and Paul L Francis, *Defense Acquisitions: Zumwalt-Class Destroyer Program Emblematic of Challenges Facing Navy Shipbuilding*, GAO-08-1061T (Washington, DC, US GAO, 2008).

3. See Director, Warfare Integration, *Report to Congress on Annual Long-Range Plan for Construction of Naval Vessels for FY 2009* (Washington, DC, Office of the Chief of Naval Operations, 2008).

2.1A FLEET REVIEW

THE UNITED STATES NAVY

The United States Navy (USN) confronts a broad spectrum of challenges in mid-2009: supporting two conflicts, maintaining 'persistent presence' in world regions of importance to the nation, dealing with the age-old scourge of piracy and modern forms of maritime terrorism, and responding to humanitarian crises in home waters and the far-abroad. Doing so with a fleet numbering only 283 ships – the smallest since 1916 – has resulted in 'red-lined' operational and personnel tempos.

For several years, the navy has articulated a requirement for a '313-Ship Fleet', tailored for the demands of the twenty-first century. Early retirements of warships during the 1990s resulted in a fleet that is a far cry from the '600-Ship Navy' of the mid-1980s. At the same time, the average age of navy ships has risen during the past decade – from about fifteen years to more than twenty years old – as ships built during the 1980s reach the ends of their service lives and replacements have been delayed or procured in fewer numbers than originally planned. Although today's new-construction warships are far more capable than the ships that have been retired, 'quantity has a quality all its own' and a ship cannot be in two places at the same time. Successive thirty-year shipbuilding plans required by the US Congress and annual shipbuilding budget requests showed the yawning gap between what was needed to reach the 313-ship target by c.2025 and the reality of what could be afforded.

In mid-May 2009, the chief of naval operations outlined the FY2010 shipbuilding programme that called for eight ships at a cost of US$14.9bn:

- 1 – *Virginia* (SSN-774) class attack submarine
- 1 – *Arleigh Burke* (DDG-51) guided-missile destroyer
- 3 – *Freedom* (LCS-1) class littoral combat ships
- 2 – *Lewis and Clark* (T-AKE-1) class replenishment ships
- 1 – JHSV joint high-speed vessel

Assuming an average ship service life of thirty years, this programme – if sustained – would deliver a fleet of only 240 ships. The FY2010 shipbuilding total of nearly US$15bn looks to be the high-water mark for the navy during the first Obama Administration. Already, indications are that there will be significant funding retrenchment, perhaps no more than US$12bn each year, beginning in FY2011.

Getting to the 313-ship navy thus looks to be too hard. Speaking at a symposium sponsored by the Hudson Institute in May 2009, Dr Eric Labs, senior naval analyst at the US Congressional Budget Office, noted that it would require about U$26bn per year to reach the navy's goal. This begs the question about the proper mix of ships: if not quantity then quality? Indeed, at the Hudson symposium US Representative Joseph Sestak, a retired navy vice admiral, argued that '... it's not the numbers. It's the capabilities we have at sea ... the navy doesn't have the right mix of forces to do today's much less tomorrow's jobs.'

Secretary of Defense Robert M Gates all-but presaged that sentiment in his 2009 testimony to the US Congress, noting, 'We must examine our blue-water fleet and the overall strategy behind the kinds of ships we are buying.'

AIRCRAFT CARRIERS

America's carriers deploy throughout the world in direct support of US strategy and commitments. Their mission is to support and operate the approximately seventy embarked aircraft that conduct attack, early warning, fleet air-defence, anti-submarine/surface, surveillance and electronic missions against seaborne, airborne and land-based targets in support of joint and coalition forces.

Author: Scott C Truver

Dr Scott C Truver is Director, National Security Programmes, at Gryphon Technologies LC, specialising in national and homeland security, and naval and maritime strategies, programmes and operations. Since 1972, Dr Truver has participated in many studies and assessments – most notably supporting the inter-agency task force drafting the US *National Strategy for Maritime Security* (2005) – and has also written extensively for US and foreign publications. He has lectured at the US Naval Academy, Naval War College and Naval Postgraduate School, among other venues. His further qualifications include a Doctor of Philosophy degree in Marine Policy Studies – the first PhD in this field ever awarded by an institution of higher education –and an MA in Political Science/International Relations from the University of Delaware.

Scott Truver was assisted by Mark Robinsky, a research analyst at Gryphon Technologies, in the preparation of his two chapters for the *Seaforth World Naval Review* 2010.

The tenth and final *Nimitz* class aircraft carrier, *George H W Bush* (CVN-77), pictured on initial sea trials from Northrop Grumman's Newport News facility in January 2009. The USN is currently mandated to operate a total of eleven aircraft carriers but this might fall to ten when *Enterprise* (CVN-65) decommissions in November 2012. *(Northrop Grumman)*

Navy leaders have stated that eleven carriers are needed to meet peacetime, crisis and wartime needs, a requirement enshrined in US law. But they also acknowledge that there will be gap of several years between the scheduled November 2012 decommissioning of the navy's first nuclear-powered carrier, *Enterprise* (CVN-65), which entered service in 1961, and the commissioning of the first of the next-generation carriers in September 2015, resulting in a ten-carrier force for about thirty-three months. A congressional waiver is needed for the navy to operate less than eleven carriers. Otherwise, keeping CVN-65 in service to maintain eleven would cost more than US$2bn and delay the refuelling and complex overhaul for the USS *Abraham Lincoln* (CVN-72). But, at the May 2009 Hudson Institute conference, retired Vice Admiral Sestak mentioned, almost in passing, 'I could live with nine'.

In addition to CVN-65, ten *Nimitz* (CVN-68) class nuclear-powered carriers are currently in active service. The *Nimitz* was commissioned in 1975, based on an initial design completed in 1964. The

last of the class, the *George H W Bush* (CVN-77), commissioned on 10 January 2009 and is expected to serve until 2059, *ceteris paribus*. Naval historian Norman Polmar notes: 'This is a remarkable and unique lifespan for a warship design. The *Nimitz* class also represents the largest number of carriers built to the same basic design since World War II by any nation.' Newport News Shipbuilding (now Northrop Grumman Ship Systems Newport News) has constructed all US nuclear-powered carriers.

The follow-on to the *Nimitz* class is *Gerald R Ford*, a new CVN-21 design that has upgraded hull, mechanical and electrical (HM&E) capabilities (although dubbed the 'CVN-21' class, the hull-numbering system will continue from the *Nimitz* class; the first 'CVN-21' will thus be CVN-78). CVN-21 carriers will incorporate new, more efficient life-of-ship/fifty-year nuclear propulsion plants; electro-magnetic aircraft launch systems (EMALS); advanced arresting gear (AAG); and a nearly three-fold increase in electrical-generation capacity compared to a *Nimitz*-class carrier to accommodate

EMALS and AAG and for electrical load margin to support future technologies. Development of EMALS has proven difficult, but the navy believes that the technical issues can be overcome. These improvements, coupled with a slightly expanded flight deck and other topside changes designed to increase operational efficiency, will enable significantly higher aircraft sortie rates. Human systems integration principles have shaped manpower requirements, which will be greatly reduced from today's crews. This will allow the navy to reap more than US$5bn in lifecycle cost-avoidance per ship compared to CVN-77.

Including research and development, the cost of the first three CVN-21 carriers is approximately US$35.1bn. The programme envisages procuring carriers on a five-year build cycle, with *Ford* to be delivered in 2015.

SURFACE COMBATANTS: AEGIS-EQUIPPED SHIPS

The navy operates twenty-two *Ticonderoga* (CG-47) class Aegis guided-missile cruisers that have combat systems centred on the Aegis weapon system (AWS) and associated SPY-1 A/B multi-function, phased-array radar. Three cruisers are also outfitted with the Aegis ballistic missile defence (ABMD) engagement capability (see below). The remaining nineteen cruisers are ABMD candidates.

Originally twenty-seven Aegis cruisers were acquired from Bath Iron Works and Ingalls Shipbuilding (now Northrop Grumman Ship Systems Pascagoula). The navy retired the first five 'Baseline 1' non-VLS (vertical-launching system) equipped cruisers in the early 2000s because of high operational costs and design constraints that made upgrades impractical. The remaining Aegis VLS cruisers are receiving a Cruiser Modernisation (CG MOD) programme that includes HM&E and combat systems upgrades. A particularly important element is the open-architecture computing environment that will facilitate future 'technology insertion'. Upgrades include:

- Air dominance: co-operative engagement capability (CEC), SPY radar enhancements.
- Maritime force protection: Phalanx close-in weapons system (CIWS-1B), Evolved Sea Sparrow Missile (ESSM), Mk53 Nulka active expendable decoy system, SPQ-9B radar set, Mk-45 Mod 4 5-inch/62-caliber gun system, and undersea warfare capabilities (SQQ-89A(V)15).

■ Mission life extension: ship control, all-electric auxiliaries, weight and moment modifications.

As of mid-2009, five ships had undergone the HM&E upgrades and, in spring 2009, *Bunker Hill* (CG-52) completed the first combined HM&E/CS refit.

The *Arleigh Burke* (DDG-51) Aegis guided-missile destroyers have combat systems centred on the Aegis weapon system and the SPY-1D (V) radar. The Flight IIA variants currently under construction incorporate facilities to support two embarked helicopters, significantly enhancing their capabilities compared to the Flight I destroyers.

By the end of FY2010, Bath Iron Works and Northrop Grumman Ship Systems Pascagoula will have delivered sixty-one of sixty-two ships in the original *Arleigh Burke* programme. The newest ships will field Aegis combat system Baseline 7 Phase 1R, which incorporates CEC, ESSM and the improved SPY-1D (V) radar, as well as advanced open-architecture combat systems using commercially-developed processors and displays. Future mods will replace the Aegis Baseline 7.1R with the open-architecture advanced capability build (ACB) 12 Aegis combat system, which was developed for the DDG Modernisation (DDG MOD) programme (see below). Aegis destroyers and cruisers will continue to constitute the majority of the navy's surface combatants for the first half of the twenty-first century. As a result of decisions taken in 2008, which curtailed the *Zumwalt* (DDG-1000) multi-mission destroyer programme at just three ships (see below), the navy will request as many as eight additional DDG-51s as plans are put in place for a yet-to-be-defined 'future surface combatant' and the CG(X) guided-missile cruiser.

From 2010, the DDG-51 class will undergo a two-phase mid-life modernisation: DDG MOD. The first phase will concentrate on HM&E systems, including gigabit ethernet connectivity in the engineering plant, a digital video surveillance system, an integrated bridge system, an advanced galley and other habitability and manpower-reduction modifications. A complete open-architecture computing environment will be the foundation for warfighting improvements in the second phase. The upgrade plan includes an improved multi-mission signal processor to accommodate Aegis Ballistic Missile Defence capability and improvements to radar performance in littoral regions. The single integrated

The *Arleigh Burke* class destroyer *Roosevelt* (DDG-80) pictured in front of the amphibious transport dock *Carter Hall* (LSD-50) whilst operating as part of the Iwo Jima expeditionary strike group in September 2008. The class forms the core of the USN surface fleet now and into the future *(US Navy)*

The twenty-two remaining *Ticonderoga* class Aegis guided-missile cruisers are receiving a cruiser modernisation programme. This is *Normandy* (CG-60) docked alongside *Ashland* (LSD-48) on a visit to Malta in 2005. *(Susan Waters)*

The *Arleigh Burke* class destroyer *Winston Churchill* (DDG-81). By the end of FY2010 Bath Iron Works and Northrop Grumman Ship Systems Pascagoula will have delivered sixty-one of sixty-two ships in the original *Burke* class programme. *(US Navy)*

The US Navy's Aegis-equipped ships are being progressively modernised to support ballistic missile defence (BMD) capabilities. Here *Decatur* (DDG-73) fires a Standard SM-3 missile at a ballistic missile target during a June 2007 test. *(US Navy)*

air picture architecture behaviour model and naval integrated fire control-counter air will provide better joint battlespace awareness, enabling weapons to be utilised to the full extent of their capabilities.

The DDG MOD HM&E and combat system phases will be accomplished separately on each ship, approximately two years apart. Although modernisation concentrates initially on Flight I and II ships (hulls 51–78), the intent is to extend the programme to the entire class. The HM&E upgrades have already been included in the latest new-construction *Arleigh Burke* destroyers (DDG-111 and 112) and, along with other combat system improvements, will be incorporated into the additional DDG-51s acquired in lieu of continued construction of the DDG-1000s.

Modernising the first eight CG-47s will cost an average of c.US$221m per ship, while modernising the DDG-51s will cost c.US$185m each (in FY2008 dollars).

Aegis BMD includes modifications to the Aegis weapons system and a hit-to-kill kinetic warhead for the Standard SM-3 surface-to-air missile. This gives

Aegis-equipped ships the capability to intercept short and medium-range ballistic missiles in the late-ascent, mid-course, and early-descent phases of exo-atmospheric trajectories. ABMD also provides surveillance and tracking capability against longer-range ballistic missile threats for cueing the national ballistic missile defence system. The US Missile Defense Agency and the navy first deployed the ABMD long-range surveillance and tracking capability as an element of the national BMD system in October 2004. On 20 February 2008, in Operation 'Burnt Frost', the *Lake Erie* (CG-70) launched a single modified SM-3 missile that intercepted an inactive US reconnaissance satellite at an altitude of 153 nautical miles and a closing speed greater than 22,000 miles per hour. Since the first Aegis BMD intercept test in January 2002 through to early 2009, the navy's element of the overall US BMD system has enjoyed outstanding success: sixteen target missile intercepts – fourteen with advanced mid-course-phase SM-3s and two with terminal-phase SM-2s – against only four misses.

As of mid-2009, three Aegis cruisers and fifteen destroyers have the latest iteration of the weapon system, Aegis BMD 3.6.1. The Aegis cruiser/destroyer modernisation programme will provide ABMD capability to all of the remaining Aegis destroyers and to selected Aegis cruisers beginning in 2012. On 6 April 2009, Secretary Gates confirmed the decision to add US$700m in FY2010 to field more of 'our most capable theater missile defense systems', the terminal High Altitude Area Defense System and SM-3 programmes, and US$200m to fund ABMD conversions in six additional Aegis warships.

SURFACE COMBATANTS: *ZUMWALT* (DDG-1000) AND CG(X) CLASSES

The DDG-1000 multi-mission destroyers are designed to provide precision strike and sustained volume fires to support joint forces inland and conduct independent attacks against land targets. Named after former Chief of Naval Operations Admiral Elmo R Zumwalt, DDG-1000s will be armed with the advanced gun system, which fires precision-guided long-range land-attack projectiles. For even longer-range strike missions, DDG-1000s will carry Tactical Tomahawk missiles housed in a peripheral vertical launch system (PVLS) that enhances the ships' passive protection compared to the legacy Mk-41 VLS. The PVLS is also capable of launching Standard and Evolved Sea Sparrow missiles.

DDG-1000's capabilities in undersea, surface and air warfare will provide enhanced performance in the littoral environment and the ship will have multi-spectral (radar, infrared, acoustic, magnetic and visual) signature reduction to render it significantly less detectable to adversaries than currently in-service surface warships of any navy. The design features an integrated power system to provide power for advanced electric-drive propulsion systems as well as high-powered combat systems and ship-service loads. This will be important once the navy begins to field electro-magnetic rail guns.

The ship's dual-band radar suite comprises the SPY-3 multi-function (MFR) and volume-search (VSR) phased-array radars. The SPY-3 is an X-band radar designed to meet all horizon-search and fire-control requirements for future ship classes, including CVN-21 carriers. The MFR can target the most advanced anti-ship cruise missiles and support fire-control requirements for the SM-2, ESSM and future missiles. The VSR is an S-band radar designed to meet all above-horizon detection and tracking requirements, replacing the functions of in-service three-dimensional and two-dimensional radars.

Other DDG-1000 features include an advanced hull form, optimal manning based on comprehensive human-systems integration and human-factors engineering and design studies, extensive automation, and advanced apertures. An open-architecture distributed combat system will support a 'plug-and-fight' environment. Once validated onboard DDG-1000, key technologies will be incorporated into future other surface combatants. By mid-2009, the programme had successfully completed nine out of ten engineering development models for new technologies and is transitioning those technologies into production.

At a 31 July 2008 US Congressional hearing, however, the USN announced a major change in the service's destroyer programmes: the service no longer wanted to acquire additional *Zumwalt* destroyers beyond the first two or three and, instead, sought procurement of eight more *Arleigh Burke* destroyers

An impression of two DDG-1000 (*Zumwalt* class) destroyers in company. Designed to provide precision strike and sustained fire support for forces ashore, only three will be built. (*US Navy*)

through to FY2015. Up to mid-summer 2008, the navy had been steadfast in its support for the DDG-1000. An initial objective of thirty-two DDG-1000s had been planned. However, as fiscal realities and force structure reassessments subsequently reshaped the navy's programmes, the buy dwindled to twenty-four, twelve, and ultimately just seven ships.

In February 2008, the navy awarded US$1.3bn contracts to each of Northrop Grumman and Bath Iron Works to build the two lead ships under a unique approach that would have seen as much competition as possible for the five ships then remaining in the programme. Partial funding was later approved for the third ship. Now that the programme has been curtailed at three ships, the navy wants to build all three at Bath Iron Works, whilst Northrop Grumman will build the additional DDG-51s. The approximate delivery cost of the first two *Zumwalt*s is US$3.2bn each. The third DDG-1000 should cost approximately US$2.8bn, only slightly more than the new DDG-51s.

The Next-Generation Guided Missile Cruiser, CG(X), is envisaged as a highly capable, multi-mission combatant tailored for air and missile defence and joint-service air-control operations. Programme materials also note that CG(X) is to provide maritime dominance, independent command and control and forward presence and will operate both 'independently and as an integral component of joint and combined forces'. As many as nineteen ships had been identified as follow-ons to the *Ticonderoga* class cruisers that will reach the end

of their thirty-year service lives from 2016. The navy continues to refine the concept and has directed an Analysis of Alternatives (AoA), which reportedly identifies a preferred hull alternative – based on the DDG-1000 hull – and examines trade-offs among propulsion, defence systems, sensors, other combat systems, employment and cost, including a nuclear-powered variant.

In spring 2009, however, the Chief of Naval Operations explained his decision to slow the CG(X) programme. 'The whole thing is, what does this ship have to be?' Admiral Gary Roughead asked reporters in late April. 'To me, to go charging off designing a ship that's not going to be inexpensive – because ships of that nature are not going to be inexpensive – without a full appreciation of the architecture in which it has to fit, which then drives your radar capability, which then drives the amount of power you need to be able to put in the ship, which then gets down to fundamental questions of how you provide that energy.' He continued, 'I mean, here we were charging off to design a ship that we didn't even know how it was going to fit in the whole scheme.'

In addition to slowing down the CG(X), the navy has also begun studies to address a 'future surface combatant' that might be pursued after the final DDG-51s are funded.

SURFACE COMBATANTS:
LITTORAL COMBAT SHIP (LCS)

This is another element of what the USN has called the 'SC-21' surface combatant 'family of ships' for the twenty-first century. As the service refocused attention in the littorals, it became apparent that various 'anti-access' capabilities – quiet diesel submarines, naval mines, and small, highly manoeuvrable surface-attack craft – offered great potential for many less-capable countries and non-state actors to prevent US forces from unhindered use of littorals. The LCS programme has thus been designed to address these and other threats in several 'focused-mission' concepts. (See the author's article on LCS-1 *Freedom* for more discussion.)

EXPEDITIONARY WARSHIPS:
MAJOR UNITS

The *Wasp* (LHD-1) class lies at the heart of the USN's and Marine Corps' expeditionary capability. It comprises eight multi-purpose amphibious assault ships whose primary mission is to provide embarked commanders with command and control capabilities for sea-based manoeuvre/assault operations, as well as deploying elements of a landing force through a combination of helicopters and amphibious vehicles. The class has several secondary missions, including power projection, sea control and humanitarian assistance and disaster response. The ships increase total lift capacity by providing a flight deck for helicopters and vertical/short take-off or landing (V/STOL) aircraft, such as the AV-8B Harrier and the MV-22 Osprey and a well deck for both air-cushioned and conventional landing craft.

Seven LHDs have been commissioned to date. In April 2002, a construction contract was awarded for the *Makin Island* (LHD-8), which incorporates significant design changes including gas-turbine propulsion and all-electric auxiliary equipment. Built by Northrop Grumman Ship Systems Pascagoula, *Makin Island* was delivered on 16 April 2009. Commissioning is planned for October 2009.

The *Wasp* class is supplemented by the *San Antonio* (LPD-17) amphibious transport dock, which is optimised for operational flexibility and designed to meet Marine Air-Ground Task Force (MAGTF) lift requirements. Characteristics include 25,000 square feet of space for vehicles (more than twice that of the *Austin* LPD-4 class it replaces), 34,000 cubic feet for cargo, accommodation for c.720 troops (800 in surge conditions) and a medical facility. The aft well deck can launch and recover traditional surface assault craft, as well as two landing craft air cushion (LCAC) vehicles that can transport cargo, personnel, Marine vehicles and tanks. Aviation facilities include a hangar and flight deck to operate and maintain a variety of aircraft, including current and future rotary-wing aircraft. Other advanced features include the advanced composite-material enclosed mast/sensor for reduced signatures and sensor maintenance, other stealth enhancements, state-of-the-art C4ISR and self-defence systems, a Shipboard Wide-Area Network (SWAN) that links shipboard systems and embarked Marine Corps platforms, and significant quality of life improvements.

The initial contract award to design and build the lead unit of the ten-ship class was awarded to the Avondale-Bath Alliance in December 1996. Because of cost increases, poor workmanship and schedule delays, the navy transferred LPD-17 class workload to then-Ingalls Shipbuilding (now part of Northrop Grumman) in June 2002. The navy commissioned the lead ship on 14 January 2006, awarding a

The *Wasp* class amphibious assault ships are at the heart of the United States' expeditionary capability. This is the seventh class member, *Iwo Jima* (LHD-7), in September 2008. *(US Navy)*

An early graphic of the LHA(R) amphibious assault warship replacement design. Now designated *America* (LHA-6), more recent images suggest she will be closer to the final modified *Wasp* class ship, *Makin Island* (LLHD-8), in general appearance – but without the LHD's well-deck. *(US Navy)*

The *Wasp* class is supplemented by the *San Antonio* class amphibious transport dock. The lead ship, *San Antonio*, suffered from serious quality problems but the programme is now seeing some improvement. *(US Navy)*

Expeditionary warfare requires substantial investment in support capabilities. This is *Lewis and Clark* (T-AKE-1), the first of fourteen dry cargo and ammunition replenishment vessels. *(US Navy)*

contract to Norfolk Shipbuilding and Drydock Company on 27 January for post-shakedown availability. Work was expected to be complete by April. However, on 22 June 2007, the Secretary of the Navy wrote to Northrop Grumman outlining numerous problems with the ship, stating: 'Twenty-three months after commissioning of LPD-17, the Navy still does not have a mission-capable ship.'

Rear Admiral William Landay, Programme Executive Officer Ships, acknowledged the challenges in May 2009: '... We're starting to really get the benefit of what we've learned in those early ones, and we are seeing some improvements there.' As of early 2009, LPD-17, 18 and 19 had been delivered, with LPDs 20 through to 24 under construction.

The next-generation LHA(R) amphibious assault warship replacement will provide forward-presence and power-projection capabilities as elements of US expeditionary strike groups and strike forces. The LHA(R) will embark, deploy, land, control, support and operate helicopters, landing craft and

amphibious vehicles in support of sustained operations. It will also support contingency-response, forcible-entry and power-projection operations as an integral part of naval, joint, interagency and multinational maritime expeditionary forces. The first LHA(R) is being designed as a variant of the *Makin Island* and will include LHD-8 enhancements (e.g., a gas-turbine propulsion plant and all-electric auxiliaries) and other significant improvements (e.g. upgraded aviation facilities, space for a staff group and greater survivability). The lead LHA(R) was designated LHA-6 in August 2005. The navy began procurement of long-lead time fiscal year 2005, and LHA-6 construction started in December 2008 at Northrop Grumman Ship Systems, Pascagoula. Delivery is scheduled for FY2012.

The LCC(R) command ship replacement will replace the afloat command and control (C^2) capability provided by the two current *Blue Ridge* (LCC-19) class ships. It will support the full range of C^2 missions and functions of a maritime operations

centre in support of the forward-deployed fleet commanders, joint force maritime component commander, and combined joint task force. The in-theatre C^2 capability this programme will provide will be key to supporting commanders' staff's presence, persistence and speed of decision.

In similar fashion to the Aegis cruiser/destroyer modernisation programmes, the navy has put in place a series of mid-life improvements for its expeditionary forces. In almost every instance, it is more cost-effective to upgrade an in-service ship than it is to construct a new one. The *Whidbey Island* (LSD 41) / *Harpers Ferry* (LSD-49) classes will therefore be subject to major upgrades, with the goal of keeping the ships in service through to 2038. Ultimately, all twelve LSD-class ships will undergo a nine-month availability that includes major upgrades to the ship-control system, local area network, and machinery-control system, as well as replacement of the ships' boilers and evaporators with an all-electric services systems. The ships will be joined by the *Wasp* class and remaining *Tarawa* class (LHA-1) amphibious assault ships in a similar mid-life upgrade programme.

EXPEDITIONARY WARSHIPS AND VESSELS: OTHER UNITS

Effective mine-countermeasures capabilities are a key requirement of expeditionary amphibious warfare. The USN is particularly mindful of the fact that fifteen of the nineteen US warships sunk or severely damaged since October 1945 have been victims of naval mines. As the fleet transitions from a 'dedicated' mine-countermeasures force to an 'organic' capability focused on the LCS, it is important to keep 'in-service' ships capable of countering these 'weapons that wait'. Speaking at the May 2009 Mine Warfare Association conference, Admiral Jon Greenert, Commander, US Fleet Forces Command, stated, '...the bottom line is: mines are relevant and mines are a threat. The way ahead is one of going from platform-centric to organic systems. And the littoral combat ship is the means by which we're going to employ this. We have to sustain, but we have to maintain our current assets too. And most importantly, we cannot lose sight of the progress we've made.' The navy's fourteen *Avenger* (MCM-1) class surface mine countermeasures (SMCM) ships are one element of the current US mine-countermeasures 'triad' that also includes mine-countermeasures helicopters and explosive ordnance disposal divers.

The SMCM MOD programme is correcting the most significant maintenance and obsolescence issues in order to maintain the ships through their full thirty-year service lives. The MCM-1 class modernisation programme commenced in FY2004 and will complete during 2010.

Expeditionary warfare also requires substantial investment in support capabilities and prepositioning capabilities.[1] The *Lewis and Clark*-class (T-AKE-1) dry cargo and ammunition ships replace the *Kilauea* (T-AE-26), *Mars* (T-AFS-1) and *Sirius* (T-AFS-8) fleet auxiliary classes, all of which are nearing the ends of their service lives. T-AKEs provide logistic lift of supplies, transferring cargo at sea to station ships that serve the combat forces; they also work in concert with a fleet oiler (T-AO) as a substitute station ship. T-AKE ships are built to commercial standards and crewed by MSC civilian mariners, augmented by military personnel as required. An embarked aviation detachment provides vertical underway replenishment capability. In December 2008 the navy awarded General Dynamics National Steel and Shipbuilding Company a contract for long-lead-time material for the last two of fourteen hulls, which are to be fully funded in FY2010.

The Joint High-Speed Vessel (JHSV) is an intra-theatre lift capability. The programme resulted from the merger of the US Army's Theatre Support Vessel (TSV) and the navy's High-Speed Connector programmes to maximise common capabilities and form a joint platform solution, with the navy designated as lead department. Experiments, exercises and real-world operations using leased high-speed vessels – *Joint Venture* (HSV-X1), *Swift* (HSV-2) and *West Pac Express* (HSV-4676) – have demonstrated their ability to embark and transport combat forces rapidly. The JHSV is not an assault platform, but provides intra-theatre lift capability for company-sized units, including personnel, equipment and supplies in support of global crisis-response and combat operations and theatre security co-operation plans. Design and cost analysis of the JHSV is ongoing, but the leased vessels are capable of speeds in excess of 40 knots and ranges greater than 1,200 nautical miles fully loaded. In addition, the shallow draft will enable the JHSV to operate effectively in littoral areas and access small, austere ports. A lead-ship ship design and construction contract will be awarded in 2009 for a 2011 delivery; in the meantime, the navy plans to increase the commercial charter of JHSVs from two to four.

SUBMARINES

The *Ohio* (SSBN-726) class Trident fleet ballistic missile submarine (SSBN) is the navy's contribution to the US strategic deterrent strategy that includes US Air Force long-range manned bombers and land-based intercontinental ballistic missiles. Eighteen of the class were built by General Dynamics Electric Boat, entering service from November 1981. The final boat, *Louisiana* (SSBN-743), joined the fleet in September 1997. The first four *Ohio* SSBNs have subsequently been converted to enhanced land-attack, strike and special-forces platforms (see below).

Each of the fourteen in-service SSBNs is armed with the Trident II/D5 Submarine-Launched Ballistic Missile (SLBM) system. Trident SLBMs are capable of carrying Multiple Independently Targeted Re-entry Vehicles (MIRVs), with the total number of MIRVs and penetration aids governed by strategic arms control treaty requirements. The SSBNs are being recapitalised via a 27-month engineered refuelling overhaul that replenishes the nuclear reactor and refurbishes all major systems, allowing them to operate for an additional twenty years. The last SSBN refuelling/overhaul will begin in 2018.

Beginning in 2027, the fourteen *Ohio* class SSBNs will reach the ends of their useful lives at a rate of about one per year. The navy intends to replace the *Ohio* submarines with a follow-on SSBN, which will have strategic nuclear deterrence as the primary mission. An AoA is scheduled for completion in 2009.

The first four *Ohio* class submarines have been converted to nuclear-powered guided-missile submarines (SSGNs). They can carry up to 154 Tomahawk land attack missiles (TLAMs) for covert, large-volume precision strikes. Additionally, these submarines can support clandestine insertion and retrieval missions for as many as sixty-six special operations forces for extended periods of time. Operating with two 'Blue/Gold' crews, each SSGN can generate a 70 per cent in-theatre presence. With large payload capability and the flexibility of twenty-two, 7ft (2.1m) diameter reconfigurable missile tubes, these submarines will be able to transform

The first four *Ohio* class Trident ballistic missile submarines have been converted into nuclear-powered guided missile submarines. This is *Ohio* (SSGN-726). *(US Navy)*

Virginia (SSN-774) is the first of the US Navy's post-Cold War generation of nuclear-powered attack submarines. They are specifically designed for littoral and regional operations as well as traditional 'blue water' missions. *(General Dynamics Electric Boat)*

rapidly as a host for future payloads and sensors to combat the future threats. The *Ohio* (SSGN-726) completed the maiden fifteen-month SSGN deployment in December 2008.

In 2009 the US embarked on a Nuclear Posture Review, complementing the 2010 Quadrennial Defense Review, to address all aspects of the nation's strategic nuclear requirements and capabilities. This will, for example, provide significant input into the design and engineering of the next-generation SSBN. It might, as well, conclude that fewer than the current fourteen SSBNs are required to sustain effective nuclear deterrence – perhaps as few as ten. If so, there will certainly be calls for a follow-on SSGN programme to build on the success of the initial effort and convert the other – perhaps as many as four – SSBNs that could be retired earlier than previously planned.

The *Virginia* (SSN-774) class attack submarines are specifically designed for littoral and regional operations, as well as the performance of traditional open-ocean anti-submarine and anti-surface missions. They have advanced acoustic technology and are configured to conduct intelligence-collection and surveillance missions, special operations forces insertion/extraction, irregular/hybrid warfare, sea control, land attack and mine reconnaissance. The *Virginia* class is also configured to adapt easily to special missions and emerging requirements. A modular design facilitates technology insertion both in future ships during new-construction and existing ships, enabling the *Virginia* class submarines to keep pace with emerging threat capabilities throughout their thirty-year service lives.

The boats are built under a teaming arrangement between General Dynamics Electric Boat and Northrop Grumman Newport News. Using the modular construction process, each shipyard builds portions of each ship, with integration and delivery of completed submarines alternating between the two yards. Construction of *Virginia* began in fiscal year 1998, and the ship was commissioned in October 2004. Four additional *Virginia* class submarines were commissioned through to 2008 and SSN-779 will be delivered in 2009. Four more boats (SSNs 780 – 783) are under construction for delivery by 2013. In FY2009, the navy awarded a multi-year procurement contract for the *Virginia* class 'Block III' ships. These incorporate 'design for affordability' changes – the unit cost has been reduced to US$2bn – that include a redesigned bow replacing the spherical sonar array

with a large aperture bow array and substitutes twelve VLS tubes with two large-diameter launchers that can carry Tomahawk missiles or other payloads.

Two other attack submarine classes are in service. The *Los Angeles* (SSN-688/688I) class is the backbone of the submarine force. A total of sixty-two *Los Angeles* submarines were built in three successive designs: (1) SSNs 688 – 718, the original *Los Angeles* class; (2) SSNs 719 – 750 with twelve vertical-launch tubes for the Tomahawk missile, along with an upgraded reactor core; and (3) SSNs 751-773 – dubbed '688I' for 'improved' – that are quieter, incorporate an advanced BSY-1 sonar suite combat system, can launch mines from their torpedo tubes (although the USN's obsolete submarine-launched mines have been taken out of inventory) and are configured for under-ice operations.

The USN also has three *Seawolf* (SSN-21) class submarines, designed as a replacement to the *Los Angeles* submarines and as a response to the high-speed/deep-diving Soviet 'Akula' class. Commissioned in July 1997, *Seawolf* is exceptionally quiet (said to be quieter at tactical speeds than a *Los Angeles* SSN pierside), fast, well armed, and equipped with advanced sensors. Though lacking vertical launch systems, the class has eight 26in (660mm) torpedo tubes that can also launch Tomahawk cruise missiles and can hold up to fifty weapons in the torpedo room. The third ship of the class, *Jimmy Carter* (SSN-23), has a 100ft (48m) hull extension called the multi-mission platform. This hull section provides for additional payload to accommodate advanced technology for classified research and development and for enhanced warfighting capabilities. Originally twenty-nine SSN-21s were planned but with the end of the Cold War and a search for 'peace dividends' in the US defence budget, the US$3.5bn unit cost was unaffordable. The USN therefore turned to the smaller and less expensive 'post-Cold War' *Virginia* class submarines.

CONCLUSION: THE WAY AHEAD

With its electoral mandate for far-reaching change, the still-new administration of President Barack Obama has challenged the US Department of Defense to 'take this moment both to rebuild our military and to prepare it for the missions of the future'. For the navy, there are growing tensions and fault lines within and outside the service – particularly with the US Congress – with regard to in-service and future assets needed for traditional, irregular, and 'hybrid' conflicts and all the other capabilities that a modern naval force can provide, from ballistic missile defence of the homeland to humanitarian assistance halfway around the world.

Should the needed funding not become available for defence, as a result of a deepening recession and trillions of dollars going to stimulate the domestic economy, the course for the USN will be uncertain, at best... and the '313-Ship Fleet' ultimately consigned to history.

Notes

1. The Maritime Prepositioning Force (Future) (MPF(F)) squadron will be a key component of the USN's overall global prepositioning posture, providing capabilities beyond that of the in-service MSC maritime prepositioning squadron (MPSRON). Each full MPF(F) squadron will include three mobile landing platforms, three MPF(F) large medium-speed roll-on/roll-off ships, three auxiliary dry cargo/ammunition ships (T-AKE), three aviation-capable large-deck amphibious ships (LHA/D), and two legacy sealift ships.

2. The following are just some of a wide range of additional sources that provide useful supplementary information on current US Navy programmes:

– Frank Hoffman, *From Preponderance to Partnerships: American Maritime Power in the 21st Century* (Washington, DC, Center for a New American Security, November 2008).

– Hans Ulrich Kaeser, *Abandon Ships: The Costly Illusion of Unaffordable Transformation* (Washington, DC, Center for Strategic and International Studies, August 2008).

– Statement of Ronald O'Rourke, Specialist in Naval Affairs, Congressional Research Service, before the House Armed Services Committee, Subcommittee on Seapower and Expeditionary Forces, Hearing on Future Requirements and Capabilities of US Maritime Forces, 26 March 2009 (Washington DC, United States House of Representatives, 2009).

– Robert O Work, *The US Navy: Charting a Course for Tomorrow's Fleet* (Washington, DC, Center for Strategic and Budgetary Assessments, 2008).

– Fiscal Year 2010 Budget Request (Washington, DC, United States Department of Defense, Office of the Under Secretary of Defence (Comptroller), May 2009).

2.2 WORLD FLEET REVIEWS
ASIA AND THE PACIFIC
Regional Review

Author: **Conrad Waters**

See page 12

As heralded in the Introduction, it is the major Asian navies that have achieved the most significant progress of all the regional naval forces in recent years. To a large extent this reflects increased local prosperity arising from the wholesale outsourcing of manufacturing from the developed economies to 'low-cost' producers, a shift that has also significantly enhanced the importance of Asia's maritime trade routes. Local tensions have also played a part. Widespread regional concerns about the potential threat posed by a resurgent China are one aspect of these but the impact of other longstanding rivalries should not be overlooked. For example, neighbours Japan and South Korea have not always shared a happy history, whilst the unpredictable intentions of nuclear-armed North Korea are also a material factor. To date, the influence of increased expenditure on enhanced naval capabilities has been largely felt at a regional level, with global presence limited to the occasional flag-waving training cruise. However, this is starting to change. A notable development was China's decision at the end of 2008 to send a naval task group comprising the Type 052B destroyer *Wuhan*, her Type 052C half-sister *Haikou* and the replenishment ship *Weishanhu* to the Horn of Africa to combat pirate attacks on Chinese merchant shipping. The initial deployment – followed by a successor in April 2009 – has proved the People's Liberation Army Navy's (PLAN) ability to operate at distance from its home bases and could herald a broader shift in policy. The Somali pirate threat has also provided the catalyst for other leading Asian fleets to spread their wings. For example, Malaysia, Singapore and South Korea have all recently supplemented Japan's longer standing regional presence with their own anti-piracy deployments.

The Introduction also referenced the fact that – to date – the majority of fleet modernisation in the Asia-Pacific area has relied on imported technology. This has included such cutting-edge weaponry as the US Aegis combat system and German air-independent propulsion (AIP) equipment. However, much construction has taken place in local yards, with the larger naval powers such as China and Korea joining Japan in adapting their market-leading merchant shipbuilding expertise for construction of increasingly sophisticated warships. Other countries, for example Singapore and Malaysia, are also actively encouraging local fabrica-

tion. The proficiency of the region's shipyards has certainly resulted in some rapid building times for simpler designs, although there is evidence that more experience might be needed before the construction of the most complex warships is wholly successful. It also seems likely that the next decade will see greater attention being given to the development of indigenous designs and associated weapons systems, an area where China – with its limited access to Western technology – appears to be taking the lead.

Table 2.2.1 provides details of regional fleet strengths as at the middle of 2009.

Opposite, above: South Korea is one of a number of Asian navies that have been steadily building up 'blue water' naval capabilities. Pictured here is the Aegis-equipped KDX-III *Sejongdaewang-Ham* class destroyer, arguably the most advanced and powerful warship to have been constructed in Asia to date. *(Hyundai Heavy Industries)*

Table 2.2.1: FLEET STRENGTHS IN ASIA AND THE PACIFIC – LARGER NAVIES (MID-2009)

COUNTRY	AUSTRALIA	CHINA	INDONESIA	JAPAN	KOREA S	SINGAPORE	TAIWAN	THAILAND
Support/Helicopter Carrier (CVS/CVH)	–	–	–	1	–	–	–	1
Strategic Missile Submarine (SSBN)	–	3	–	–	–	–	–	–
Attack Submarine (SSN)	–	5	–	–	–	–	–	–
Patrol Submarine (SSK/SS)	6	55	2	16	11	4	4	–
Fleet Escort (DDG/FFG)	12	45	6	43	19	6	26	8
Patrol Escort/Corvette (FFG/FSG/FS)	–	30	24	8	28	6	–	11
Missile Armed Attack Craft (PGG/PTG)	–	65	4	6	1	–	50	6
Mine Countermeasures Vessel (MCMV)	6	20	12	29	9	4	12	6
Major Amphibious Units (LHD/ LPD/ LSD)	–	1	3	3	1	4	1	–

Note: Chinese numbers approximate

MAJOR REGIONAL NAVAL POWERS – AUSTRALIA

The smallest but arguably the most proficient of the major Asian naval powers, the Royal Australian Navy (RAN) is currently centred on a balanced fleet of surface escorts and patrol submarines. These front-line units are supplemented by an extensive flotilla of patrol vessels used to police the country's vast offshore waters. Principal units are listed in Table 2.2.2. The fleet awaits a significant upgrade to its capabilities that will emerge as a result of decisions first taken almost a decade ago under the 2000 Defence White Paper and subsequently affirmed in the 2006–16 Defence Capability Plan. The key

elements of this enhancement are the domestic construction of three air-defence destroyers under project SEA 4000 and the acquisition of two new amphibious assault ships under project JP2048 (phase 4A/B), the latter meeting an enhanced amphibious requirement first defined in the 2003 Strategic Review. Both of these projects are being implemented in close collaboration with Spanish shipbuilder Navantia.

The three destroyers will be built to a modified version of the *Armada Española*'s F-100 air-defence frigate design, with delivery planned between 2013 and 2017 under a contract reported to be worth around A$8bn (US$6.4bn equivalent). The overall

project is in the hands of the Air Warfare Destroyer (AWD) Alliance of ASC and Raytheon Australia. It was decided at an early stage that the US Aegis system would provide the heart of the ships' air-defence capabilities, with a competition subsequently being run between an evolved version of the USN's *Arleigh Burke* (DDG-51) destroyer designed by Gibbs & Cox and the existing F-100 type to determine the most effective solution for Australia's needs. Although the RAN reportedly favoured the modified *Burke* on the basis of its enhanced air-defence missile and helicopter capacity, the lower costs and risks associated with the existing ship eventually won the day. The selection of the Navantia design was announced on 20 June 2007 and the relevant technology transfer agreements – worth €285m to the Spanish shipyard – were subsequently signed in October of that year. The new destroyers, to be named *Hobart*, *Brisbane* and *Sydney,* will have a full load displacement of around 6,000 tons and incorporate a number of detailed improvements over the Spanish vessels. A decision on whether to exercise an option on a fourth vessel remains pending.

The new LHD-type amphibious assault ships are based on Navantia's 27,000-ton *Juan Carlos I* strategic protection ship. Designed to transport and deploy a landing force of c.1,000 troops by helicopter or watercraft, the ships feature a full-length helicopter deck and aft well dock. In contrast to the AWD build strategy, the majority of work under the A$3bn (US$2.4bn) contract will be carried out at the Spanish company's Ferrol shipyard. BAE Systems Australia will fabricate the superstructure and conduct final outfit at their Williamstown facility. Construction of the initial ship – to be named *Canberra* – commenced on 23 September 2008, with delivery scheduled for early 2014. Under current plans she will be followed by sister-ship *Adelaide* in the following year.

The RAN's longer-term future was set out in the Australian government's defence white paper – 'Defending Australia in the Asia-Pacific Century: Force 2030' – published on 2 May 2009.[1] Intended principally to respond to the emergence of new regional rivals to the pre-eminence of Australia's key ally – the United States – it commits to funding sustained increases in the country's defence capabilities over the next decades. Key elements of an ambitious forward maritime programme included formal confirmation of plans to double the size of the submarine fleet to twelve boats through construction

The most significant Australian naval construction project is the A$8bn programme for the *Hobart* class air warfare destroyer. Navantia's F-100 design has been chosen for this three-ship class, which will be built in Australia by the AWD Alliance. *(AWD Alliance)*

Table 2.2.2: ROYAL AUSTRALIAN NAVY: PRINCIPAL UNITS AS AT MID-2009

TYPE	CLASS	NUMBER	TONNAGE	DIMENSIONS	PROPULSION	CREW	DATE
Principal Surface Escorts							
Frigate – FFG	ADELAIDE (FFG-7)	4	4,100 tons	138m x 14m x 8m	COGAG, 30 knots	220	1980
Frigate – FFG	ANZAC	8	3,600 tons	118m x 15m x 4m	CODOG, 28 knots	175	1996
Submarines							
Submarine – SSK	COLLINS	6	3,350 tons	78m x 8m x 7m	Diesel-electric, 20 knots	45	1996

Submarines form an important part of the Royal Australian Navy's capabilities. This image shows three of the six *Collins* class submarines on surface passage. *(Royal Australian Navy)*

Table 2.2.3: PROJECTED ROYAL AUSTRALIAN NAVY DEVELOPMENT (2010-30)

SHIP TYPE	NUMBER: 2010	NUMBER: 2030
Destroyer – DDG	0	3 (+1 option)
Frigate – FFG	12	8
Patrol Submarine – SSK	6	12
Multirole Offshore Patrol Vessel – OPV	0	20
Major Amphibious Vessel – LHD	0	2
Other Amphibious Vessel	3	1
Coastal Patrol Vessel– PB	14	0
Mine Warfare & Survey Vessels	8	0

of a new class of patrol submarine in replacement for the existing *Collins* vessels. In addition, the current *Anzac* class patrol frigates will eventually be replaced by larger escorts optimised for anti-submarine operations on a one-for-one basis. A new class of around twenty modularised offshore combatant vessels will also be built to rationalise the current disparate fleet of mine-countermeasures, hydrographic and patrol forces. The latter will displace up to 2,000 tons and appear remarkably similar in concept to the British Royal Navy's C3 variant of the FSC future surface combatant.[2] By 2030 the RAN should have evolved

The Royal Australian Navy operates an extensive force of patrol vessels to oversee its vast offshore waters. Here the *Armidale* class vessels *Maryborough* and *Albany* are seen operating in company. They will ultimately be replaced by a class of larger, modularised offshore combatants. *(Royal Australian Navy)*

towards the force structure set out in Table 2.2.3.

Although the outlook for Australia's maritime power is therefore broadly positive, the current day is not without its challenges. Somewhat ironically given the future focus on underwater assets, the state of the existing submarine force has, in particular, given rise to considerable public concern. A significant shortage of trained submariners has resulted in a marked decline in overall force readiness, whilst the influential *Jane's Defence Weekly* has reported problems with the availability of pressurised submarine escape training and deep-sea rescue assets. The current surface flotilla is also seeing heavy utilisation given ongoing commitments to the maintenance of stability in the Persian Gulf as a broader part of the largely Afghanistan-focused Operation 'Slipper', commitments which have recently been extended to support a contribution to international anti-piracy operations off the Horn of Africa. Some respite is being provided by the long-awaited return to the fleet of the remaining four FFG-7 class frigates. These have been upgraded with the installation of new surveillance, fire control and sonar systems, a vertical launch system for the Evolved Sea Sparrow Missile (ESSM) and modification of the existing Mk13 launcher to allow use of the Standard SM-2 anti-aircraft missile under Project SEA 1390. The final ship in the programme, *Newcastle*, was subject to provisional acceptance on 29 May 2009, paving the way for project completion at the year-end. Focus will then shift to modernisation of the *Anzac* class's anti-missile defences. This will begin with commencement of work on *Perth* in 2010.

MAJOR REGIONAL NAVAL POWERS – CHINA

The PLAN appears to be experiencing something of a pause in its long-term development plans after a previous phase of rapid technological and capability expansion. After commissioning no less than six new destroyers in three classes over a three-year period, the focus of attention in respect of the surface fleet appears to have turned to recapitalising the lower-profile but more numerically significant frigate fleet with series production of the Type 054A 'Jiangkai-II' frigate design. Four of this class had entered service by the end of 2008 and additional units are under construction at shipyards in Shanghai and Guangzhou. This will doubtless allow withdrawal or re-designation of the increasingly obsolescent earlier Type 053H and Type 053H1 members of the

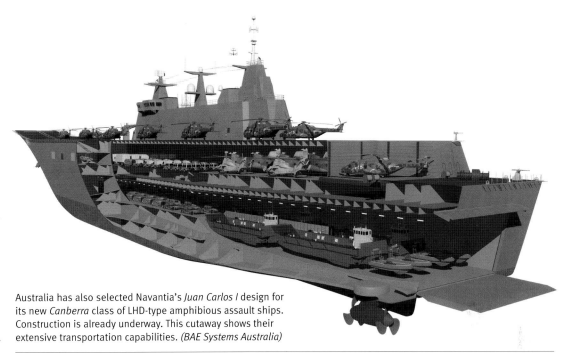

Australia has also selected Navantia's *Juan Carlos I* design for its new *Canberra* class of LHD-type amphibious assault ships. Construction is already underway. This cutaway shows their extensive transportation capabilities. *(BAE Systems Australia)*

'Jiangu' class, two of which have already been transferred to coast guard service. Whilst additional destroyers are expected in due course, the current hiatus could be explained by a desire to assess the relative effectiveness of the recent designs that have been put into service.

The 60th anniversary fleet review on 23 April 2009 provided an opportunity for China to showcase its submarine technology, including the first public appearance of its nuclear boats. New designs of nuclear-powered ballistic missile (SSBN), nuclear-powered attack (SSN) and conventionally-powered patrol (SSK) submarines have all entered service over the last decade and ongoing construction is reported. Public pronouncements also make it clear that China intends to deploy aircraft carriers in due course, albeit the status of the former Soviet carrier *Varyag* remains subject to considerable conjecture. Reports at the start of May 2009 indicated that, after a considerable period of inactivity, the ship had been returned to dry dock in the Dalian facility where she has been berthed for the last few years. This could herald a new phase in the ship's refurbishment, including the possible installation of propulsion machinery.

Also subject to conjecture are the longer-term aims behind China's broadly expansionary maritime strategy. The current emphasis on anti-piracy operations certainly suggests that improved Sea Lines of Communication (SLOC) protection capabilities are an important consideration. This certainly ties in with the fundamental importance of maritime trade to China's export-driven economy. However, incidents such as the harassment of the unarmed US ocean surveillance ship *Impeccable* by Chinese naval vessels in international waters off Hainan Island suggest the possibility of a more assertive stance being taken by certain elements in the military in due course.

Chapter 2.2A provides an in-depth assessment of

Whilst China's naval expansion is currently focused on protecting its trade routes, it is capable of taking a more assertive role. This is a picture of the US ocean surveillance ship *Impeccable* (T-AGOS-23) being harassed by Chinese 'fishing vessels' in international waters. *(US Navy)*

Table 2.2.4: PEOPLE'S LIBERATION ARMY NAVY: PRINCIPAL UNITS AS AT MID-2009

TYPE	CLASS	NUMBER	TONNAGE	DIMENSIONS	PROPULSION	CREW	DATE
Principal Surface Escorts							
Destroyer – DDG	Type 051C SHENYANG ('Luzhou')	2	7,100 tons	155m x 17m x 6m	Steam, 29 knots	Unknown	2006
Destroyer – DDG	Type 052C LANZHOU ('Luyang II')	2	6,500 tons	154m x 17m x 6m	CODOG, 28 knots	280	2004
Destroyer – DDG	Type 052B GUANGZHOU ('Luyang I')	2	6,000 tons	154m x 17m x 6m	CODOG, 29 knots	280	2004
Destroyer – DDG	Project 956E/EM HANGZHOU (Sovremenny)	4	8,000 tons	156m x 17m x 7m	Steam, 32 knots	300	1999
Destroyer – DDG	Type 051B SHENZHEN ('Luhai')	1	6,000 tons	154m x 16m x 6m	Steam, 31 knots	250	1998
Destroyer – DDG	Type 052 HARBIN ('Luhu')	2	4,800 tons	143m x 15m x 5m	CODOG, 31 knots	260	1994
Plus c. 12 additional obsolescent destroyers of Type 051 JINAN ('Luda') class							
Frigate – FFG	Type 054A XUZHOU ('Jiangkai II')	4	4,100 tons	132m x 15m x 5m	CODAD, 28 knots	190	2008
Frigate – FFG	Type 054 MA'ANSHAN ('Jiangkai I')	2	4,000 tons	132m x 15m x 5m	CODAD, 28 knots	190	2005
Frigate – FFG	Type 053 H2G/H3 ANQING ('Jiangwei I/II')	14	2,500 tons	112m x 12m x 5m	CODAD, 27 knots	170	1992
Frigate – FFG	Type 053 H/H1/H1G/H2 CHANGDE ('Jianghu')	28	1,800 tons	103m x 11m x 3m	Diesel, 26 knots	200	1974
Submarines							
Submarine – SSBN	Type 094 ('Jin')	2	9,000 tons	133m x 11m x 8m	Nuclear, 20+ knots	Unknown	2008
Submarine – SSBN	Type 092 XIA ('Xia')	1	6,500 tons	120m x 10m x 8m	Nuclear, 22 knots	140	1987
Submarine – SSN	Type 093 ('Shang')	2	6,000 tons	107m x 11m x 8m	Nuclear, 30 knots	100	2006
Submarine – SSN	Type 091 ('Han')	3	5,500 tons	106m x 10m x 7m	Nuclear, 25 knots	75	1974
Submarine – SSK	Type 039A/Type 041 ('Yuan')	2	2,500 tons	75m x 8m x 5m	AIP, 20+ knots	Unknown	2006'
Submarine – SSK	Type 039/039G ('Song')	16	2,300 tons	75m x 8m x 5m	Diesel-electric, 22 knots	60	1999
Submarine – SSK	Project 877 EKM/636 ('Kilo')	12	3,000 tons	73m x 10m x 7m	Diesel-electric, 20 knots	55	1995

Plus c. 25 obsolescent patrol submarines of the Project 033 ('Romeo' Class) and Type 035 ('Ming' Class) designs.

the PLAN's recent development and current key force structure. An overview of current principal units is set out in Table 2.2.4.

MAJOR REGIONAL NAVAL POWERS – JAPAN

Although forced to maintain a broadly low-key role by nature of Japan's post-war pacifist constitution, the Japan Maritime Self Defence Force (JMSDF) has historically been the dominant local Asian naval power. Traditionally focused on anti-submarine warfare in defence of Japan's extensive maritime trade, the JMSDF has increasingly assumed a wider range of responsibilities, not least a theatre ballistic missile defence (TBMD) role as a result of the emergence of North Korea's nuclear weapons ambitions.

Current fleet structure is governed by the *Mid Term Defense Program (FY2005-FY-2009)*. This was published in December 2004 and is therefore due for imminent review. The programme places particular emphasis on the four eight-strong fleet escort flotillas. Each of these includes one helicopter-carrying destroyer (DDH) and at least one Aegis-equipped air-defence vessel. It is envisaged that these

vessels will form the core components of two more deployable four-ship sub-units in each flotilla. The remaining surface escorts are allocated to the regional escort squadrons, which also have responsibility for the vast bulk of amphibious and mine-countermeasures assets. The submarine force comprises sixteen operational submarines, divided into two flotillas. A small number of additional submarines and surface ships are designated as training vessels, allowing the front line forces to be reinforced or replaced should the need arise. Table 2.2.5 provides a summary of principal fleet units.

The highlight of 2009 was undoubtedly the commissioning on 18 March of the helicopter-carrying destroyer *Hyuga* (DDH-181), essentially a through-deck helicopter carrier. Although heralded by some as marking a major extension of Japan's naval aviation capabilities, her primary mission is to act as a powerful anti-submarine command ship for an escort flotilla. Displacing around 18,000 tons at full load, she can operate up to eleven helicopters. However, her initial air group is more likely to comprise three SH-60 Seahawks in the anti-submarine role, together with an EH-101 Merlin for mine-countermeasures

duties. Other anti-submarine equipment includes a bow-mounted sonar and two triple 324mm torpedo tubes. *Hyuga* also has considerable close range air-defence capabilities in the form of a sixteen-cell Mk41 launcher for ESSM and two 20mm Phalanx close-in weapons systems (CIWS). The former is controlled by a locally-produced Melco FCS-3 phased array that shares much technology with the Thales APAR. Propulsion is by means of four GE LM-2500 gas turbines, which can produce a top speed in excess of 30 knots through two shafts. A sister-ship is already under construction for commissioning in 2011. It would seem that there will be a requirement for a total of four ships in the medium term given the need to replace the existing elderly *Haruna* (DDH-141) and *Shirane* (DDH-143) classes.

Although drawing less attention than *Hyuga*'s arrival, 2009 also saw a major reinforcement of the submarine flotillas with the commissioning of the first of a new class of air-independent propulsion (AIP) equipped boats, *Soryu* (SS-501), on 30 March. Essentially an improved and slightly enlarged variant of the previous *Oyashio* (SS-590), the new submarine is fitted with a licence-built version of Kockums'

Above: Traditionally focused on an anti-submarine warfare role, Japan's JMSDF continues to deploy considerable numbers of escort vessels, many of which are assigned to the fleet escort flotillas. Pictures here are the destroyers *Umigiri* and *Asagiri* – the latter re-designated as a training vessel – on a training cruise in European waters. *(Conrad Waters)*

Below: Japan commissioned its helicopter-carrying destroyer *Hyuga* (DDH-181) on 18 March 2009. Essentially a through-deck helicopter carrier, she is intended to act as a command ship for one of Japan's escort flotillas. *(JMSDF)*

Table 2.2.5: JAPAN MARITIME SELF-DEFENCE FORCE: PRINCIPAL UNITS AS AT MID-2009

TYPE	CLASS	NUMBER	TONNAGE	DIMENSIONS	PROPULSION	CREW	DATE
Support and Helicopter Carriers							
Helicopter Carrier – DDH	HYUGA (DDH-181)	1	18,000 tons	195m x 32m x 7m	COGAG, 30 knots	350	2009
Principal Surface Escorts							
Helicopter Destroyer – DDH	SHIRANE (DDH-143)	2	7,500 tons	159m x 18m x 5m	Steam, 31 knots	350	1980
Helicopter Destroyer – DDH	HARUNA (DDH-141)	1	6,900 tons	153m x 18m x 5m	Steam, 31 knots	370	1973
Destroyer – DDG	ATAGO (DDG-177)	2	10,000 tons	165m x 21m x 6m	COGAG, 30 knots	300	2007
Destroyer – DDG	KONGOU (DDG-173)	4	9,500 tons	161m x 21m x 6m	COGAG, 30 knots	300	1993
Destroyer – DDG	HATAKAZE (DDG-171)	2	6,250 tons	150m x 16m x 5m	COGAG, 30 knots	260	1986
Destroyer – DDG	TACHIKAZE (DDG-168)	1	5,500 tons	143m x 14m x 5m	Steam, 32 knots	250	1976
Destroyer – DDG	TAKANAMI (DD-110)	5	5,250 tons	151m x 17m x 5m	COGAG, 30 knots	175	2003
Destroyer – DDG	MURASAME (DD-101)	9	5,000 tons	151m x 17m x 5m	COGAG, 30 knots	165	1996
Destroyer – DDG	ASAGIRI (DD-151)	6 (2)	4,250 tons	137m x 15m x 5m	COGAG, 30 knots	220	1988
Destroyer – DDG	HATSUYUKI (DD-122)	11 (1)	3,750 tons	130m x 14m x 4m	COGOG, 30 knots	200	1982
Frigate – FFG	ABUKUMA (DE-229)	6	2,500 tons	109m x 13m x 4m	CODOG, 27 knots	120	1989
Frigate – FFG	YUBARI (DE-227)	2	1,750 tons	91m x 11m x 4m	CODOG, 25 knots	95	1983
Submarines							
Submarine – SSK	SORYU (SS-501)	1	4,200 tons	84m x 9m x 8m	AIP, 20 knots+	65	2009
Submarine – SSK	OYASHIO (SS-590)	11	4,000 tons	82m x 9m x 8m	Diesel-electric, 20 knots+	70	1998
Submarine – SSK	HARUSHIO (SS-583)	5 (2)	3,250 tons	77m x 10m x 8m	Diesel-electric, 20 knots+	75	1990
Major Amphibious Units							
Landing Platform Dock – LPD	OSUMI (LST-4001)	3	14,000 tons	178m x 26m x 6m	Diesel, 22 knots	135	1998

Note: Figures in brackets refer to trials or training ships.

Stirling AIP system. She can also be distinguished by an innovative X-shaped rudder, a design which is also Swedish in origin. At least four further boats have been authorised and the class could well prove to be an extended one.

Away from new construction, the most important current project is undoubtedly the ongoing modernisation of the four Aegis-equipped *Kongou* (DDG-173) class destroyers to enable them to deploy the Standard SM-3 missile in the TBMD role. Essentially locally built and modified versions of the USN's *Arleigh Burke* (DDG-51) vessels, the class are being updated at roughly yearly intervals to a similar specification to the United States' BMD-capable ships. *Kongou* – the first ship to be modified – carried out a successful interception of a ballistic missile target on 17 December 2007. However, a second trial involving her sister-ship *Chokai* (DDG-176) on 19 November 2008 ended in failure. According to the US journal *Defense Daily*, the mishap arose as a result of the SM-3 missile losing track of the target in the last seconds before interception. In spite of this, the combined USN/JMSDF record in ballistic missile intercept trials remains generally good and the project

is being given renewed momentum by the resumption of North Korean nuclear tests. Both *Kongou* and *Chokai* were deployed to protect the home islands alongside Japanese-based USN destroyers during North Korea's April 2009 rocket launch. Whilst the two later *Atago* (DDG-177) class Aegis ships are not yet part of the upgrade programme, it is likely that they will be added to its scope in due course.

There is some evidence that the JMSDF is suffering from a degree of strain from the recent expansion of its operations. In addition to the TBMD role described above, this broadening of the fleet's activities has included an ongoing presence in the Indian Ocean; initially in support of the US-led Operation 'Enduring Freedom' anti-terrorism mission but more recently also encompassing the anti-piracy crusade off the Horn of Africa. A series of mishaps during 2007–8 culminated in a fatal collision between the newly-commissioned *Atago* and a fishing boat that resulted in the dismissal of the then service head, Chief of Staff Admiral Eiji Yoshikawa. Disciplinary measures against other officers involved in the incident were confirmed in May 2009. Part of the problem appears to relate to difficulties in

recruiting sufficient personnel in a country where less prestige is attached to military service than elsewhere. Increasing the presence and duties of women in the force is seen as part of the solution. It is interesting to note that seventeen of *Hyuga*'s crew are female – a first for a JMSDF destroyer.

MAJOR REGIONAL NAVAL POWERS – SOUTH KOREA

The Republic of Korea Navy possibly suffers from the lowest profile of all the four major regional Asian powers. However, its transition to achieving 'blue water' maritime power has been the most marked. Assisted by a world-leading shipbuilding infrastructure, it has been steadily transformed from a local defence force almost totally reliant on second-hand US vessels to a powerful regional fleet capable of international deployments. A particular feature of the fleet's expansion has been a progressive increase in the use of indigenous equipment. An initial focus on the use of imported technology – and often designs – in locally-constructed ships is being increasingly superseded by the substitution of weapons systems developed in South Korean. Although the most advanced

Japan has modified the destroyer *Chokai* for the theatre ballistic missile defence (TBMD) role. Whilst a missile defence intercept test using a Standard SM-3 missile on 19 November 2008 ended in failure, Japan is pressing ahead with upgrading four Aegis-equipped destroyers for this mission. *(US Navy)*

fleet units such as the KDX-III air-defence destroyers and Type 214 AIP-equipped submarines are still heavily reliant on equipment sourced from overseas, indigenisation is a trend that is likely to continue.[3] Table 2.2.6 lists principal fleet components.

The key constituent of the surface fleet is a force of ten KDX (Korean destroyer experimental) guided-missile destroyers, which will soon be reinforced by a further two vessels currently under construction. Developed under a three phase programme, the three earliest KDX-1 *Gwanggaeto-daewang* class ships were built by Daewoo to a 4,000-ton general-purpose design and delivered from 1998 to 2000. They were succeeded by the larger, 5,500-ton KDX-II class, the first of which – *Chungmugong Yi Sun-Shin* – was commissioned in November 2003. Although retaining a general-purpose configuration, this design has more powerful air-defence capabilities, including a US Mk41 vertical launch system for thirty-two SM-2 medium range anti-aircraft missiles and both RAM and Goalkeeper CIWS. The sixth and final vessel in the class – *Choi Young* – entered service in September 2008. The following KDX-III

Sejongdaewang-Ham type has progressed to the use of Aegis technology and the resulting 10,000-ton vessels are amongst the most powerful in the region. The lead ship of an initial class of three – built by Hyundai Heavy Industries (HHI) – was formally commissioned on 22 December 2008 but had earlier made its presence felt at South Korea's second international fleet review in October. It subsequently performed well in detecting and tracking North Korea's April 2009 rocket launch, leading to hopes that the navy's long-held ambition for an additional three-vessel batch might find political support.

The balance of the surface escort force comprises nine frigates of the *Ulsan* class commissioned during 1991–3 and as many as twenty-four *Po Hang* corvettes. The former are to be replaced by a new 3,200-ton FFX-design, the first of which was ordered from HHI on 26 December 2008. Intended for anti-submarine and anti-surface warfare in the littoral, images suggest that the new design is a cut-down variant of the KDX-II type featuring a locally developed radar and combat system.

The development of the surface flotillas has been

matched by significant expenditure on underwater assets, possibly in response to North Korea's substantial submarine arm. The bulk of the current force is comprised of the nine German-designed Type 209 *Chang Bogo* patrol submarines delivered by HDW and Daewoo under the KSS-I programme between 1993 and 2001. However, these are now being supplemented by AIP-equipped Type 214 boats (also of German design) that are being constructed locally under licence arrangements by Hyundai. The first vessel, *Son Won-Il*, was delivered in December 2007 and a total of three should be in service by the end of 2009. Although the Korean *Choson Ilbo* newspaper suggested that the excessive noise levels had been experienced during initial sea trials due to problems with the propeller shaft, this report was strongly denied by naval authorities who have subsequently demonstrated their faith in the programme through an order for a further six boats signed in December 2008. The first unit of this new batch will be built by Daewoo, with subsequent construction contracts subject to competitive tender between Daewoo and HHI.

Table 2.2.6: REPUBLIC OF KOREA NAVY: PRINCIPAL UNITS AS AT MID-2009

TYPE	CLASS	NUMBER	TONNAGE	DIMENSIONS	PROPULSION	CREW	DATE
Principal Surface Escorts							
Destroyer – DDG	KDX-III **SEJONGDAEWANG-HAM**	1	10,000 tons	166m x 21m x 6m	COGAG, 30 knots	300	2008
Destroyer – DDG	KDX-II **CHUNGMUGONG YI SUN-SHIN**	6	5,500 tons	150m x 17m x 5m	CODOG, 30 knots	200	2003
Destroyer – DDG	KDX-I **GWANGGAETO-DAEWANG**	3	3,900 tons	135m x 14m x 4m	CODOG, 30 knots	170	1998
Frigate – FFG	**ULSAN**	9	2,300 tons	102m x 12m x 4m	CODOG, 35 knots	150	1981
Corvette – FSG	**PO HANG**	24	1,200 tons	88m x 10m x 3m	CODOG, 32 knots	95	1984
Corvette – FS	**DONG HAE**	4	1,100 tons	78m x 10m x 3m	CODOG, 32 knots	95	1982
Submarines							
Submarine – SSK	KSS-2 **SON WON-IL** (Type 214)	2	1,800 tons	65m x 6m x 6m	AIP, 20+ knots	30	2007
Submarine – SSK	KSS-1 **CHANG BOGO** (Type 209)	9	1,300 tons	56m x 6m x 6m	Diesel-electric, 22 knots	35	1993
Major Amphibious Units							
Amph. Assault Ship – LHD	LPX **DOKDO**	1	18,900 tons	200m x 32m x 7m	Diesel, 22 knots	425	2007

South Korea has been expanding its surface fleet through series production of the three KDX classes of destroyer, each of which is progressively more capable. This image shows the KDX-II class ship *Munmu Daewang*, one of six sister-ships that have all now commissioned. Future surface ship construction is now focused on the more powerful KDX-III project, as well as the smaller FFX frigate. *(US Navy)*

Longer-term plans contained in the *Defense Reform 2020* programme call for the construction of an indigenous KSS-III submarine design of around 3,000 tons submerged displacement, with delivery originally scheduled from 2018. *The Korea Times* has reported that the new class will feature a locally-developed combat management system produced by a Samsung Thales joint venture, whilst sonar integration will be in the hands of Korean company LIG Nex1. However, some equipment will still be sourced internationally; for example weapons-handling systems are to be designed by the UK's Babcock International. A reduction in defence expenditure caused by the global economic crisis and a decision to give priority to army projects in the light of increased tensions with the North is likely to result in some slippage in timescales. As a result, it is unlikely to be the 2020s before the first KSS-III submarine enters service.

The Korean naval programme that has probably most caught global attention is the *Dokdo* class LHD-type amphibious assault ship, which was commissioned in July 2007. Although remarkably similar in appearance to Japan's *Hyuga* and with a similar full load displacement of c.19,000 tons, her primary role is significantly different from the JMSDF ship's anti-submarine orientation. There have been persistent rumours that Korea is interested in acquiring the STOVL F-35B variant of the Joint Strike Fighter (JSF), which would enable the formation of an amphibious ready group with limited power-projection capabilities similar to the US concept. However, *Dokdo* is probably too small to operate more than a handful of jet fighters and there have been reports that at least one of two planned sister-ships will be enlarged for this purpose.

Although recent investment has concentrated on 'blue water' naval capabilities, South Korea continues to maintain a powerful but increasingly elderly flotilla of coastal units as a safeguard against potential North Korean aggression. Raised tensions with the North, particularly following the Democratic People's Republic's nuclear test on 25 May 2009, have increased focus on this capability. Forces in the Yellow Sea – scene of previous skirmishes over the last decade – have been significantly increased. Amongst the vessels deployed was the new PKX fast attack craft, *Yoon Young-Ha*, which is intended to be the prototype for a new fleet of 400-ton missile armed patrol craft designed to dominate the littoral. Whilst any further clashes had – thankfully – been avoided at the time this chapter was written, it seems likely that the worsening political environment will provide additional impetus to accelerate this modernisation process.

OTHER REGIONAL FLEETS

Brunei: Essentially a small coastal defence force, the Royal Brunei Navy planned a substantial enhancement to its capabilities through the construction of three *Nakhoda Ragam* type corvettes at the Scotstoun-based Yarrow shipyard of the then GEC (now part of BVT Surface Fleet) under a contract signed in 1998. Although trials of the first of class commenced as early as 2002, a long-running contractual dispute that was eventually settled through arbitration ended in the ships being put up for sale after their final acceptance in 2007. It has been claimed that a key influence on Brunei's reluctance to take delivery of the ships was a growing perception of the practical difficulty of operating such sophisticated vessels. It is understood that Brunei subsequently approached German shipbuilder Lürssen to produce a less complex design to replace its existing 1970s-vintage fast attack craft. Meanwhile, the three Scotstoun-built ships remain laid up awaiting a buyer.

Indonesia: The Indonesian Navy's primary task is policing the extensive territorial waters of the vast and diverse Indonesian archipelago, home to the world's fourth largest population. Given a relatively weak economic performance compared with leading South East Asian nations and the need to combat low level instability resulting both from regional separatist movements and a significant level of piracy, naval budgets have been channelled towards the construction of unsophisticated coastal patrol and amphibious vessels. An increasing proportion of these have been built in local shipyards, of which PT PAL of Surabaya is the most significant. The facility has demonstrated a capability to fabricate a relatively broad range of vessels, with two 11,000-ton *Makassar* LPDs probably being the most significant constructed to date. These ships form the second pair of a four ship class built in conjunction with South Korea's Daesun Shipbuilding and represent a significant boost to Indonesia's amphibious capabilities. The first of the Indonesian-built ships was launched on 28 August 2008.

Korea is replicating expansion of its surface fleet with the acquisition of more powerful underwater capabilities. This is a Type 214 AIP-equipped submarine licence-built by Hyundai Heavy Industries. *(Hyundai Heavy Industries)*

The construction of principal combatants is still in the hands of overseas shipyards, with four *Diponegoro* class Sigma type corvettes the most significant recent addition to the fleet. Built by the Schelde Naval Shipbuilding subsidiary of the Dutch Damen Shipyards Group at Vlissingen, they were ordered in two equal batches in 2004 and 2006. Displacing 1,700 tons, the class is orientated towards anti-surface operations. Armament includes four Exocet surface-to-surface missiles, close-range Mistral Tetral surface-to-air missiles and an Oto Melara 76mm gun. The final ship, *Frans Kaisiepo*, was handed over in March 2009 before departing for her new homeport of Surabaya on 11 April. The class will supplement three older Dutch-built corvettes of the *Fatahillah* class delivered some thirty years ago, as well as the six second-hand *Leander/Van Speijk* type frigates transferred from the Royal Netherlands Navy in the late 1980s. Additional surface ships are urgently needed to replace the sixteen obsolescent former East German 'Parchim I' coastal escorts acquired following German reunification. However, the priority for limited funds appears to be expansion of the submarine flotilla, which currently comprises just two Type 209/1300 German-built boats. Options include the acquisition of new-build 'Kilo' class submarines or acquisition of refurbished South Korean Type 209 units as they are replaced by the new Type 214 AIP-equipped boats. South Korea's Daewoo Shipbuilding has already been involved in the modernisation of Indonesia's existing members of the class so the latter course might be the more likely option.

Malaysia: Indonesia's smaller neighbour has benefited from more stable economic conditions in recent years. This has helped fund a relatively small but technically-advanced navy that celebrated its diamond jubilee on 27 April 2009. Central to the Royal Malaysian Navy's acquisitions plans has been the establishment of a submarine force, with contracts for two *Scorpène* class boats placed with a consortium of DCNS and IZAR (now Navantia) in 2002. The first of these conventionally-powered patrol submarines, *Tunku Abdul Rahman*, was built at the former's Cherbourg facility from sections produced by both companies prior to formal handover at Toulon on 27 January 2009. She should be followed by *Tun Razak*, the other class member that is currently undergoing sea trials from Navantia's Cartagena yard, before the end of the year. Displacing c.1,700 tons and with a length of 67.5m,

Malaysia is commissioning her first submarines: two boats of the Franco-Spanish *Scorpène* class. This is the Navantia-built *Tun Razak* during trials in spring 2009. *(Navantia)*

the new class is amongst the most technically advanced in the region and can be deployed for up to forty-five days by a 31-strong crew.

The core of the surface fleet is comprised of two Yarrow-built *Lekiu* class frigates delivered towards the end of 1999. Although long-delayed by combat systems integration problems, they have proved successful ships in Malaysian service. A letter of intent for two modified versions – to be assembled locally – was signed with Britain's BAE Systems in 2006. However, a formal contract has not yet materialised and the state of the project must be considered as uncertain.

The other major construction programme is for an initial batch of six MEKO A-100 type *Kedah* class offshore patrol vessels. Although currently lightly armed with a 76mm Oto Melara gun and smaller calibre weapons, provision for installation of surface-to-surface and surface-to-air missiles gives scope for these 1,700-ton ships' capabilities to be upgraded to a level approaching that of a light frigate. Designed by the German Naval Group that has now metamorphosed into Thyssen Krupp Marine Systems, it was envisaged that the class would eventually extend to as many as twenty-seven units. These were to be completed at the local Penang PSC-Naval Dockyard after delivery of two initial hulls from Germany. All six ships in the first batch were scheduled to enter service by the end of 2008. However, significant technical and financial problems at the Malaysian shipyard delayed delivery of the class and threatened the entire project. A government-sponsored restructuring of the shipyard under the local Boustead group seems to have turned the situation around and three of the four locally-built hulls had been launched by the end of 2008. It is anticipated that all the ships will have entered service by the end of 2009, at which time additional orders may be considered.

New Zealand: The small Royal New Zealand Navy (RNZN) is currently receiving a major upgrade to its constabulary capabilities with the progressive delivery of ships contracted under Project Protector. This NZ$500m (US$315m) project to deliver one multi-role support vessel (MRV), two large offshore patrol vessels and four smaller inshore patrol vessels was agreed with Tenix Defence (now part of BAE Systems Australia) in 2004. Although beset by delays and technical problems, the programme now appears to be back on track and all bar the offshore patrol vessels had been delivered as of June 2009.

The first ship to be handed over is the MRV *Canterbury*, which was constructed to a commercial Ro-Ro ferry design by the Dutch Merwede Shipyard before being fitted out in Australia. Of c.9,000 tons full load displacement, she is effectively a cut-price amphibious transport capable of deploying and landing a force of 250 troops from two personnel landing craft or embarked helicopters.[4] The largely commercial specification has resulted in some operating difficulties, with the exposed location of the alcoves for her rigid-hulled inflatable boats (RHIBs) a particular problem. This caused the loss of one boat in heavy weather shortly after delivery and will result in design revisions. Although an enquiry into the ship's safety found no correlation between her basic design and the tragic drowning of a crewmember when one of the boats capsized during launch in October 2007, the RHIBs are also being replaced by

Below: The Royal New Zealand Navy has embarked on a major upgrade to its constabulary capabilities under Project Protector. Pictured here is the offshore patrol vessel *Otago* whilst on sea trials – acceptance by the RNZN is said to be imminent *(BAE Systems Australia)*

The RNZN's multi-purpose vessel *Canterbury* has seen a rather chequered introduction into service and provides a good indication of the limitations inherent in adapting commercial designs for military use. Nevertheless, the concept is attracting considerable attention from other fleets wishing to increase their flexibility. *(NZDF Official)*

a new type.[5] Whilst *Canterbury*'s ability to operate in extreme weather conditions is likely to be limited, the overall concept is seen as a success and is attracting attention from other fleets.

Operationally, the RNZN remains extremely busy for a small-ship navy. Recent deployments have seen one of the navy's two *Anzac* class frigates, *Te Mana*, patrolling the Persian Gulf in support of the coalition security activities – a mission that has been carried out on an occasional basis throughout the last decade. *Te Mana* and the replenishment vessel *Endeavour* were also amongst ships of some twenty nations that participated in the PLAN's 60th anniversary review at Qingdao in April 2009.

Singapore: Possibly the most potent regional force outside of the 'big four' Asian navies, the Republic of Singapore Navy (RSN) consists of a well-balanced force of surface, amphibious and underwater units. The fleet has been steadily upgrading its capabilities for 'blue water' operations over recent years and has become more active in international waters, most notably in the Indian Ocean. This has included participation in the Indo-American Malabar series of exercises, as well as a contribution to anti-terrorist and anti-piracy missions in the Persian Gulf and off the African coast.

A major factor supporting this more evident regional presence has been the recapitalisation of the surface fleet with six French-designed *Formidable* class multi-role frigates, which were commissioned between 2007 and 2009. Displacing c.3,200 tons in full load condition, these ships are derived from the *Marine Nationale*'s stealthy *La Fayette* design but have significantly enhanced anti-aircraft and anti-submarine capabilities. These include an advanced Thales Herakles multifunction radar coupled with Aster surface-to-air missiles and a towed array sonar. Whilst the lead ship was built by DCNS' Lorient yard, subsequent vessels were assembled by ST Marine in Singapore, greatly strengthening indigenous shipbuilding capabilities.

ST Marine was previously responsible for construction of four *Endurance* class landing platform docks that arguably provide Singapore with the region's most coherent amphibious capability. These 8,500-ton ships are able to deploy a force of 350 troops together with supporting armour and supplies and land the same by means of helicopters or landing craft shipped in an aft dock well. The class has proved flexible in supporting international missions

The Royal New Zealand Navy inshore patrol vessel *Rotoiti* pictured off Auckland on 24 April 2009, shortly after delivery. She is the first of four sister-ships that have all now been commissioned. *(NZDF Official)*

An image of the new Republic of Singapore Navy *Formidable* class frigate *Steadfast* during landing trials with a USN SH-60B Seahawk helicopter in April 2008. Note the distinctive appearance of the Thales Herakles multifunction radar. *(US Navy)*

and *Endurance* was the first RSN vessel to circumnavigate the globe when she visited New York in 2000. The class were also active in relief efforts following the Boxing Day 2004 tsunami and have undertaken several deployments in the Persian Gulf.

Singapore still relies on overseas yards for subsurface forces, with the current submarine flotilla currently comprising four second-hand Swedish *Sjöormen* class patrol submarines. They will soon be reinforced by two A-17 *Västergötland* class boats – to be named *Archer* and *Swordsman* – that are being retrofitted with Stirling AIP equipment under a deal that was signed with Kockums of Sweden in November 2005. In the longer term, Sweden hopes that Singapore will be a participant in its A-26 submarine project, which is essential for Kockums to retain a domestic submarine construction capability. Design work on this new AIP-equipped submarine was authorised in 2007 but it seems unlikely that production will be viable unless international partners can be attracted to the programme.

Taiwan: Although still numerically strong, Taiwan's Republic of China Navy is becoming increasingly qualitatively outclassed by the larger PLAN. Much-needed modernisation plans are being stalled both by political infighting and difficulties in finding suitable suppliers in the face of hostility from the People's Republic of China. As a result, the only significant advance in recent years has been the acquisition of four former USN destroyers of the *Kidd* (DDG-993) type that were commissioned as the *Kee Lung* class during 2005 and 2006. Other principal surface forces are largely comprised of US-designed frigates of the FFG-7 and *Knox* classes, the former all being locally built between 1993 and 2004. There are also six *La Fayette* type *Kang Ding* stealth frigates purchased from France in a controversial arms deal during the 1990s. The Republic of China Navy would like to acquire Aegis-based combat systems to counterbalance recent improvements in the technology fielded by the PLAN but the United States has consistently refused to support transfer of the relevant equipment.

The greatest weakness in Taiwan's navy is in its submarine arm, where two *Hai Lung* variants of the Dutch *Zwaardvis* design are the only operational units. An offer by the United States to assist acquisition of up to eight new patrol submarines has failed to make progress against numerous hurdles, not least the difficulty in finding a country that will provide relevant design expertise given the USN's sole focus on nuclear-powered boats. Modernisation of anti-submarine forces has largely been confined to the purchase of twelve surplus P-3C Orion maritime patrol aircraft from the US government. They are currently being upgraded by Lockheed Martin under a US$650m contract prior to delivery from 2012 onwards.

Some progress appears to have been made in revitalising all-important coastal forces, which are becoming increasingly obsolescent. The first of a new *Kuang-Hua* (KH-6) class of missile-armed fast attack craft commenced trials in 2003 and, although the prototype was severely damaged after grounding in a storm in September 2008, the design has been approved for series production. The US journal *Defense News* has reported that a further twenty-nine of the 170-ton vessels will be constructed by the state-owned China Shipbuilding Corporation for delivery from late 2009 onwards.[6] They will be armed with the indigenously produced HF-2 surface-to-surface missile and be capable of speeds in excess of 30 knots from three MTU diesels.

Thailand: The only Asian nation to operate a fully-fledged aircraft carrier, political instability has been one of a number of factors delaying the Royal Thai Navy's expansion plans. As a result, upgrades such as construction of modern patrol frigates by the United Kingdom's BAE Systems have been put on hold in favour of less sophisticated corvette-type offshore patrol vessels built in low-cost Chinese yards.

The most significant recent development has undoubtedly been the award of a US$200m contract to ST Marine announced in November 2008 to build a landing platform dock to the RSN's existing *Endurance* design. Work on the ship has already commenced with delivery scheduled for the later part of 2012. However, tentative plans for a second member of the class look set to be delayed by funding cutbacks. The same difficulty might delay the construction of a locally-built offshore patrol vessel, which could be based on the two *Pattani* class vessels built to a Thai-design in China. These 1,400-ton vessels are lightly armed with a 76mm gun but are capable of being upgraded to light frigate standard with the addition of surface-to-surface missiles and embarkation of an anti-submarine helicopter. More ships are urgently needed to supplement the Chinese-built frigates that form the core of Thailand's surface flotillas and to replace elderly US and British built designs that serve in patrol and training roles.

Singapore has purchased two former Swedish A-17 class submarines under a deal that will see them retrofitted with Stirling AIP-equipment. This is the newly-modified *Archer* shortly before its naming ceremony on 16 June 2009. *(Peter Nilsson, Kockums AB)*

Thailand's *Knox* class frigate *Phuttha Loetla Naphalai* participating in exercises with the USN during 2008. Lack of funding is preventing replacement of older ships with modern tonnage. *(US Navy)*

Vietnam: Although subject to little international attention, a steady improvement in Vietnam's economy is allowing a progressive upgrade of local naval forces. Acquisitions have largely focused on improving coastal defence capabilities, with Russia emerging as the clear supplier of choice. Reported purchases include at least two light frigates of the Project 1166.1 'Gepard' type, along with several corvettes of the Project 1241.1 'Tarantul' and Project 1241.2 'Pauk' classes. Coastal surveillance and defence equipment is also being enhanced through further investment. However, a significant expansion of the country's maritime ambitions has been heralded by reports in April 2009 of a c.US$1.8bn deal to acquire six 'Kilo' class patrol submarines from St. Petersburg's Admiralty Shipyards. If the contract is confirmed, it will provide the Vietnamese People's Navy with a significant counter to the PLAN's increasingly assertive presence in the South China Sea.

Notes

1. The Australian government's new defence white paper, *Defending Australia in the Asia-Pacific Century: Force 2030* (Canberra, Commonwealth of Australia, 2009) can be accessed in full at www.defence.gov.au/whitepaper/docs/defence_white_paper_2009.pdf

2. Please refer to Chapter 2.4A for a more detailed description of the Royal Navy's FSC project, which forms part of a broader surface fleet upgrade.

3. Mingi Hyun's 'Manoeuvre in Maritime Asia' blog spot is a good source of information on South Korean naval developments, including ongoing attempts to develop indigenous equipment. Please refer to www.maritimeasiablogspot.com for further reading.

4. A more detailed overview of *Canterbury*'s design is contained in 'Tenix delivers Multi-Role Vessel', Editor: David Foxwell, *Warship Technology* – July/August 2007 (London, RINA, 2007), p 16.

5. The Royal New Zealand Navy's review of *Canterbury*'s design, *Report of the Review of the Safety and Functionality of HMNZS Canterbury*, can be found at the navy's website under reference: http://www.defence.govt.nz/pdfs/independent-review-safety-hmnzs-canterbury.pdf

6. Please see Wendell Minnick, 'Taiwan Begins Building Fast Attack Boats', *Defense News* – 20 October 2008 (Springfield VA, Army Times Publishing, 2008), p 16.

2.2A FLEET REVIEW

CHINA: THE PEOPLE'S LIBERATION ARMY NAVY

On 23 April 2009, China held an international fleet review at Qingdao to mark the 60th anniversary of the People's Liberation Army Navy (PLAN). Sixty years ago, the PLAN grew out of a small fleet of abandoned and captured ships and craft operated by Army soldiers. Today, the PLAN is becoming one of the largest and most sophisticated naval forces in East Asia. Under the country's ocean-going naval strategy, China has embarked upon a modernisation programme to develop a 'blue water' navy that can protect the nation's interests in distant seas. As a result, the PLAN has been transformed from what was essentially a coastal defence force to a more offensively-oriented service capable of operating in high seas beyond China's continental shelf waters.

Over the last two decades, the number of the PLAN's surface combatants has expanded significantly and there also has been a slight increase in the size of its operational submarine fleet. More importantly, the PLAN has been able to phase out some of its 'legacy' vessels built before the 1990s. In the last five years there has been an intensified shipbuilding programme, which has seen the introduction of a number of relatively modern designs. The domestic building programme has also been supplemented by foreign acquisitions such as the Russian *Sovremenny* class destroyers and 'Kilo' class diesel-electric submarines. These purchases filled the gap before new indigenous designs could enter full production, and also provided access to advanced naval technologies such as the 9M38M2 (SA-N-12) SAM, 53-65KE wake-homing torpedo and 'Top Plate' long-range 3D search radar, which China has not yet been able to produce domestically.

EVOLVING MISSION

The PLAN played some minor roles during the Chinese Civil War in the late 1940s. After the founding of the People's Republic of China in 1949, the navy was modernised and reorganised after the Soviet model. Between 1954 and 1960, the Soviet

Union supplied China with a variety of combatants and Soviet advisers assisted with organisation and training. PLAN operations in this period were largely focused on defending the Chinese coastline against attacks by Nationalist forces and assisting land forces in capturing offshore islands held by Taiwan. With Soviet aid, a shipbuilding industry was also developed, with emphasis on building small and medium-sized ships, patrol craft and submarines.

Despite the Sino-Soviet split and China's internal political turmoil and economic hardship, the 1960s to 1970s saw continued expansion of the PLAN in both size and quality. During this period, the PLAN was mainly tasked with the defence of China's coastal regions against a possible amphibious assault by the United States or the Soviet Union. A defensive strategy of 'maritime guerrilla warfare' was developed, with emphasis on the deployment of a large number of inexpensive fast attack missile and torpedo boats, which were supported by conventional submarines and land-based tactical bombers. Larger missile-armed destroyers and frigates began to enter service in the 1970s.

Since the late 1980s, the role of the PLAN has been gradually shifted from pure coastal defence to

Author: Dawei Xia

Dawei Xia is a long-time researcher on the Chinese military and the Asian military balance. He is the editor and founder of SinoDefence.com, an online information source covering the latest developments in Chinese military capabilities. He is also a special correspondent for *Jane's Defence Weekly* and *Jane's Military Vehicles and Logistics*. His areas of research include China's armed forces, security policies, defence industry, WMD and space programmes, as well as the military power of China's neighbours, such as Taiwan and Japan. Dawei Xia studied at the Beijing University of Aeronautics & Astronautics (BUAA) and at the University of Sussex in the UK.

Opposite: Over the last few years the PLAN has embarked upon an intensified shipbuilding programme that has seen the introduction of a number of modern designs. Here the Type 052B ('Luyang-I') destroyer *Guangzhou* is seen departing Portsmouth Harbour in September 2007. *(Conrad Waters)*

'active offshore defence' in order to assert China's role as a regional power and protect the country's coastal economy and maritime interests.[1] One particular factor that has driven the naval modernisation process is the possibility of a conflict with Taiwan. The PLAN has been investing heavily in developing its access denial and blockade capabilities, resulting in a rapid expansion of its surface fleet and modernisation of its submarine forces. Concerns over an escalation of the dispute over the sovereign rights of the Nansha (Spratly) Islands in the South China Sea have also prompted the PLAN to develop some platforms for offshore power projection.

In its recent publications, the PLAN has outlined a two-step strategy in its modernisation process. In the first step, the navy aims to develop a 'green water' capability, which allows it to operate beyond the 'First Island Chain', an arc swung from Vladivostok to the north, via the Aleutian Islands, Japan, Okinawa, Taiwan, the Philippines and Brunei, to the Strait of Malacca to the south. In the second step, by the middle of this century the PLAN will develop a 'blue water' capability that can operate in the high seas beyond China's continental shelf, in order to ensure China's access to trade routes and economic resources throughout the region, a typical example being the navy's deployment of two surface combatants and a replenishment ship to the Gulf of Aden to protect Chinese merchant ships against Somali pirate attacks.

FORCE STRUCTURE

As one of the four service branches of the People's Liberation Army (PLA), the PLAN is controlled through the naval headquarters in Beijing, which is directly subordinated to the Central Military Commission through the four General Departments. The current PLAN Commander is Admiral Wu Sheng-Li and the current PLAN Political Commissar is Vice Admiral Liu Xiao-Jiang. The PLAN is organised into three fleets: the North Sea Fleet headquartered in Qingdao, the East Sea Fleet headquartered in Ningbo, and the South Sea Fleet headquartered in Zhanjiang. Each fleet consists of surface forces, submarine forces, naval aviation, marine corps and coastal defence forces, as well as

A Type 091 ('Han') SSN. China's first-generation nuclear submarines suffered from poor reactor reliability and noise. They are being replaced by current generation Type 093 ('Shang') boats. *(US Department of Defense)*

various training, logistics and maintenance elements.

The PLAN has a total strength of 255,000 personnel, including 26,000 in naval aviation, 10,000 marines and some 27,000 coastal defence forces.[2] Like other service branches of the PLA, the PLAN adopts a selective service system where conscripts undertake a two-year service, after which they can apply to continue their service as non-commissioned officers (NCOs). PLAN officers follow one of the five career tracks: military, political, logistics, equipment or technical. Almost all PLAN officers have received a three-year higher education or obtained a four-year Bachelor's degree and many have also received a Master's or Doctorate degree. There is roughly a 1:1:1 ratio for officers, NCOs and conscripts in the PLAN. Education of the officer corps is provided by the nine naval academies across the country.[3]

Each fleet has two or three major bases and a number of minor bases. Major naval bases include Lushun, Qingdao, Huludao, Shanghai, Zhoushan, Guangzhou, Zhanjiang, Yulin and Xisha. China's state-owned shipbuilding industry is grouped into two consortia: China State Shipbuilding Corporation (CSSC) and China Shipbuilding Industry Corporation (CSIC), both of which are capable of building naval vessels of all types. Major construction facilities for surface vessels are located at Dalian, Shanghai, Wuhu and Guanzhou.

Conventional submarines are constructed at Wuhan and Shanghai. Nuclear-powered submarines are constructed at Huludao.

SUBMARINE FORCES

The PLAN currently operates approximately fifty-five conventional attack submarines, about 40 per cent of which are obsolete Type 033 ('Romeo') and Type 035 ('Ming') designs. The rest includes sixteen members of the indigenous Type 039 ('Song') class, twelve Russian-built 'Kilos' and at least two indigenous Type 039A/B ('Yuan') class. The Type 039 was first introduced in 1994, and is comparable in performance to Western design of the 1980s. The submarine features a more hydrodynamically sleek profile, coupled with noise-reduction measures such as propulsion shock-absorbance and rubber anti-sonar protection tiles. Other features include a digital bow-mounted, medium-frequency sonar with multiple-target tracking capability, German MTU 16V diesels, Yu-3 electric-propelled acoustic-homing ASW torpedoes and YJ-82 submarine-launched anti-surface missiles.

The 'Kilo' class is the most capable conventional submarine asset of the PLAN. Ten of the twelve 'Kilo' boats in the PLAN inventory are the improved Project 636 boats, which are regarded as one of the world's quietest conventional submarines, being extremely difficult for enemy ASW systems to detect

and track. Along with the 'Kilo' class, the PLAN also obtained some of the most advanced naval weapon systems produced by Russia, including the 53-65KE wake-homing anti-ship torpedo, the TEST-71MKE wire-homing ASW torpedo, and the 3M-54E 'Klub-S' submarine-launched ASM. The purchase of the 'Kilos' not only greatly boosted the underwater capability of the PLAN, but also inspired the development of a new indigenous design referred to as the 'Yuan' class by Western intelligence.

In addition to conventional boats, the PLAN also operates a small fleet of eight nuclear-powered submarines. Two of the five Type 091 ('Han') class SSN nuclear-powered attack submarines commissioned between 1974 and 1990 have now been withdrawn from service, whilst two new-generation Type 093 ('Shang') class SSNs have been operational with the PLAN since 2006. The navy received a single Type 092 ('Xia') class SSBN in the 1980s, and is now testing two new Type 094 ('Jin') class SSBNs. The latter are designed to carry twelve JL-2 submarine-launched ballistic missiles (SLBMs), which have a reported maximum range of 8,000km and the capability to deliver up to three multiple independently targetable re-entry vehicles (MIRV). China's first generation nuclear submarines are known to have suffered from poor reactor reliability and are noisier than US and Russian designs. The PLAN will most certainly try to address these issues in its new generation designs but the slow pace of construction may suggest that some problems remain unsolved.

SURFACE FORCES

Major surface combatants of the PLAN include approximately twenty-five destroyers and fifty frigates. Retirement of the obsolete Type 051 ('Luda') class destroyers and Type 053 ('Jianghu') class frigates finally began in 2008 but is proceeding at a very slow pace. Over the past two decades, the indigenous shipbuilding programme has produced nine destroyers in five classes and twenty frigates in four classes. The most recent of these Chinese surface combatants have been fitted with advanced Russian weapons and sensors, including the 9M38M2 and S-300FM surface-to-air missiles, 'Top Plate' 3D long-range air/surface search radar, 'Front Dome' fire-control radar and the 'Band Stand' anti-surface missile supporting data-link. Some destroyers are powered by a CODOG propulsion arrangement, largely featuring two Ukrainian DA80/DN80 gas turbines.

The most notable recent development in the modernisation of the PLAN's surface fleet was the commissioning of six modern guided-missile destroyers (DDGs) during 2004–6. These comprise two 5,850-ton Type 052B ('Luyang-I') class vessels: *Guangzhou* (hull 168) and *Wuhan* (169); two 6,500-ton Type 052C ('Luyang-II') class units: *Lanzhou* (170) and *Haikou* (171); and two 7,100-ton Type 051C ('Luzhou') class ships: *Shenyang* (115) and *Shijiazhuang* (116). The three classes were each equipped with a different surface-to-air missile system. The Type 052B is fitted with two Russian 9M38M2 (SA-N-12) medium-range SAM launchers coupled with four Russian 'Front Dome' radars. The Type 052C is fitted with forty-eight indigenous HQ-9 SAMs housed in eight six-cell vertical launch system (VLS) modules guided by an indigenous, Aegis-like phased-array radar. The Type 051C is fitted with a Russian S-300FM 'Rif-M' (SA-N-20) area air-defence system comprising forty-eight missiles housed in six eight-cell revolving VLS modules and a Volna 'Tomb Stone' 3D phased-array tracking radar. Type 052C also features the new 280km-range YJ-62 (C-602) ASM.

Frustrated by its inability to prevent two US Navy aircraft carrier battle groups (CVBG) from intervening during the 1996 Taiwan Strait crisis, the

Over the past two decades China's indigenous shipbuilding programme has produced nine destroyers in five classes. Pictured here is one of the earlier ships in this programme, the Type 052 ('Luhu') destroyer *Qingdao*. *(US Department of Defense)*

Table 2.2A.1.

MODERN CHINESE DESTROYERS PRINCIPAL PARTICULARS

CLASS	TYPE 052 'LUHU'	TYPE 051B 'LUHAI'	TYPE 052B 'LUYANG I'	TYPE 052C 'LUYANG II'	TYPE 051C 'LUZHOU'
In Service Date:	1994	1998	2004	2004	2006
Number:	2	1	2	2	2
Names:	*Harbin* (112) *Qingdao* (113)	*Shenzhen* (167)	*Guangzhou* (168) *Wuhan* (169)	*Lanzhou* (170) *Haikou* (171)	*Shenyang* (115) *Shijiazhuang* (116)
FL Displacement:	4,800 tons	6,000 tons	6,000 tons	6,500 tons	7,100 tons
Dimensions:	143m x 15m x 5m	154m x 16m x 6m	154m x 17m x 6m	154m x 17m x 6m	155m x 17m x 6m
Armament:	4 x quad YJ-83 SSM 1 x octuple HQ-7 SAM 1 x Type 79A twin 100mm gun 4 x Type 76A twin 37mm AA guns 2 x triple 324mm torpedo tubes 2 x Type 75 12-tube A/S launchers 2 x helicopters	4 x quad YJ-83 SSM 1 x octuple HQ-7 SAM 1 x Type 79A twin 100mm gun 4 x Type 76A twin 37mm AA guns 2 x triple 324mm torpedo tubes 2 x helicopters	4 x quad YJ-83 SSM 2 x SA-N-12 SAM 1 x single 100mm gun 2 x Type 730 CIWS 2 x triple 324mm torpedo tubes 2 x Type 87 6-tube A/S launchers 1 x helicopter	2 x quad YJ-62 SSM 8 x sextuple VLS for HQ-9 SAM 1 x single 100mm gun 2 x Type 730 CIWS 2 x triple 324mm torpedo tubes 1 x helicopter	2 x quad YJ-83 SSM 6 x octuple SA-N-20 SAM 1 x single 100mm gun 2 x Type 730 CIWS 2 x triple 324mm torpedo tubes Flight deck only for helicopter
Main Sensors:	1 x Type 518 LR air search 1 x TSR 3004 air/surf search (112) 1 x Type 360S air/surf search (113) 1 x Type 362 surface search 1 x Type 344 SSM/gun fire control 1 x Type 345 SAM fire control 2 x Type 347G AA gun fire control 1 x DUBV-23 hull-mounted sonar 1 x DUBV-43 towed-array	1 x Type 381 LR air search 1 x Type 517H-1 LR air search 1 x Type 360S air/surf search 1 x Type 344 SSM/gun fire control 1 x Type 345 SAM fire control 2 x Type 347G AA gun fire control 1 x DUBV-23 hull-mounted sonar	1 x 'Top Plate' LR air search 1 x Type 364 air/surf search 1 x Type 344 SSM/gun fire control 1 x 'Band Stand' datalink for SSM 4 x 'Front Dome' SAM fire control 2 x Type 347G as part of CIWS 1 x hull-mounted sonar	4 x phased-array MF radar panels 1 x Type 517H-1 LR air search 1 x Type 364 air/surf search 1 x Type 344 SSM/gun fire control 1 x 'Band Stand' datalink for SSM 2 x Type 347G as part of CIWS 1 x hull-mounted sonar	1 x 'Top Plate' LR air search 1 x Type 364 air/surf search 1 x 'Tomb Stone' SAM fire control 1 x 'Band Stand' datalink for SSM 2 x Type 347G as part of CIWS 1 x hull-mounted sonar
Propulsion:	CODOG 2 x GE LM-2500 GT (112) 2 x Ukraine GT-25000 (113) 2 x MTU 12V 1163TB83 diesels 31 knots, 2 shafts	Steam Turbine propulsion[1] 31 knots, 2 shafts	CODOG 2 x Ukraine DA80 GT 2 x Shaanxi/MTU 20V 956TB92 29 knots, 2 shafts	CODOG 2 x Ukraine DA80 GT 2 x Shaanxi/MTU 20V 956TB92 28 knots, 2 shafts	Steam Turbine propulsion (N1) 29 knots, 2 shafts
Complement:	c.260	c.250	c.280	c.280	Not Known

Notes:
1 Some sources claim CODOG propulsion featuring two Ukraine gas turbines and two MTU diesels.
2 Local designations are used for Chinese supplied equipment. Russian supplied equipment uses NATO designations.

Type 052 Destroyer *Harbin*

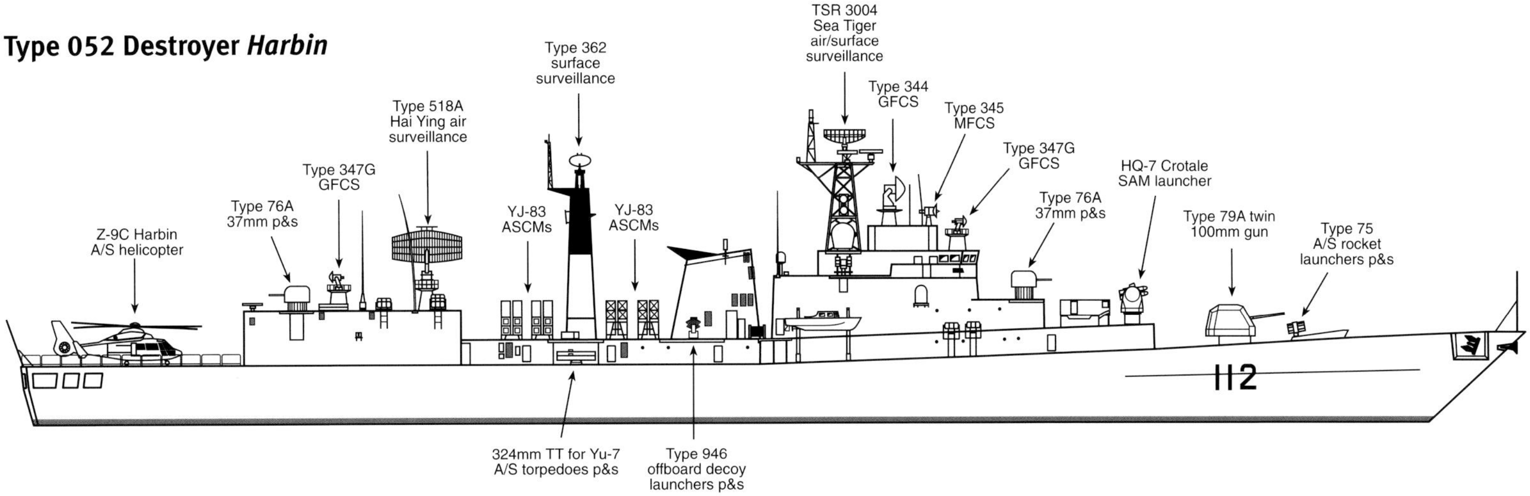

TSR 3004
Sea Tiger
air/surface
surveillance

Type 362
surface
surveillance

Type 518A
Hai Ying air
surveillance

Type 344
GFCS

Type 345
MFCS

Type 347G
GFCS

Type 347G
GFCS

HQ-7 Crotale
SAM launcher

Type 76A
37mm p&s

Type 76A
37mm p&s

Type 79A twin
100mm gun

Type 75
A/S rocket
launchers p&s

Z-9C Harbin
A/S helicopter

YJ-83
ASCMs

YJ-83
ASCMs

II2

324mm TT for Yu-7
A/S torpedoes p&s

Type 946
offboard decoy
launchers p&s

Type 051B Destroyer *Shenzhen*

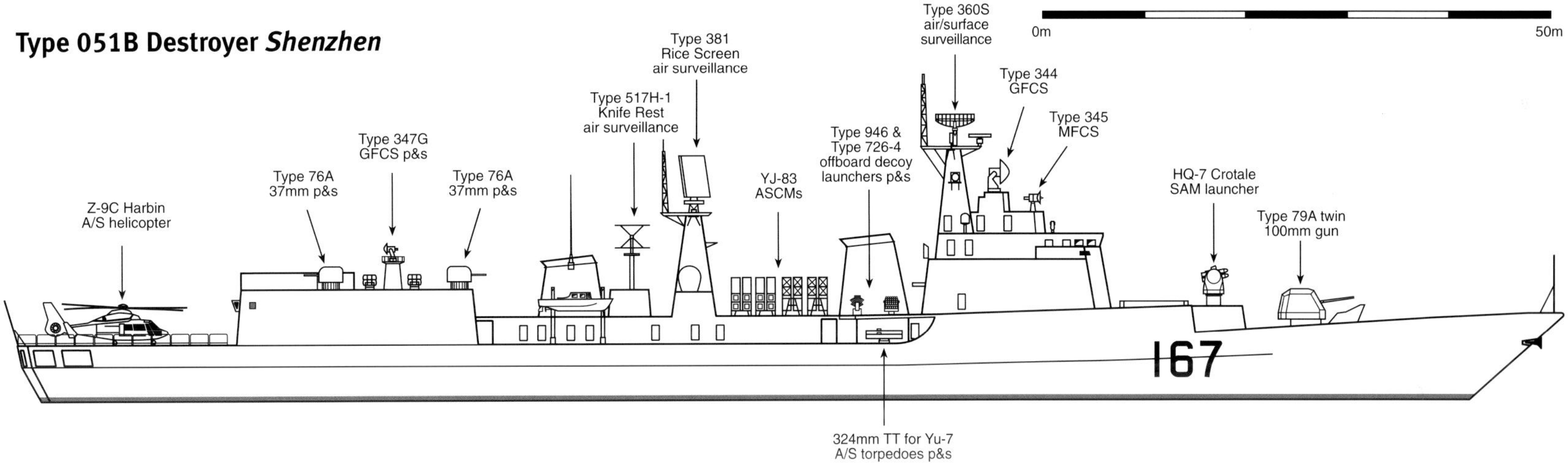

Type 360S
air/surface
surveillance

0m   50m

Type 381
Rice Screen
air surveillance

Type 517H-1
Knife Rest
air surveillance

Type 344
GFCS

Type 347G
GFCS p&s

Type 76A
37mm p&s

Type 76A
37mm p&s

Type 946 &
Type 726-4
offboard decoy
launchers p&s

Type 345
MFCS

HQ-7 Crotale
SAM launcher

Type 79A twin
100mm gun

Z-9C Harbin
A/S helicopter

YJ-83
ASCMs

I67

324mm TT for Yu-7
A/S torpedoes p&s

Type 052B Destroyer *Guangzhou*

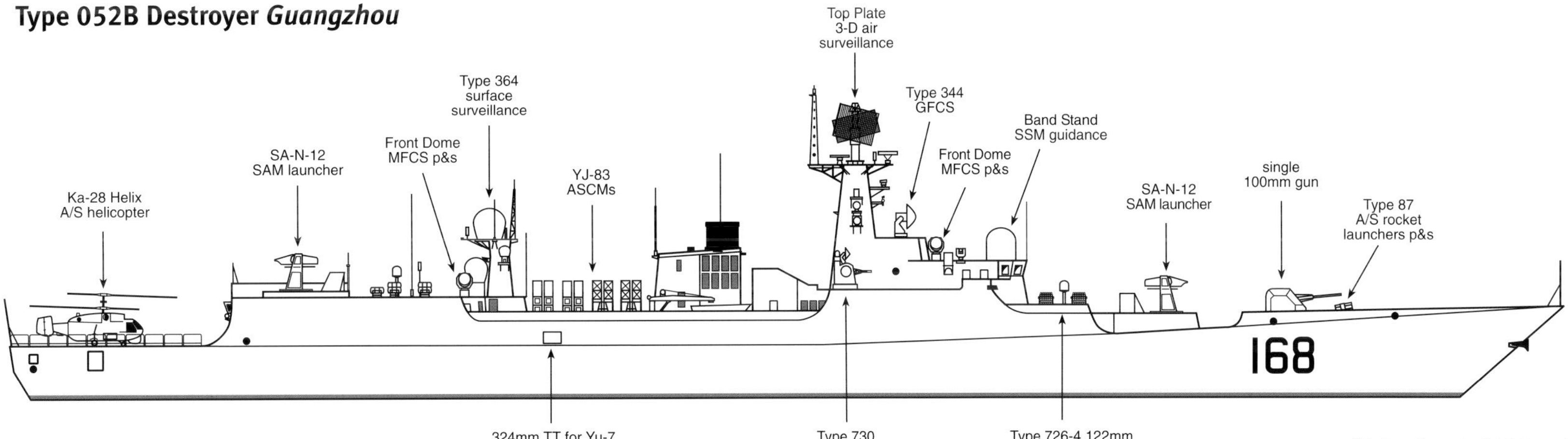

Top Plate
3-D air
surveillance

Type 364
surface
surveillance

Type 344
GFCS

Band Stand
SSM guidance

SA-N-12
SAM launcher

Front Dome
MFCS p&s

YJ-83
ASCMs

Front Dome
MFCS p&s

SA-N-12
SAM launcher

single
100mm gun

Type 87
A/S rocket
launchers p&s

Ka-28 Helix
A/S helicopter

I68

324mm TT for Yu-7
A/S torpedoes p&s

Type 730
CIWS p&s

Type 726-4 122mm
offboard decoy
launchers p&s

All drawings to 1:700 scale
(Drawings by John Jordan, 2009)

Type 052C Destroyer *Lanzhou*

VLS launchers
for HQ-9 SAM

Type 364
surface
surveillance

Type 344
GFCS

Band Stand
SSM guidance

VLS launchers
for HQ-9 SAM

Type 517H-1
Knife Rest
air surveillance

multifunction
phased array
radars p&s

Type 730
CIWS

single
100mm gun

Ka-28 Helix
A/S helicopter

Type 730
CIWS

YJ-62
ASCMs

170

Type 726-4 122mm
offboard decoy
launchers p&s

324mm TT for Yu-7
A/S torpedoes p&s

0m 50m

Type 051C Destroyer *Shijiazhuang*

Tomb Stone
planar 3-D
radar stowed
horizontally

Type 364
surface
surveillance

Top Plate
3-D air
surveillance

Type 946 &
Type 726-4
offboard decoy
launchers p&s

Band Stand
SSM guidance

VLS launchers
for SA-N-20
SAM missiles

single
100mm gun

Ka-28 Helix
A/S helicopter
(flight deck but
no hangar)

VLS launchers
for SA-N-20
SAM missiles

Tomb Stone
planar 3-D
radar fully
elevated

YJ-83
ASCMs

116

Type 730
CIWS p&s

324mm TT for Yu-7
A/S torpedoes p&s

Drawings to 1:700 scale

HQ-9 Missile System: vertical launch silos

hinged caps
for individual
launch cells

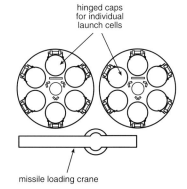

missile loading crane

Note: The Chinese HQ-9 system employs gas ejection for a 'cold launch' which takes the missile clear of the ship before the rocket motors are ignited. Each of the six missiles in the circular module is housed within its own fixed cylindrical cell and there is a hinged cap for each cell. The missiles are loaded into the silos using a crane located alongside or between each pair/group of silos.

S-300FM Missile System: vertical launch silos

circular blast
vent plates
above missiles

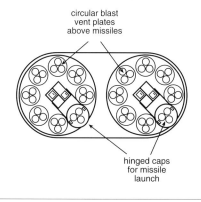

hinged caps
for missile
launch

Note: The Russian SA-N-20 system employs a revolving missile magazine in which eight S-300FM missiles are stowed vertically in each module. Each of the missile stowage positions is capped by a light circular plate designed to shatter in the event of the premature detonation of a missile, allowing the explosion to be vented upwards. The magazine ring is rotated to move each missile in turn to the launch position, which is covered by a larger-diameter hinged cap.

(Drawings by John Jordan, 2009)

PLAN also acquired four 6,200-ton Project 956 (*Sovremenny* class) DDGs from Russia as a stopgap before new-generation indigenous destroyer designs could be built in significant numbers. The *Sovremenny* class was developed in the 1980s by the Soviet navy as a counter to the US Navy's aircraft carrier battle groups and Aegis cruisers. Each *Sovremenny* class vessel is equipped with eight formidable 3M-80E (SS-N-22) supersonic surface-to-surface missiles, two 9M38 (SA-N-7) medium-range SAM launchers, 'Top Plate' 3D radar, and a Ka-28 'Helix' ASW/SAR helicopter. The second pair – delivered in 2005–6 – were constructed to an improved Project 956EM design variation, featuring two 'Kashtan' CIWS/SAM short-range air-defence systems. These replaced the four AK-630 CIWS and aft 130mm main gun in the standard design.

The latest frigate programme is the 4,000-ton Type 054 ('Jiangkai') class, which shows an obvious focus on low radar cross-section design considerations. The first two hulls, launched in 2005–6, were equipped with the older weapons and sensors found on the Type 053H3 ('Jiangwei-II') class. However, from the third hull – *Xuzhou* (530) – the design was constructed to an improved Type 054A ('Jiangkai-II') variant, featuring an indigenous 32-cell VLS to launch the HQ-16 medium-range SAM. This is a Chinese copy of the Russian 9M317/38M2 (SA-N-12). The vessel also features a Chinese-built copy of the Russian AK-176 single 76mm anti-air/surface gun, a 'Top Plate' 3D air/sea search radar, and four 'Front Dome' SAM fire-control radars. Four Type 054As had been launched by the end of 2008, and production continues at two shipyards in Shanghai and Guangzhou.

The PLAN also operates a massive fleet of several hundred patrol craft, missile boats, underway replenishment ships, mine warfare vessels, transport ships, oil and water tankers, tugs, icebreakers and surveillance ships. Two new 23,000-ton 'Fuchi' class auxiliary oiler replenishment (AOR) ships, *Qiandaohu* (886) and *Weishanhu* (887), joined the fleet in 2003, complementing the existing single AOR ship *Qinghaihu* (885) and two 'Fuqing' class fleet oilers. In 2004, the PLAN caused something of a stir when its first Type 022 ('Houbei') class cata-

Images of the Type 051B ('Luhai') destroyer *Shenzen* and the Type 052B ('Luyang-I') destroyer *Guangzhou*. Each class has now been followed into service by more modern variants. *(Conrad Waters)*

The 1990s vintage Type 053 H2G ('Jiangwei I') frigate *Huainan*. These vessels are now being supplemented by the more modern Type 054 ('Jiangkai') class. *(US Department of Defense)*

maran missile fast attack craft (FAC) was launched. The Type 022 features a Small Waterplane Area Twin Hull (SWATH) wave-piercing hull design, which provides a high-speed and yet stable platform for its onboard weapons. Each Type 022 is equipped with eight 180km YJ-83 surface-to-surface missiles, and can attack targets at 'over-the-horizon' distances with battlefield information received from airborne or surface sensors via its data-link. The PLAN has already received over forty examples of the Type 022, with the production continuing at three locations in China.

AMPHIBIOUS WARFARE

The PLAN operates a fleet of more than seventy large and medium landing ships, as well as over 300 smaller landing ships and craft. Although China possesses the ability to develop and build more modernised and sophisticated designs, the PLAN's major amphibious warfare ships are limited to the conventional tank landing ship (LST) and medium landing ship (LSM) types with design antecedents dating back to the Second World War. The backbone of the amphibious fleet includes seven Type 072 ('Yukan') class LSTs, ten Type 072-II ('Yuting') class LSTs, and nine Type 072-III ('Yuting-II') class LSTs. A single hull of the Type 071 landing platform dock (LPD), *Kunlunshan* (998), was commissioned in 2007. The vessel has an estimated displacement of

17,000–20,000 tons and is capable of carrying four LCAC-sized air cushion landing craft inside her floodable bay.

The PLAN is equipped with 300 to 500 small landing ships and landing craft, which could also play a role in an amphibious assault operation against Taiwan. The total amphibious fleet has an estimated aggregate sealift capability of 10,000 to 15,000 troops. In time of crisis, this fleet is likely to be reinforced by China's massive merchant ship fleet composed of almost every vessel type, from cargo ships, roll-on/roll-off ships, container ships, to oil tankers. Some of these vessels can be easily converted for vehicle/personnel transport, helicopter carrier or hospital ship roles.[4] The PLAN Marine Corps has two combined-arms brigades, with a total strength of 10,000 men. Additionally, the People's Liberation Army (PLA) ground forces have two amphibious mechanised infantry divisions, where are specifically equipped and trained for maritime amphibious assault operations.

NAVAL AVIATION

The PLAN's fixed-wing aircraft are all shore-based, with limited numbers of helicopters operating from onboard the major surface units. The most capable aircraft operational with the naval aviation forces are twenty-four Russian-built Sukhoi Su-30MKK2 'Flanker' two-seater, twin-engine fighter-bombers.

These have a maximum combat radius of 1,600km without refuelling, or 3,500km with multiple refuellings. There are also 60 – 70 indigenous Xi'an JH-7 fighter-bombers and some Xi'an H-6 (Tu-16 'Badger' copy) medium bombers. The air-defence role is carried out by the indigenous Chengdu J-7 (MiG-21 'Fishbed') and Shenyang J-8 fighters. The PLA has also received small numbers of fixed-wing maritime patrol, surveillance, and intelligence aircraft, most of which were based on the four-engine Shaanxi Y-8 turboprop transport airframe.

The PLAN's helicopter force is small but growing in capability and numbers. It consists of about 20 – 30 examples of the Changhe Z-8 (AS 321Ja 'Super Frelon' copy) and Harbin Z-9C (AS 365 'Dauphin-II' copy), as well as eight examples of the Russian Ka-28 'Helix' ASW/SAR helicopter. The Z-9Cs and Ka-28s are mostly operated from onboard destroyers and frigates, while the larger Z-8s have been deployed to transport marine commandos in the amphibious assault role and to ferry supplies from land bases to large vessels at sea. Almost all destroyers and frigates built by the Chinese after 1990 are fitted with a helicopter hanger and flight deck as standard and have data-link capabilities with their embarked helicopters.

AIRCRAFT CARRIER PROGRAMME

One subject that has constantly caught people's imagination in respect of China's naval modernisation programme is the possibility of the PLAN acquiring one or more aircraft carriers. China has made several efforts to acquire or develop an aircraft carrier but these have produced no results to date. The PLAN revealed its aircraft carrier ambitions as early as 1987 by launching a 'Pilot Warship Captain' programme to train naval pilots to command warships. This was said to have been inspired by the US Navy's practice of appointing naval pilots to captain their aircraft carriers. In 2007, China announced that fifty students were to be trained at the Dalian Naval Academy to become the country's first naval aviators that could operate fixed-wing aircraft from an aircraft carrier.[5]

China has purchased four decommissioned aircraft carriers from Australia (HMAS *Melbourne*), Russia (*Minsk* and *Kiev*) and Ukraine (*Varyag*) for examination and study. The most recent acquisition was that of the unfinished 65,000ton ex-Soviet Navy aircraft carrier *Varyag* from Ukraine. The vessel has been docked at the Dalian Shipyard since 2002 for restoration and refurbishment. Unconfirmed reports suggested that the PLA may have planned to turn *Varyag* into a fully-operational carrier or for use in a training role but the navy's lack of knowledge and technology in propulsion and relevant aircraft take-off and landing equipment would make this a difficult proposition. China also lacks any aircraft suitable for operations from a conventional take-off and landing (CTOL) carrier, though it is in negotiation with Russia on a possible deal of up to fifty Sukhoi Su-33 naval fighters worth US$2.5 billion.[6]

AREAS FOR FUTURE DEVELOPMENT

In order for the PLAN to perform Sea Lines of Communication (SLOC) protection missions in blue waters, it will need to increase significantly its current limited inventory of major surface combatants and underway replenishment ships. However, the increase in the quantity of these vessels over the past decade has been modest and far less aggressive compared with the Soviet Navy in the 1970s–80s. As a result, a large number of pre-1990 combatants, patrol craft and associated equipment have had to be retained in operational service. Furthermore, the older generation 'Luda' and 'Jianghu' classes are obsolete and incapable of front-line operations by any standards and desperately need replacement. Therefore the PLAN will have to construct over fifty major surface combatants simply to maintain current overall force levels.

Another major weakness of the PLAN is its limited anti-submarine capability. Only three of the PLAN's major surface combatants are equipped with the variable depth sonar (VDS). ASW weapons onboard these combatants are limited to anti-submarine rocket launcher and active/passive acoustic-homing torpedoes. Despite having devoted considerable budget and training to learning the difficult and expensive art of ASW operations in a blue water environment, the PLAN still lacks effective anti-submarine systems, including ASW helicopters, maritime patrol aircraft and long-range ASW weapons (such as ASROC and SUBROC). Effective anti-submarine warfare also requires the effective and co-ordinated use of nuclear-powered attack submarines, a capability the PLAN has yet been able to demonstrate.

Other limitations include an inadequate overseas power-projection capability, sub-standard personnel training and readiness, and continued reliance on foreign sources for advanced weapons, sensors and

The PLAN is steadily developing a fleet replenishment capability to support longer range operations. This is the 'Fuchi' class AOR *Weishanhu*. *(Conrad Waters)*

propulsion technology. For now, the PLAN appears to remain focused on improving its ability to conduct access-denial operations for a Taiwan scenario. However, China's ability to quickly build large classes of ships should not be underestimated.

Indeed, the PLAN's recent history of development suggests that China possesses the financial strength and industrial capability to develop a sizeable naval force for all types of missions within a short period of time.

Notes

1. Please see Chapter V of the white paper *China's National Defence in 2008* (Beijing, People's Republic of China, 2009). The paper, published in January 2009, stated 'the Navy is a strategic service of the PLA, and the main force for maritime operations. It is responsible for such tasks as safeguarding China's maritime security and maintaining the sovereignty of its territorial waters, along with its maritime rights and interests'. Also in the same chapter it stated 'since the 1980s, the Navy has realised a strategic transformation to offshore defensive operations'.

2. Anthony H Cordesman and Martin Kleiber, *The Asian Conventional Military Balance in 2006* (Washington DC, Centre for Strategic and International Studies, 2006), p.25. The strength of the Coastal Defence Forces was an estimate by the author based on the units identified so far.

3. *China's Navy 2007* (Maryland, Office of Naval Intelligence, 2007), p 58.

4. Inspired by the example of the British RFA *Argus*, the PLAN experimentally converted a container ship, *Huayuankou*, into a training vessel for helicopter take-off and landing in the 1980s. The project provided the PLAN with experience in converting merchant ships for military purposes. In 2008, an oil tanker was converted to become a hospital ship (hull number 865). Fishing vessels have been frequently used for troop transport and minesweeping roles in exercises since the mid-1990s.

5. Please see Dawei Xia, 'China Starts Training 50 Carrier Pilots', *Jane's Defence Weekly* – 15 September 2008 (Coulsdon, Jane's Information Group, 2008).

6. 'Russia to Deliver Su-33 Fighters to China', *Kommersant* – 23 October 2006 (Moscow, Kommersant Publishing): www.kommersant.com/p715509/r_528/China_jet_fighters_export/. The article suggested that two planes for trial could be delivered to the PLAN as early as 2008.

THE INDIAN OCEAN, AFRICA AND THE MIDDLE EAST Regional Review

Author: Conrad Waters

See page 12

The Indian Ocean region is fast becoming a global focal point for naval operations. The importance of the neighbouring Persian Gulf as a key conduit for international oil supplies, coupled with tensions relating to Iran and Iraq, has meant that the region has long been subject to a relatively heavy naval presence. However, the increasing asymmetric threat posed by piracy – particularly off the Horn of Africa – has given this presence a new dimension. Piracy off the Somali coast has been an increasing thorn in the side of merchant shipping throughout the duration of that country's protracted civil war. However, incidents such as the seizure of the French luxury yacht *Le Ponant* in April 2008 and, most notably, that of the Ukrainian-owned *Faina* with her cargo of thirty-three T-72 tanks in September of that year served to increase the threat's profile dramatically. The outcome has been a significant increase in naval resources allocated to combat the menace, including the United States-initiated Combined Task Force 151 and the European Union's first ever naval mission, Operation 'Atalanta'.[1] This heightened presence has produced some results, most notably the successful outcome to the *Maersk Alabama* hijacking in April 2009. However, legal limitations on the actions that can be taken against the pirates, coupled with an inability to take the war to the enemy and strike at their Somali bases, means that the current situation is, at best, an unsatisfactory stalemate.

It is also difficult to avoid being a little cynical about the motivations of some of the nations involved in anti-piracy operations, particularly given the Indian Ocean's broader strategic importance as a major transit route for trade in manufactured goods and raw materials. The Chinese PLAN's anti-piracy mission has certainly provided an opportunity to test the country's ability to protect one of its key Sea Lines of Communication (SLOC) under the cloak of international co-operation. It is interesting to speculate how India, which is on its own long-term mission to achieve regional maritime pre-eminence in the Indian Ocean, views this increased activity in its own backyard. One reaction appears to have been something of a restructuring of international alliances. For example, India's links with 'Western' navies such as those of Australia, Japan, Singapore and the US are now seemingly closer than hitherto.

The broader African continent also seems to be subject to greater interest from the major maritime nations than previously. This is partly because of anti-terrorism considerations but doubtless also because of the growing importance of the region's vast mineral wealth. The activation of a new US Africa Command on 1 October 2008 was one indication of this trend. This appears to have been complemented by a general increase in USN and NATO deployments to the continent's waters.

Opposite: An increased Chinese presence in the Indian Ocean is giving rise to new alliances. Here the Indian Project 61ME *Rajput* class destroyer *Ranvir* refuels from the Royal Australian Navy replenishment vessel *Success* in April 2009. *(Royal Australian Navy)*

Table 2.3.1: FLEET STRENGTHS IN THE INDIAN OCEAN, AFRICA AND THE MIDDLE EAST – LARGER NAVIES (MID-2009)

COUNTRY	ALGERIA	EGYPT	INDIA	IRAN	ISRAEL	PAKISTAN	SAUDI ARABIA	SOUTH AFRICA
Support/Helicopter Carrier (CVS/CVH)	–	–	1	–	–	–	–	–
Patrol Submarine (SSK/SS)	2	4	16	3	3	5	–	3
Fleet Escort (DDG/FFG)	–	6	20	–	–	6	6[2]	4
Patrol Escort/Corvette (FFG/FSG/FS)	6	4	8	6	3	–	4	–
Missile Armed Attack Craft (PGG/PTG)	12	30[1]	12	24	10	6	9	3
Mine Countermeasures Vessel (MCMV)	–	14	10	–	–	3	7	4
Major Amphibious (LPD)	–	–	1	–	–	–	–	–

Notes:

1 Egyptian fast attack craft numbers approximate

2 Status of one Saudi Arabian fleet escort doubtful following grounding damage.

Meanwhile, the Middle East has been mercifully quiet since the last Israeli incursion into Lebanon in 2006. However, the maritime task force component of the United Nation's UNIFIL peacekeeping mission continues to remain active off the country coast in support of its mission to combat illicit arms shipments. The naval force has provided Germany with a good opportunity to demonstrate its new-found willingness to engage in international security operations and the *Deutsche Marine* took charge of the task group between October 2006 and February 2008. Current command is in the hands of Italy's *Marina Militare* following a handover from Belgium on 1 June 2009. Elsewhere, the embryonic Iraqi Navy is taking increasing responsibility for the country's coastal waters as the drawdown of allied coalition forces continues. Nonetheless, the major Western powers remain keen to maintain a military presence in the region. This was demonstrated by the visit by France's President Sarkozy to Abu Dhabi on 26 May 2009 to inaugurate the first French bases in the Gulf. Other nations are also said to be interested in bolstering their presence in the Middle East. For example, Russia has been reported as eyeing the possibility of naval facilities in Libya or Syria as part of a return to a more assertive Mediterranean presence.

Table 2.3.1 provides details of regional fleet strengths as at the middle of 2009.

INDIAN OCEAN NAVIES

Bangladesh: Home to the world's seventh largest but one of the world's poorest populations, Bangladesh has ambitious plans for military modernisation that have yet to achieve much in the way of tangible results. Current naval forces are focused on a core of five patrol frigates, three of which are former Royal Navy Type 41 and Type 61 diesel-powered escorts built in the 1950s. Plans to replace them with more modern ships were confirmed in February 2009, with local construction of Turkish-designed Milgem corvettes one possible way forward. In the meantime, the most modern frigate – the South Korean-built derivative of the *Ulsan* class, *Khalid Bin Walid* – is to be refitted with Chinese surface-to-surface and surface-to-air missiles.

India: By far the strongest and most influential of the region's fleets, the Indian navy continues along its slow but steady path to become one of the world's

The Indian frigate *Beas* departs Portsmouth Harbour in June 2009 prior to exercises in the North Atlantic with the British Royal and French navies. *(Conrad Waters)*

Table 2.3.2: INDIAN NAVY: PRINCIPAL UNITS AS AT MID-2009

TYPE	CLASS	NUMBER	TONNAGE	DIMENSIONS	PROPULSION	CREW	DATE
Aircraft Carriers							
Aircraft Carrier (CV)	**VIRAAT** (HERMES)	1	29,000 tons	227m x 27/49m x 9m	Steam, 28 knots	1,350	1959
Principal Surface Escorts							
Destroyer – DDG	Project 15 **DELHI**	3	6,900 tons	163m x 17m x 7m	COGAG, 32 knots	360	1997
Destroyer – DDG	Project 61 ME **RAJPUT** ('Kashin')	5	5,000 tons	147m x 16m x 5m	COGAG, 35 knots	320	1980
Frigate – FFG	Project 1135.6 **TALWAR**	3	4,000 tons	125m x 15m x 5m	COGAG, 30 knots	180	2003
Frigate – FFG	Project 16A **BRAHMAPUTRA**	3	4,000 tons	127m x 15m x 5m	Steam, 30 knots	350	2000
Frigate – FFG	Project 16 **GODAVARI**	3	3,850 tons	127m x 15m x 5m	Steam, 30 knots	315	1983
Frigate – FFG	**NILGIRI** (LEANDER)	3	3,000 tons	114m x 13m x 5m	Steam, 28 knots	300	1974
Corvette – FSG	Project 25A **KORA**	4	1,400 tons	91m x 11m x 5m	Diesel, 25 knots	125	1998
Corvette – GSG	Project 25 **KHUKRI**	4	1,400 tons	91m x 11m x 5m	Diesel, 25 knots	110	1989
Submarines							
Submarine – SSK	Project 877 EKM **SINDHUGHOSH** ('Kilo')	10	3,000 tons	73m x 10m x 7m	Diesel-electric, 17 knots	55	1986
Submarine – SSK	**SHISHUMAR** (Type 209)	4	1,900 tons	64m x 7m x 6m	Diesel-electric, 22 knots	40	1986
Submarine – SSK	Project 641 **VELA** ('Foxtrot')	2	2,500 tons	91m x 8m x 6m	Diesel-electric, 16 knots	75	1967
Major Amphibious Units							
Landing Platform Dock – LPD	**JALASHWA** (AUSTIN)	1	17,000 tons	173m x 26/30m x 7m	Steam, 21 knots	405	1971

leading 'blue water' forces. Although adequate financial resources are being made available to fund a significant modernisation and expansion programme, a desire to support indigenous construction capabilities is slowing delivery of new capabilities due to the need to upgrade existing infrastructure. The Indian navy's reliance on imported Russian technology is also proving to be somewhat problematic. The highest-profile example of this is the ongoing delay to the refurbished Russian aircraft carrier *Vikramaditya* (ex-*Admiral Gorshkov*), which was initially due to be delivered in 2008 as a much-needed replacement for the elderly *Viraat* (ex-British Royal Navy *Hermes*) but which will not now be in Indian hands until 2012. The original cost of the upgrade was said to be around US$1bn but recent press reports suggest that a series of demands from Russia has raised the cumulative total to as much as US$2.9bn as more and more problems have emerged with the refurbishment. Although agreement had yet to be agreed between the Indian and Russian authorities as of June 2009, the project looks increasingly bad value for the Indian navy given the broadly similar cost associated with a brand new British Royal Navy *Queen Elizabeth* class CVF. However, with over US$600m already handed over to Russia in progress payments, the Indian bargaining position looks weak.

India is also heavily reliant on Russia for the provision of submarine equipment, particularly in support of its secretive advanced technology vessel (AVT) nuclear submarine programme. However, there have been problems here as well. The planned lease of the Project 971 'Akula' class nuclear-powered attack submarine *Nerpa* to act as an interim training vessel has been delayed due to the accidental activation of the vessel's fire-fighting system during November 2008 sea trials that killed twenty personnel onboard. Recent reports suggest that repairs have now been effected and that the submarine will be delivered before the end of 2009. In spite of these difficulties, India appears determined to maintain defence co-operation with Russia. An order for a third batch of Project 1135.6 *Talwar* class frigates is one of a number of additional contracts that are being discussed.

Operationally, the Indian navy is becoming increasingly ambitious in the scope of its activities. A much-heralded deployment to Lebanon to protect Indian nationals during the 2006 Israeli incursions attracted widespread domestic support. More recently, a powerful Indian task group comprising the Project 15 destroyer *Delhi*, the Project 16A frigates *Brahmaputra* and *Beas* and the fleet replenishment tanker *Aditya* travelled as far as the North Atlantic in June 2009 for anti-submarine exercises with the British Royal Navy and France's *Marine Nationale*. According to reports in the Indian newspaper *The Hindu*, the deployment is intended to give the task group direct experience of operating and fighting in the different hydrographic and meteorological conditions prevailing in the Atlantic.

Chapter 2.3A provides an in-depth assessment of the Indian Navy's recent development and current force structure. An overview of current principal units is set out in Table 2.3.2.

Pakistan: Traditionally India's major regional rival in the Indian Ocean, the Islamic Republic of Pakistan's navy has become increasingly outclassed by its neighbour's naval forces in recent years. To some extent, this reflects significant disparity in the two countries' economies, although instability in Pakistan and the consequent need to focus on internal security has also played a part. Whilst efforts are being made to remedy this situation, Pakistan's navy has been shrinking in size. In addition, much of its equipment is obsolescent. A summary of principal units is provided in Table 2.3.3.

The heart of the surface fleet is a relatively homogenous flotilla of six modernised Type 21 frigates of 1970s vintage that were acquired from Britain's Royal Navy during 1993-4. They are to be joined by four Chinese-designed F22P *Zulfiqar* patrol frigates that are reported to be a much-modernised variant of the Type 053H3 'Jiangwei II' class. Displacing around 2,500 tons in full load condition and with an

Table 2.3.3: PAKISTAN NAVY: PRINCIPAL UNITS AS AT MID-2009

TYPE	CLASS	NUMBER	TONNAGE	DIMENSIONS	PROPULSION	CREW	DATE
Principal Surface Escorts							
Frigate – FFG	**TARIQ** (Type 21)	6	3,600 tons	117m x 13m x 7m	COGOG, 32 knots	180	1974
Submarines							
Submarine – SSK	**HAMZA** (AGOSTA 90B/AIP)	1	2,050 tons	76m x 7m x 6m	AIP, 20 knots	40	2008
Submarine – SSK	**KHALID** (AGOSTA 90B)	2	1,750 tons	68m x 7m x 6m	Diesel-electric, 20 knots	40	1999
Submarine – SSK	**HASHMAT** (AGOSTA)	2	1,750 tons	68m x 7m x 6m	Diesel-electric, 20 knots	55	1979

overall length of 118m, they will be capable of 29 knots from a CODAD power arrangement. A contract reported to be valued at US$750m was signed for the ships' acquisition in 2006. Construction of the first three units is now well advanced at China's Hudong Zhonghua shipyard in Shanghai, from where the third was launched on 28 May 2009. The first two should have entered service by the start of 2010. The final ship is to be built at Karachi Shipyard & Engineering Works, where the first steel was cut on 5 March 2009. Pakistan also hopes to supplement this contract with the purchase of surplus second-hand units. Greek *Elli* (ex-Dutch *Kortenaer*) and US *Oliver Hazard Perry* (FFG-7) class frigates, as well as surplus British Type 42 destroyers, have all been touted as potential candidates. As many

as six vessels might be acquired to replace the Type 21 class on a one-for-one basis.

Modernisation of the submarine force is a little more advanced. All three 'Agosta 90B' *Khalid* class boats ordered from France as long ago as 1994 are

finally in service following the commissioning of the final vessel, *Hamza*, on 26 September 2008. Along with the second class member, *Saad*, she was locally built in Karachi, marking a major achievement for local industry. In contrast to the two earlier boats she is fitted with the DCNS MESMA AIP-system, which allows around three weeks uninterrupted underwater operation. The system, which requires

---

The Pakistan Navy's Type 21 frigate *Tippu Sultan* in the Arabian Sea. Pakistan urgently needs to upgrade its surface fleet with new construction. *(US Navy)*

insertion of an 8.7m hull-plug, will be retrofitted to the two earlier boats when they fall due for major refit. Additional submarines are required to replace the former *Daphne* class units decommissioned in 2006, as well as the two 1970s-vintage *Agosta* boats that remain in service. Reports suggest that the German Type 214 AIP-equipped design is front-runner for the contract, possibly reflecting Pakistan's disquiet at France's sale of *Scorpène* technology to regional rival India.

Sri Lanka: The small Sri Lanka navy is celebrating success after the 25-year-long civil war with the Liberation Tigers of Tamil Eelam (LTTE) was brought to a close with the official announcement of an end to the insurgency by Sri Lanka's president in May 2009. The navy is likely to reconfigure itself to facilitate a broader range of operations now the conflict appears to be over.[2]

AFRICAN NAVIES

With the notable exception of South Africa, Sub-Saharan Africa is a virtual desert so far as material local developments are concerned, with most significant naval activity being driven by non-indigenous navies. On the west coast of Africa, there are some signs that the overall readiness of **Nigeria's** naval forces is being upgraded, with previously non-operational warships being returned to service and new patrol vessels and helicopters being acquired as part of a response to unrest in the oil-rich Niger delta. On the other side of the continent, **Kenya** has signed a contract with Italy's Fincantieri to conduct midlife refits of the two *Nyayo* fast attack craft, which were first delivered by the UK's Vosper Thornycroft in the late 1980s. The Italian company expects a substantial increase in demand for patrol vessels from the African Continent to provide a more effective response to piracy and low-level insurgency and this might result in greater news-flow in years to come.

North Africa: The fleets along Africa's northern coast-line have been stepping up naval acquisitions in recent years, in part reflecting greater purchasing power as commodity prices have increased. One country benefiting from this trend has been **Algeria**, which is currently awaiting the delivery of two additional 'Kilo' class submarines from Russia to join the existing pair commissioned in the 1980s. Algeria has also ordered AW-101 Merlin and Super Lynx helicopters from Augusta-Westland and is said to be in

Above: The AIP-equipped submarine *Hamza* pictured shortly after launch at Karachi Shipyard & Engineering Works in August 2006. Pakistan will retrofit AIP equipment to its two other Agosta 90B type boats. *(DCNS)*

Right: Nigeria is making progress in returning previously non-operational units to service. The MEKO 360 frigate *Aradu* is seen here visiting the UK in the aftermath of the Trafalgar 2005 naval review. *(Alexander Waters)*

the market for new surface escorts. The French FREMM design is said to be the most likely contender for the deal, although shipyards in Germany and the United Kingdom are also bidding.

Neighbouring **Morocco** has also been bolstering its naval forces, with two major contracts announced in the course of 2008. France has traditionally been one of the country's major suppliers and has achieved further success with a contact for a FREMM type frigate, representing the Franco-Italian design's first export order. Morocco has also forged a new relationship with the Netherlands' Schelde Naval Shipbuilding for the supply of three enlarged variants of the Sigma class corvette already sold to Indonesia under a contract estimated to be worth c.US$1.2bn. The agreement envisages the delivery of two 98m and one 105m diesel-powered ships between 2011 and 2013. All will be equipped with a state-of-the-art

combat system and sensors manufactured by Thales Nederland, with armament including Exocet surface-to-surface and Mica surface-to-air missiles, as well as a 76mm gun.

Libya and **Egypt** are other North African nations looking to bolster their naval capabilities, with both seeking new fast attack craft. Libya is reportedly discussing a deal for three Russian Project 1241.1/8 'Tarantul' missile boats, whilst Egypt has concluded lengthy negotiations for three US-built 'Ambassador III' vessels. Delivery of the latter is scheduled for the 2012–13 timeframe.

South Africa: The post-apartheid era South African Navy has emerged as a significant and capable force that is well-equipped to exert considerable regional influence. The navy's increasing diplomatic presence has been demonstrated by lengthy deployments to Europe and Asia, as well as increased interaction with other leading navies.

The most significant naval units are three 'Heroine' class Type 209 patrol submarines and four

Morocco has ordered two 98-metre and one 105-metre (pictured here) Sigma corvettes from Schelde Naval Shipbuilding. The ships feature command & control and sensor systems from Thales Nederland, including the increasingly popular SMART-S Mk2 surveillance radar. *(Thales Nederland)*

Four 'Valour' class MEKO A-200 frigates form the core of South Africa's surface forces. Here *Spioenkop* is pictured with two of her sisters before being fitted with combat systems. *(Thyssen Krupp Marine Systems)*

Table 2.3.4: PROJECTED SOUTH AFRICAN NAVY DEVELOPMENT (2010-25)

SHIP TYPE	NUMBER: 2010	NUMBER: 2025
Frigate – FFG	4	4
Patrol Submarine – SSK	3	3
Fast Attack Craft	3	0
Multirole Offshore Patrol Vessel – OPV	0	3
Inshore Patrol Vessel – IPV	0	3
Coastal Patrol Vessel – PB	3	0
Mine Warfare Vessels	4	0
Major Amphibious Vessel – LHD/LDS	0	1

'Valour' class MEKO A-200 frigates, which were ordered from German shipbuilders during 1999–2000. The latter are equipped with newly-acquired Super Lynx helicopters. The programme was completed with the arrival of the final Type 209, *Queen Modjadji*, at Simon's Town on 22 May 2008. Although there has been some debate within South Africa whether the navy has the operational funding or personnel expertise to deploy such sophisticated warships to maximum effect, operational availability appears to be improving as greater attention is paid to retaining key staff.

Future force structure is set out in the Defence Update 2025 plan, which should be approved by the end of 2009. The most eye-catching item on the navy's wish list is the acquisition of a strategic support ship, which could be a variant of the French *Mistral* LHD type. Other significant purchases will include three offshore and three inshore patrol vessels, the former being one-for-one replacements of the remaining 'Warrior' fast attack craft that have been re-assigned to the patrol role. Both patrol ship programmes are being managed under Project Biro, which envisages the offshore vessels being around 85m in length and equipped with a 76mm gun and helicopter. The inshore ships will be smaller, 55m vessels with a 30mm main armament. It is anticipated that both types will be built locally in South Africa and be marketed to meet the requirements of other regional forces.[3]

Please refer to Table 2.3.4 for the likely evolution of South African naval strength.

MIDDLE EASTERN NAVIES

Iran: Whilst the Islamic Republic of Iran Navy continues to adopt an assertive public stance, not least the dispatch of warships as far as the Gulf of Aden in what has been claimed to be an anti-piracy mission, hard information on the fleet's recent devel-

opment has been scarce. With only restricted access to overseas weaponry given concerns over the country's nuclear ambitions, there has been increased reliance on local production, most notably a series of mini-submarines. It also appears that the remaining three *Alvand* (Vosper Mk5) frigates that form the core component of the surface fleet have been reinforced by at least one similar locally-built ship.

Israel: Undoubtedly the most effective regional navy, Israel's fleet is awaiting reinforcement by new submarines and surface vessels. The submarine flotilla currently comprises three German-built Type 800 *Dolphin* class boats that were constructed with the benefit of considerable subsidies from the German government. They are to be joined early in the coming decade by a further two boats currently being built by Germany's Thyssen Krupp Marine Systems under a secretive US$1.3bn contract signed in 2006. The new submarines will be AIP-equipped variants of the existing class and are reported to incorporate a number of other improvements. There have been rumours that at least some of the submarines have the ability to carry out nuclear strikes by means of 'Popeye turbo' cruise missiles.

The most potent surface vessels are the three heavily-armed 1,300-ton SAAR 5 *Eilat* corvettes completed by the then Ingalls, Pascagoula yard between 1994 and 1995. They are supplemented by a range of smaller vessels, including ten SAAR 4.5 and SAAR 4 missile-armed fast attack craft and increasing numbers of 'Super Dvora' and 'Shaldag' patrol craft. The next significant acquisition is likely to be for a new class of slightly larger surface combatant. Extensive discussions have been held with Lockheed Martin for the construction of up to

The centre section of an Israeli SAAR 5 corvette. Israel is currently considering designs for a new class of surface combatant. *(US Navy)*

four enhanced *Freedom* (LCS-1) type littoral combat ships. This plan would provide welcome commonality with USN technology and assist future support arrangements but recent reports suggest that cost considerations are likely to prove problematic. As a result, other design options are now being explored.

Oman: The Royal Navy of Oman is a small but efficient force whose main constituents are currently two *Qahir* class corvettes and three smaller *Al Bushra* class offshore patrol vessels built in the mid-1990s, as well as four *Dhofar* fast attack craft of slightly older vintage. They will soon be joined by three larger, 100m ocean patrol vessels currently under construction at BVT's Portsmouth facility under a £400m (US$650m) contract signed in January 2007 to meet the requirements of Project Khareef. Scheduled for delivery from 2010, these vessels will be outfitted with armament and systems – including 76mm and 30mm guns, surface-to-surface and surface-to-air missiles, helicopter and a Thales SMART-S Mk2 surveillance radar and TACITOS combat management system – that place them close to a light frigate in terms of capabilities.

Saudi Arabia: The Royal Saudi Naval Forces are relatively weak in comparison with the other branches of the Saudi armed services and face the additional geographical complication of having to maintain separate forces on the Red Sea (Western Fleet) and Persian Gulf (Eastern Fleet). The Western Fleet is traditionally comprised of the largest vessels and includes the four *Madina* and three *Al Riyadh* frigates constructed by France under the Sawari I and Sawari II arms programmes. The latter are particularly capable 4,700-ton developments of the *La Fayette* design with potent anti-air defences built around a combination of the Aster 15 missile and Arabel radar.[4] However, the status of the second ship of the class – *Makkah* – remains uncertain following a high-speed grounding off the Western Fleet's main naval base at Jeddah in December 2004 shortly after delivery. The influential *Jane's Fighting Ships* indicates that the fleet spends little time at sea and this incident certainly suggests a need to improve basic seamanship.

The Eastern Fleet is home to most of the navy's corvettes and patrol forces, including four 1,000-ton members of the *Badr* class delivered by the United States between 1980 and 1983 and the bulk of the

navy's inventory of nine 500-ton *Al Siddiq* class fast attack craft of similar vintage. These are now quite elderly in comparison with many of their counterparts in the fleets of other countries bordering the Persian Gulf and their replacement can be expected within the next few years.

United Arab Emirates: Home of one of the smaller Gulf navies, the United Arab Emirates is currently focused on the construction of six compact missile-armed corvettes under the *Baynunah* programme contracted to Abu Dhabi Shipbuilding in conjunction with France's CMN. An order for four ships was first placed on 28 December 2003, with an option for a further two exercised in July 2005. The French yard is building the lead ship, which was scheduled for launch during the summer of 2009. The other five vessels are in the course of construction in Abu Dhabi, with work on the sixth and final vessel commencing on 26 October 2008. The ships are extremely heavily armed for their size, with a 76mm main gun, eight Exocet surface-to-surface missiles, a VLS for Sea Sparrow surface-to-air missiles, a RAM close-in weapons system and helicopter deck and hangar all being squeezed into a 70m hull.[5]

Three light frigate-like offshore patrol vessels are being built by the UK's BVT Surface Fleet for the Royal Navy of Oman. They are another modern class that feature Thales Nederland's SMART-S Mk 2 surveillance radar. *(Thales Nederland)*

Notes

1. Briefing notes on the EU's anti-piracy mission can be found on the Council of Europe's website at: www.consilium.europa.eu/showpage.aspx?id= 1521&lang=EN

2. An interesting overview of the Sri Lanka Navy's important role in bringing the LTTE insurrection to an end can be found in Tim Fish's 'Sri Lanka learns to counter Sea Tigers' swarm tactics', *Jane's Navy International* – March 2009 (Coulsdon, HIS Jane's, 2009), pp 20–5.

3. A good source of information on the little-reported African defence market is the South African defenceWEB site. It can be found at www.defenceweb.co.za

4. French speaking readers should refer to Michel Perchoc, 'Le tour du bord ... en 80 jours d'essais à la mer' *Marines et Forces Navales* – Juin-Juillet 2002 (Nantes, Marines Editions, 2002), pp 4-17 for an excellent review of the class's design and development.

5. The best available description of this class is contained in the Naval Technology website – please refer to www.naval-technology.com/projects/baynunah

THE INDIAN NAVY

India's Mahanian quest for control of the seas in the Indian Ocean region has seen its navy assume a central and visible role in recent years as the country's stature grows internationally. To realise this aspiration, about a decade ago the Indian Navy set about formulating a number of policy papers and a maritime doctrine, whilst initiating an ambitious fleet renewal programme. This was aimed at arresting declining force levels, whilst – at the same time – transforming the fleet into a three-dimensional, high technology and networked force with aircraft carrier strike groups and a seaborne nuclear deterrent equally capable of protecting India's 'blue water' maritime interests and projecting power in littoral regions. At the time of writing, the plan is to have a 160-warship fleet along with 300 aircraft by 2022. This article provides a brief introduction to the Indian Navy's organisation and composition, as well as giving an overview of the fleet renewal programme.

Author: Mrityunjoy Mazumdar

Mrityunjoy Mazumdar, whose father served in the Indian Navy, has been writing on naval matters since 1999. His words and pictures have appeared in many naval and aircraft magazines around the world. He is a regular contributor to *Jane's Fighting Ships*, *Flotes des Combat*, *Combat Fleets of the World* and *Weyers Flotten Taschenbuch*. He also maintains a comprehensive website on the Indian Navy at www.bharat-rakshak.com. Mr Mazumdar lives in Alameda, California with his wife.

THE INDIAN NAVY: A BRIEF OVERVIEW

The Indian Navy (IN), with a strength of some 95,000 service and civilian personnel, around 135 commissioned ships and submarines and c.200 aircraft in its Fleet Air Arm, is a major navy. In terms of tonnage and number of platforms, it ranks around fifth amongst navies of the world. In recent years, in keeping with India's rising global stature and great-power aspirations, the IN has rapidly emerged from its relative isolation during the Cold War era to become a significant world player. The IN is now recognised by its government as an effective instrument for promoting India's foreign policy along Mahanian lines and its share of the defence budget has accordingly increased from 13 per cent to c.18 per cent in recent years. The navy's formally stated vision is 'to create and sustain a three-dimensional, technology-enabled and networked force capable of safeguarding India's maritime interests on the high seas and projecting combat power across the littoral'.

Operationally the IN is organised into three commands. Western Naval Command, controlling the Western Fleet, is based primarily at Mumbai and Karwar. Eastern Naval Command, with the Eastern Fleet, is based at Vishakapatnam. The Southern Naval Command at Kochi is responsible for all ashore and afloat training assets – including First Training Squadron (1TS) with up to four naval ships and a Coast Guard offshore patrol vessel on detachment. A large local flotilla is also assigned to the tri-service Andaman and Nicobar Command. The Navy's Fleet Air Arm (FAA) is headquartered at Goa. It controls close to 200 aircraft in eighteen squadrons

The Project 16A frigate *Beas*. Built in India by Garden Reach Shipbuilders & Engineers in Kolkata (Calcutta), she was commissioned in July 2005 as the newest steam turbine powered frigate in the world. The ship's lineage can be traced back to the *Leander* – and even the Type 12 – frigates. *(Conrad Waters)*

from at least eight bases around the country. The Submarine Service operates sixteen submarines under a Flag Officer Submarines (FOSM), with a number of submarine squadrons distributed amongst both fleets.

Even though the IN's heritage is steeped in Royal Navy traditions, the prevailing geopolitical situation in the 1960s left the IN no choice but to embrace the Soviet Russian offer of warships and submarines because the British and American governments of the day would not supply the ships that the Indians wanted. Consequently, the IN has uniquely evolved into a navy with a dual heritage: one that embraces both Western and Russian naval practices, doctrine, tactics and technologies. At one time, the IN was practically two separate navies: the Western Fleet with ships of British lineage and the Eastern Fleet with Russian-supplied ships and submarines. Today, this dual heritage is still very much evident in fleet composition: there is a mixture of warships from the West, Russia and locally-developed hybrid platforms mixing Western and Russian technologies.

The IN took an early lead in becoming a builder's navy by setting up an in-house Corps of Naval Constructors on 23 November 1956 to undertake indigenous repair, design and construction of warships. In the early days, the naval architects were primarily trained in the UK, then in India (at the faculty of Naval Architecture at IIT Kharagpur) and later in Russia. Starting with the design of auxiliary craft, a survey vessel (*Darshak*) and seaward defence boats, the naval architects gradually progressed to the construction of larger combatants. A notable step was commencement of work on *Nilgiri*, an Admiralty Broad Beam *Leander* design, at Mazagaon Docks Ltd (MDL), Bombay (now Mumbai) in the late 1960s. Six *Leander* frigates were ultimately ordered, the last two being significantly different from the original design. This, in turn, set the stage for the first major indigenous warship design in early 1975 when conceptual design work on the Project 16 (P-16) *Godavari* class frigates commenced. The P-16 used a scaled-up *Leander* hull form with a mix of Russian and Western weapons and sensors. The design is actually faster than the *Leander*s in spite of using the same Yarrow Y160 propulsion package and having a 35 per cent greater displacement. The latest evolution of the *Leander* design is represented by the three P-16A *Brahmaputra* class frigates, the last of which commissioned in July 2005 as the newest steam powered warship in the world.

The Directorate of Naval Design (DND), as it is known today, has since produced over seventeen designs and is working on several more projects. It is rapidly acquiring the necessary experience and maturity to produce state-of-the-art warships and submarines. The present trend is for the DND to offload detailed design work to the shipyards, thus freeing up the organisation to concentrate more on conceptual and preliminary designs.

India's fleet includes an extensive flotilla of sixteen patrol submarines, of which ten are Russian-built 'Kilo' types. This is the newly modernised *Sindhuvijay* with much Indian-built equipment including the USHUS sonar suite, communications suite and the Porpoise ESM system. Significantly, the submarine now fires the Klub family of missiles, including the land attack 3M-14E variant. *(Conrad Waters)*

India's navy is assuming an increasingly visible role as the country grows in international stature. Here the aircraft carrier *Viraat* (the former Royal Navy *Hermes*) takes centre stage during a PhotoEx involving 42 ships shortly after the 2006 Fleet Review. The next decade should see India's full transition to eminence as a leading 'blue water' fleet. *(Mrityunjoy Mazumdar)*

FLEET COMPOSITION

At the time of writing, it is estimated that the IN has c.135 commissioned vessels and submarines in service, along with several dozen auxiliaries and yard craft. This tally includes sixteen diesel submarines and nearly thirty so-called 'principal surface combatants comprising one carrier *Viraat* (ex-HMS *Hermes*), eight guided-missile destroyers, twelve frigates and eight missile corvettes. These are supplemented by six large offshore patrol vessels, some of which have been converted to carry the seaborne 'Dhanush' cruise missile. Other significant units include twelve Project 1241RE 'Tarantul I' missile boats and four Project 1241PE 'Pauk II' anti-submarine patrol ships, each displacing c.450 tons. The large Project 266ME 'Natya I' class minesweepers and eight indigenous *Sandhayak* armed survey ships – the latter equipped with an organic helicopters and interceptor boats – serve as a useful adjunct to these ships in the patrolling role. Amphibious ships include a large landing platform dock, *Jalashwa* (ex-USS *Trenton*), as well as tank landing ships of the *Shardul*, *Magar* and Project 773 'Polnochny' types. Fleet replenishment assets have dwindled down to two dedicated vessels and there are some other auxiliaries.

The Indian Naval Air Arm has c.200 aircraft in its inventory. This includes around ten remaining upgraded Sea Harrier FRS51 fighters and four T60 trainers; thirteen long-range maritime patrol aircraft (eight gigantic Tu-142MKE 'Bears' and five IL-38SD 'Mays'); about twenty Dornier 228 short-range patrol aircraft and approximately 100 helicopters of various types. Other types operated include twelve indigenous 'Kiran' Mk1/II jet trainers and over a dozen Israeli 'Searcher' and 'Heron' unmanned aerial vehicles (UAVs) and a few PTA target drones.

FLEET EXPANSION PLANS

To achieve the goal of a 160-ship navy, the IN has been working on a fleet renewal programme over the last decade. Naval planners have been relatively successful in making up shortfalls in platforms from the so called 'lost decade' between 1985 and 1995, when no new major warships were ordered and block obsolescence of platforms threatened to reduce force levels to unacceptable numbers. They have done so with a judicious mix of foreign acquisitions and domestic production using five-, ten- and fifteen-year building plans that are reviewed every five years or as the situation demands. Over seventy-five major

The Indian Naval Air Arm has c. 200 aircraft in its inventory. This is a HAL Chetak (Aérospatiale Alouette III) light utility helicopter. Several of these helicopters will be converted to unmanned aerial vehicles under the joint HAL-IAI NRUAV project. *(US Navy)*

and minor naval vessels were sanctioned by the Indian Government for completion during the 10th and 11th Five Year Plan periods (2002–12). Several of these have entered service. A total of twenty-one ships and fourteen aircraft were inducted during the 9th Five Year Plan period (1997–2002) with another twelve ships and twenty-four aircraft (including twelve UAVs) entering service during the 10th Five Year Plan (2002–7). Since then, two amphibious ships and two patrol craft have been commissioned. A frigate and another tank landing ship should be delivered before the end of 2009. The naval air arm has received new Dornier Do 228 aircraft, whilst delivery of the first batch of Mig-29K 'Fulcrum' fighters, along with further 'Heron' UAVs, should be completed by early 2010. In what is the biggest arms deal with the USA thus far, eight Boeing P-8I Poseidon maritime patrol aircraft were ordered on 4 January 2009.

In 2007, the IN outlined a requirement of 132 ships and twelve submarines in the form of a fifteen-year Maritime Capability Perspective Plan (MCPP), now referred to as the Long Term Integrated Perspective Plan (LTIPP 2007–2022). A very large portion of these vessels will be of indigenous construction. The LTIPP 2007–2022 document is

expected to be formally approved by India's Defence Acquisition Council by 31 October 2009 – some two years after the navy formulated it.

In the LTIPP, Indian naval planners have sought to strike a balance between 'brown water' and 'blue water' forces, whilst keeping in mind budgetary constraints. Recent events such as 2008's '26/11' terror attacks in Mumbai have shown the need to focus on smaller ships and enhanced co-ordination with various coastguard and marine agencies for effective coastal patrolling, so some changes to the fleet composition are likely. Central to the 'blue water' navy will be three aircraft carriers and around sixty major warships, including submarines. Having three carriers would enable simultaneous operation of two carrier strike groups with a suitable mix of multi-mission capable destroyers, frigates, and corvettes – one for each coast. The last time India operated two carriers simultaneously was in the late eighties, when the elderly *Vikrant* (ex-HMS *Hercules*) was joined by the then newly-acquired *Viraat*. A submarine-based nuclear deterrence capability will be established with a small number of nuclear-powered submarines carrying missiles. According to the Chief of Naval Staff, Admiral Sureesh Mehta: 'We are looking at a submarine force not much larger than our present one in terms of numbers, but certainly one that is adequately equipped to meet the operational requirements of the future.' Amphibious capability is also to be upgraded to include LPD/LPH type platforms. Likewise, fleet replenishment assets will be increased.

A precise breakdown of projected force levels has not been publicly released. However, using data from known construction plans, it is estimated that by 2022 there should be at least ten guided-missile destroyers, twenty-two frigates, up to fifteen corvettes and at least nine large, well-armed OPVs in service, along with three/four LPDs and up to five fleet oilers. In net terms, fleet size will increase by around 20 per cent from current levels, with the naval air arm seeing a 50 per cent expansion.

DELAYS IN INDIGENOUS PROGRAMMES

Warship construction in India is largely in the domain of state-owned Public Sector Unit (PSU) yards such as Garden Reach Shipbuilders & Engineers (GRSE), Goa Shipyard Ltd (GSL), Mazagon Docks Ltd (MDL), Hindustan Shipyard Ltd. (HSL) and Cochin Shipyard Ltd (CSL). A few privately-owned yards deliver most minor patrol and yard craft. It was in only in 2004 that India's largest privately-owned shipbuilder, ABG Shipyards, won a contract to build three large pollution-control vessels for India's Coast Guard. Other private players include Indian engineering giant, Larsen and Toubro (L&T). L&T, actively involved in India's defence aerospace market and the ATV nuclear submarine programme, has obtained licenses for warship and submarine construction.

Naval vessels built in Indian yards tend to be either of indigenous design (with foreign input) from the IN's Directorate of Naval Design (DND) or adapted from foreign models. Warship projects are primarily managed by the Navy's Directorate of Ship Production (DSP) in conjunction with the Warship Overseeing Team (WOT) at Naval Headquarters. These agencies work with the shipyards and various other related agencies. Letters of Intent (LOI) are issued by the navy to shipyards once a preliminary design is ready, but long before equipment, weapon and sensor selection is finalised. Contracts tend to be signed with shipyards on a cost plus basis.

Unfortunately for the navy, extensive delays with indigenous shipbuilding programmes has meant keeping existing platforms in service much longer

India's fleet expansion plans include investment in new replenishment assets. The Garden Reach-built *Aditya* is one of just a handful of replenishment assets currently in commission. *(Conrad Waters)*

Project 15A destroyers under construction at Mazagon Dock, Mumbai. Indian fleet expansion has been delayed by lack of capacity in its shipyards but upgrades are underway. *(Ajai Shulka, Broadsword)*

than originally planned through mid-life upgrades to sustain adequate force levels. In the past decade or so, almost all frigates and destroyers have undergone very significant combat system capability enhancements. Plans are advanced for similar upgrades to Project 25 missile corvettes and other warships.

The reality is that there is a disconnect between the IN's stated plans and the actual shipbuilding output capacity of Indian yards. Simply put, the navy needs at least five to six ships each year and the government-owned shipyards simply cannot deliver at the required rates. The ambitious fleet renewal programme has therefore been slow to deliver. The more the indigenous yards delay, the more the navy resorts to ordering some vessels from foreign yards.

Indian PSU shipyards, for a number of reasons, have been quite unable to deliver ships to the contracted timelines. Some of the major reasons are:

■ A lack of suitable infrastructure at shipyards, such as adequate draft to launch ships that are more than 30 per cent complete (just the hull) and a lack of suitable large cranes.

■ Lack of familiarity and expertise with modular construction methods.

■ An inadequate supplier base for ancillary equipment.

■ Lack of suitable shipbuilding steel or sourcing problems from Russia.

■ Breakdown of the Commonwealth of Independent States (CIS) based supply chain.

■ Ongoing changes to weapons and sensor designs

Table 2.3A.1: INDIAN NAVY – KEY NEW CONSTRUCTION PROGRAMMES

SHIP CLASS	PROJECT 71	PROJECT 15A/15B	PROJECT 17/17A	PROJECT 28	NEW OPV	WJFAC
Type:	Aircraft Carrier	Destroyer (DDG)	Frigate (FFG)	Corvette ASW (FSG)	Offshore Patrol Vessel	Fast Patrol Craft
Building (Planned):	1 (1)	3 (4)	3 (7)	4 (8)	4 (5)	4 built +6
Shipyard:	Cochin Shipyard	Mazagon Docks	Mazagon Docks	Garden Reach SE	Goa Shipyard	Garden Reach SE
Displacement:	40,000 tons	6,800 tons	5,300 tons	2,500 tons	2,250 tons	300 tons
Dimensions:	260m x 60m x 8m	163m x 17m x 7m	143m x 17m x 5m	109m x 15m x 4m	105m x 13m x 5m	50m x 8m x 4m
Propulsion:	COGAG 4 x LM-2500 120,000 hp	COGAG 4 x Zorya DT-59 >64,000 hp	CODOG 2 x LM-2500 2 x Pielstick 16 PA6 STC 64,000 hp	CODAD 4 x Pielstick 12 PA6 STC 23,000 hp	Diesel 2 x Pielstick 20 PA6 STC 22,000 hp	Diesel 3 x HM811 waterjets 3 x MTU 16V 4000 M90 12,000 hp
Speed;	28+ knots	30+ knots	32 knots	25 knots	25 knots	35 knots
Complement:	c. 1,600	c.350	257	123	118	29
Armament:	Surface-to-air missiles (Barak NG), 76mm guns, CIWS	16 x BrahMos VLS SSM 48 x Barak NG VLS SAM 32 x Barak-1 VLS SAM 1 x 127mm gun 4 x AK-630M CIWS 2 x twin 533mm TT 2 x RBU-6000 ASW lhr	8 x SS-N-27 Klub VLS SSM 1 x SA-N-7 Shtil SAM 16 x Barak-1 VLS SAM 1 x 76mm gun 2 x AK-630M CIWS 2 x twin 533mm TT 2 x RBU-6000 ASW lhr	16 x Barak-1 VLS SAM 1 x 76mm gun 2 x AK-630M CIWS 2 x twin 533mm TT 2 x RBU-6000 ASW lhr	1 x 76mm gun 2 x AK-630M CIWS	1 x 30mm gun Igla MANPADs Light machine guns
Aircraft:	30 jets & helicopters	2 helicopters	2 helicopters	1 helicopter	1 helicopter	Nil
Principal Sensors:	Elta EL/M 2248 MF-STAR Thales SMART-L variant	Elta EL/M 2248 MF-STAR BEL RAWL-02 search Garpun Ball TI Fire control radars Humsa-NG bow sonar Active towed-array sonar	'Top Plate' search BEL RAWL-02 search Garpun Ball TI 'Front Dome' fire control Humsa-NG hull sonar Active towed-array sonar	'Revathi' search Lynx fire control Humsa-NG bow sonar Active towed-array sonar	Radar & EO fire control	Furuno search/nav. EO fire control
Electronic Warfare:	Not Known	Ellora EW suite	Ellora EW suite	Ellora EW suite	Sanket Mk2	N/A
Combat Systems Control:	Not Known	AISDN-15A network CAIO-15A	AISDN-17 network CMS-17	CMS-28	Not Known	N/A

Notes:

Given ships are under construction, details of armament and sensors are partly speculative; only principal sensors and systems are listed. P15B & P17A will have differences from P15A/P17.

to fit alternate equipment as a result of supply chain issues and consequent delays in finalising production drawings.

- Introduction of new state-of-the-art technologies: for example, new combat management systems or stealth – and the resulting time required to achieve maturity in local industries.
- Selecting as yet undeveloped weapons and sensors.
- Underestimating project management challenges.

On the plus side, more and more work packages are being outsourced as local industry gains experience. Shipyards have devised new ways to mitigate draft related launching problems by using pontoon-assisted launches to enable at least 50 per cent ship completion prior to launching. There are major yard-modernisation programmes ongoing that will see installation of new large-capacity Goliath cranes, modular construction halls and painting facilities. Recently, both GRSE and MDL have set up joint venture design organisations with France's DCNS to absorb new technologies and apply them in the design of the P-17A frigate. Protracted delays from the broken-down Russian supply chain have forced the development of suitable indigenous raw material such as D40S shipbuilding steel.

The upshot is that – in a decade or less – India's naval shipbuilding industry should have been modernised and matured to a point where ships are built to timescales comparing favourably to Western shipyards. Thus the next group of programmes should benefit considerably from these ongoing projects coming to fruition. The entry of private shipyards should further speed the process, breaking the stranglehold that the comparatively inefficient state-owned yards have had on the navy until now.

OVERVIEW OF CONSTRUCTION PROGRAMMES

Today, there are approximately forty-five ships and submarines on order and at various stages of construction at a number of domestic yards and in foreign facilities in Italy and Russia. Over fifty additional vessels have been sanctioned but not yet formally ordered. Recently, at the keel laying of the P-71 Indigenous Aircraft Carrier on 28 February 2009 at Cochin Shipyard, the Chief of Naval Staff Admiral Sureesh Mehta said that 'over the next 10-12 years, we hope to place orders for something like sixty platforms'. The principal programmes are described below.

AIRCRAFT CARRIERS

Presently, there are two aircraft carrier projects: the indigenous Project 71 (P-71) at Cochin shipyard and the modernisation of the former *Admiral Gorshkov* at Sevmash in Russia. Readers may be only too familiar with the *Gorhskov* saga so it will suffice to say that the Indians literally find themselves over a barrel: Russia continually escalates the price and India acquiesces. Whether the ship – to be named *Vikramaditya* – will actually perform as expected remains to be seen. But by far the more ambitious project is the P-71 and the planned follow-on carriers. At the time of the carrier's keel-laying, officials announced that up to two subsequent vessels, possibly displacing around 60,000 tons, are on the cards. However, some basic truths regarding suitable infrastructure such as bigger berths, cranes and other facilities would need to be resolved before larger ships could be built at Cochin. But this is certainly within the realms of possibility within the next decade or so.

The 40,000-ton P-71 Indigenous Aircraft Carrier (IAC) is undoubtedly the highest-profile naval project in India. Under construction at Cochin Shipyard Ltd (CSL) in technical partnership with Italy's Fincantieri for propulsion system integration and Russia's Nevskoye Design Bureau for the aircraft facilities complex, estimated cost is in excess of US$800m. The ship's design has changed considerably since fabrication commenced: for example, the ship is now larger with an overall length of 260m (252m) and a beam of 60m (57m). Graphics released during the keel-laying ceremony also show a redesigned ski jump along the lines of *Gorshkov* and changes to sensors.

Powered by a COGAG propulsion system similar in layout that is similar to Italy's Fincantieri-built carrier *Cavour*, the IAC will be capable of speeds greater than 28 knots. Renk, through its Indian partner Elecon Engineering, was selected to provide the two main propulsion gearboxes and associated thrust bearings for the COGAG power plant, which features four licence-built GE LM 2500 gas turbines driving two shafts. The gearboxes incorporate double helical teeth for low noise radiation and weigh around 90 tons each.

The planned maximum size of the embarked air wing is thirty aircraft, comprising Mig-29K multi-role fighters, the naval variant of the HAL 'Tejas' light combat aircraft (LCA) and helicopters. Up to seventeen aircraft will be stowed in the hangar. One unique feature is the covered elevators in sponsons,

The Project 71 indigenous aircraft carrier is the Indian Navy's current prestige project. The new carrier's keel was laid on 28 February 2009 and it should be in service around the middle of the coming decade. *(Cochin Shipyard Ltd)*

which provide protection from the elements. The flight deck has a short take-off but arrested recovery (STOBAR) configuration. This will feature two take-off runways and a landing strip with three arrester wires but will not permit simultaneous take-off and landing operations. Defensive systems are likely to encompass a long-range surface-to-air missile system directed by multi-function radar, possibly of Israeli origin, as well as a 'last-ditch' CIWS. Air-warning and control-approach radar arrays are also specified. Integration of all weapon systems onboard the carrier will be through an indigenous combat management system.

Officially sanctioned in January 2003, progress with the IAC after the ceremonial steel cutting on 11 April 2005 was slow. This was due to a lack of Russian-sourced D40S steel, ongoing design changes and technology absorption issues at CSL rather than through any funding constraints. Effective construction only commenced in November 2006 after D40S equivalent steel, DMR 249A, could be developed and sourced locally. The ship is being built in general accordance with the integrated hull outfit and painting (IHOP) method and – at the time of keel laying – CSL had fabricated c.400 of the ship's total 874 blocks. However, outfitting will still take several years, as more than 1,800 compartments will require completion and hundreds of systems need to be installed. Approximately 2,500km of piping, 5,000km of cabling and about 20,000 tonnes of steel

The first Project 17 frigate *Shivalik* is now close to completion and should commission before the end of 2009. Bearing some outward resemblance to the Project 1135.6 *Talwar* class frigates, she is fitted with a mix of Russian, Western and indigenous equipment, including an Oto Melara 76mm gun and SA-N-7 surface-to-air missiles. *(Ajai Shulka, Broadsword)*

will be required for the ship's construction. Launch is currently scheduled for December 2010, with delivery slated four years later. Realistic estimates place the 'in service' date at 2016 at the earliest.

SUBMARINES

Ten years into a thirty-year plan to build twenty-four submarines, the only concrete development is the six boat Project 75 *Scorpène* programme underway at MDL in conjunction with France's DCNS. This originally envisaged delivery of the first boat in 2012 and the last in 2017. The project is being delayed as a result of the steep learning curve and consequent reworking of hull sections and plating. India plans to introduce progressive modification and indigenisation into each successive boat starting with the third boat.

Consequently the first boat is not likely to be delivered by 2012, although the experience gained will be crucial in developing a second production line for submarines and further indigenous development. A second line of submarine construction is planned but the selection of the relevant design has not yet been made. In any event, given that a yard other than MDL is likely to be awarded the contract, significant time will be needed to build up the requisite infrastructure. It will therefore be a few years before construction of the boats can commence and – optimistically – eight to ten years from contract award before the first submarine commissions. It is known that the DGND has been working on a 3,000-ton submarine but whether this will form the basis for a completely new submarine design is not yet clear.

Meanwhile, recent reports indicate that repairs to the Russian Project 971 'Akula II' submarine *Nerpa* are complete and the submarine is set to resume sea trials. The boat is expected to be the transferred to the Indian Navy before the end of 2009. Several dozen lives were lost following the accidental discharge of the fire-fighting system during the boat's first submerged sea trial on 8 November 2008.

Although much has been written about the advanced technology vessel (ATV) nuclear-powered submarine project, other than that the first boat is

expected to enter service in 2011 official information has been scant. However, it is believed that the first of three hulls currently under construction will soon be launched at the secret SBC facility at Visakhapatnam. Built with Russian assistance, there has been widespread participation amongst Indian industry, including that of well-known engineering giant L&T. It is expected that the first vessel will commence trials in late 2009 or 2010. The K-15 missile system for these submarines has been successfully tested, so one major hurdle has been overcome. Ultimately, up to five hulls armed with a mix of ballistic and cruise missiles may become operational.

PROJECT 15A DESTROYER

Three units of this much-modified version of the existing Project 15 *Delhi* class are currently under construction at MDL. They use the proven hull form and COGAG propulsion system of the earlier ships, with changes including a different internal layout, dedicated accommodation for female officers and the incorporation of several stealth features found on the Project 17 *Shivalik* class frigates. The design has evolved from featuring a predominantly Russian anti-air warfare suite to a system derived from Israel's Barak SAM. Untried radars and weapons mean more delays are likely but the ships should be powerful anti-air assets for the navy when completed. Other equipment will include 'BrahMos' surface-to-surface missiles, as well as bow-mounted sonar along with a towed array. The choice of gun system is believed to be between the Italian Oto Melara 127mm mounting and the US BAE Systems version of the same calibre after problems arose with sourcing A-190E 100mm gun mounts from Russia.

Scheduled delivery dates of May 2010, May 2011 and May 2012 appear to have slipped to late 2012/early 2013 for the first unit, which was launched six months behind schedule on 30 March 2006. The second and third ships will be launched with pontoon assistance, thus allowing over 50 per cent hull completion against 30 per cent for the lead ship *Kolkata*. Launch of the second vessel, Yard 12702, is expected sometime in 2009.

Four units of a follow-on design, the Project 15B, have been approved for construction at MDL. The choice of power plant is still undecided between the LM 2500 and the Ukrainian Zorya M36E plants fitted in the earlier ships, although it is believed that the latter lobby may be prevailing.

PROJECT 17 SHIVALIK 'STEALTH' FRIGATE

Also under construction at MDL, these three 5,300-ton frigates are the first stealth warships to be built in India so the learning curve has been steep. First of class, *Shivalik*, should commission before the end of 2009. Although outwardly bearing some resemblance to Russian Project 1135.6 *Talwar* class frigates, the actual design is very different even though a mix of Russian, Western and indigenous equipment means that some weapons and sensors are similar. Propulsion is by means of a CODOG system using the US-designed GE LM 2500 gas turbines also specified for the IAC and French Pielstick diesels. Other Western equipment includes an integrated platform management and battle damage control system supplied by Canada's L3-MAPPS.

The IN has yet to select a foreign partner for the follow-on, seven-ship P-17A programme. The navy wanted two of the seven ships to be built abroad so that Indian technicians could gain knowledge of modular construction techniques but the Indian MoD has mandated that all seven ships be built at MDL and GRSE. Construction of the first P-17A frigate at MDL is expected to commence end 2011 with delivery by 2017. While details have not been released, it is believed that this design will use the Project 17 hull form, with appropriate changes to reflect state of the art design practices, weapons and sensors.

PROJECT 28 ASW CORVETTE

Designed as a relatively low-cost dedicated ASW platform, GRSE's highly-regarded design team has been responsible for jointly designing this class with the navy's DGND. The first of an initial batch of four ships currently on order is due to launch in early 2010 for entry into service by mid 2012. The remainder will follow at yearly intervals.

The vessels have an X-shaped cross section much like the German K-130 class corvettes. They are intended to be relatively cheap, dedicated ASW platforms, with only limited air defences in the form of Barak VLS supplemented by a pair of AK-630M CIWS and a 76mm Oto Melara 'Super Rapid' gun mount. However, they have a good ASW suite supplemented by raft-mounted CODAD machinery to attenuate acoustic signature. There has been particular emphasis on incorporating a high percentage of locally-developed equipment, including the Bharat Electronics 'Revathi' 3D surveillance radar. Much overseas-designed equipment is also built locally under licence.

PATROL FORCES

The IN has embarked on a relatively large-scale recapitalisation of patrol forces. No less than nine large 2,250-ton *Saryu* class offshore patrol vessels (OPVs) designed by GSL and ten 288-ton water-jet powered fast patrol craft from GRSE are planned.

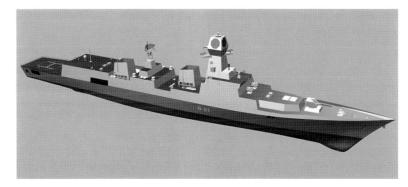

Three Project 15A destroyers – a much modified version of the existing Project 15 *Delhi* design – are currently under construction. (*Directorate of Naval Design, India*)

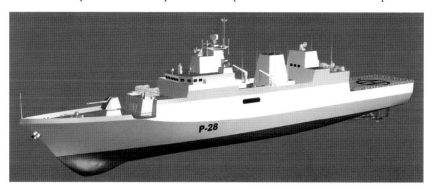

The Project 28 corvette is designed as a relatively low-cost specialised ASW platform. (*Directorate of Naval Design, India*)

GSL is building four of the OPVs, with five others approved for construction by one or more suitable private shipyards. The first Goa-built OPV should commission in early 2011. The first two *Car Nicobar* class fast patrol craft from Garden Reach commissioned in early 2009 and GRSE expects to deliver all ten by early 2011.

CONCLUSION

In conclusion, the IN is well on its way towards realising its objective of being a prime instrument of Indian state policy – as well as being the dominant navy in the Indian Ocean region – through a process of transformation into a modern force. One can certainly see a growing American influence in doctrinal and policy statements as it embraces change management as part of this transformation process. Shedding its largely insular attitude from the 1970s and 1980s, it has been regularly interacting with major world navies through exercises such as

Left: The Indian Navy *Rajput* class destroyer *Ranvir* at sea early in 2009. The next decade should see India's full transition to eminence as a leading 'blue water' fleet. *(Royal Australian Navy)*

Malabar with the US and others, Konkan with the UK, Varuna with France and INDRA with Russia. It has also engaged regional navies through initiatives such as MILAN and, more recently, the Indian Ocean Naval Symposium (IONS). Operationally, the IN has been actively involved in successful anti-piracy missions off the Horn of Africa. Even though its extensive recapitalisation programme is proceeding slower than planned, the induction of new platforms, including satellites, and a gradual

Above: *Car Nicobar* and *Chetlat* are the first of a class of ten fast patrol craft being built by Garden Reach for the Indian Navy. *(Indian Navy)*

shift to a network-centric concept of operations represent major gains in maintaining maritime domain awareness and provide the ability to respond rapidly to emerging threats in a constantly evolving geo-political environment. Thus, the next decade will see the IN's full transition to eminence.

Notes

1. The following sources provide much additional useful information on the IN's development:

– The Indian Navy's website at www.indiannavy.nic.in contains a wealth of information. Particularly relevant from a historical perspective are web versions of two excellent books by Vice Admiral G M Hirananadani, *Transition to Triumph* and *Transition to Excellence*. The site also contains doctrinal and similar information such as Freedom to use the Seas: India's Maritime Military Strategy (September 2007).

– Bharat Rakshak's Indian Navy website is a good complement to the official site, containing detailed ship descriptions and a large image gallery. It can be found at: http://www.bharat-rakshak.com/NAVY/ .

– A broad photographic overview of the IN is provided by Raja Menon, R. K. Dhowan, Kunal Vermal, Jasjit Mansingh, *The Indian Navy: A Photo Essay* (New Delhi, Director of Ex-Servicemen's Affairs, 2000).

– A good summary of India's naval air arm can be found in Pushpindar Singh, *Fly Navy – An Illustrated History of Indian Naval Aviation* (New Delhi, The Society of Aerospace Studies, 2006).

2.4 WORLD FLEET REVIEWS

EUROPE AND RUSSIA
Regional Review

Author: Conrad Waters

See page 12

Of all the world's navies, it is probably the European and Russian fleets that have faced the most significant challenges in adapting to the post-Cold War environment. Many of the missions that the European NATO and Warsaw Pact navies had been designed to undertake, be they mass-scale anti-submarine warfare in the North Atlantic or high-intensity littoral operations in the Baltic, were effectively rendered redundant. In their place came an increased emphasis on expeditionary activities and the need to develop forces that could counter the new demands of asymmetric warfare. An additional challenge was the fact that these changes required substantial investment at a time when politicians were either seeking to reduce military expenditure to gain a so-called 'peace dividend' or, in the case of the former Soviet Russia, facing significant economic dislocation. As a result, the overall pace of change has been relatively slow and it is only now that new capabilities are emerging. Change has also been accompanied by very substantial reductions in force levels as overall unit numbers have been cut to fund relevant new equipment such as amphibious assault ships or multi-mission frigates. There have also been significant variations in the extent to which individual countries have been successful in responding to the new order.

In general terms, it seems that the former colonial powers of France, Spain and the United Kingdom have gone furthest in embracing the necessary transformation. To some extent this is a reflection of the fact that the relative size of their defence budgets has made it easier for them to fund changes in equipment. However, it is also arguable that a cultural legacy of global operations has also facilitated change. All have invested significant sums in expanding expeditionary assets and the fruits of this expenditure are starting to become apparent with the arrival of potent and flexible warships such as the *Mistral* and *Juan Carlos I* classes of amphibious assault ships, as well as the *Daring* class Type 45 destroyers. Other European countries – most notably the Netherlands – also have a history as players on the world stage but have seen their ability to adapt weakened by a lack of will-power, most usually demonstrated by shrinking defence budgets.

Conversely, a number of nations that have traditionally adopted a largely continental outlook in foreign affairs have become much more global in their vision. Germany, which appears finally to be shaking off its unfortunate legacy as the aggressor state in two world wars, is a particularly good example of a country that is developing its maritime capabilities as an effective force for international stability. This has extended to the design of a new frigate – the F-125 class – with a particular emphasis on long-distance stabilisation missions. The Scandinavian navies are also expanding the scope of their deployments against generally tight cost constraints.

There has been much focus on the resurgence of Russian maritime ambitions as part of that country's generally more assertive political stance. However, the extent to which the Russian Federation's navy can return to its former role as a leading maritime player needs to be regarded with a degree of scepticism. As referenced in the Introduction, progress made with the delivery of new construction has been feeble, with efforts to increase levels of fleet activity therefore placing increasing strain on a relatively modest force of obsolescent Soviet-era units of doubtful reliability. With priority being given to the construction of new strategic missile submarines to maintain the effectiveness of Russia's nuclear deterrent, it is doubtful whether enough is being done even to maintain current conventional maritime forces at the present level. It should also be noted that the global 'credit crunch' has done much to weaken the previous commodity-driven improvement in Russian finances. This suggests the recent upsurge in the country's defence outlays might not be sustainable.

Table 4.1.1 summarises the strengths of the leading Western European fleets as at mid-2009.

MAJOR REGIONAL NAVAL POWERS – FRANCE

France's armed forces are currently in the middle of a major restructuring following publication of a new White Paper on defence and national security on 17 June 2008. Attempting to provide an overall framework for the country's military in the uncertain environment that has followed the 9/11 terrorist attacks, the new strategy is intended to create more effective and flexible forces that are better able to provide a swift response to emerging threats than hitherto. In addition to reducing overall personnel numbers and levels of equipment – the former are to fall from 320,000 to 266,000 by 2015 – to fund additional investment in communications, space technology and homeland defence, the White Paper aligned France more closely with its traditional allies by returning France within NATO's integrated command structure. Reflecting a growing rapprochement between France and the alliance in recent years, the decision is indicative of a realisation of the need to adopt a multilateral approach to securing France's military interests. It should therefore be seen in conjunction with the country's similar moves to bolster European defence co-operation as an aid to mutual security.

To some extent, France's defence restructuring is also a reflection of the fact that commitments towards new military projects had lost connection with likely future resources during the later years of the Chirac regime. The newly-elected President Sarkozy therefore wanted to bring the two back into balance. As a result, the White Paper was not entirely good news for France's *Marine Nationale* and will result both in some longer-term reductions to the current force levels set out in Table 2.4.2 and a scaling-back of future ambitions.

An artist's impression of the French version of the Franco-Italian FREMM multi-mission frigate. The leading European navies are slowly reconfiguring their fleets through the addition of warships more suited to the current-day needs of expeditionary warfare. *(DCNS)*

The most significant casualty of the Sarkozy regime was the postponement of a decision as to whether to construct a second aircraft carrier (*deux-ième porte avions* or PA2) to supplement the existing *Charles de Gaulle* to a 2012/13 timeframe. France had previously intended to adapt the British Royal Navy's CVF design for conventional take-off and landing operations. The intention was for the new 70,000-ton ship to be in service in time to cover the existing carrier's major refit and refuelling in 2015–16. However, an estimated €2.5bn (US$3.5bn) price tag was regarded as being simply unaffordable in the shorter term, particularly since the UK proved reluctant to consider a French-sponsored joint construction programme that might have reduced overall costs. Even if the PA2 project does

TABLE 2.4.1: FLEET STRENGTHS IN WESTERN EUROPE – LARGER NAVIES (MID-2009)

COUNTRY	FRANCE	GERMANY	GREECE	ITALY	NETHERLANDS	SPAIN	TURKEY	UK
Aircraft Carrier (CVN)	1	–	–	–	–	–	–	–
Support/Helicopter Carrier (CVS/CVH)	1	–	–	2	–	1	–	3
Strategic Missile Submarine (SSBN)	3	–	–	–	–	–	–	4
Attack Submarine (SSN)	6	–	–	–	–	–	–	8
Patrol Submarine (SSK)	–	10	8	6	4	4	14	–
Fleet Escort (DDG/FFG)	18	15	14	16	6	10	16	24
Patrol Escort/Corvette (FFG/FSG/FS)	15	2	3	8	–	–	6	–
Missile Armed Attack Craft (PGG/PTG)	–	10	20	–	–	–	26	–
Mine Countermeasures Vessel (MCMV)	16	19	10	12	10	6	19	16
Major Amphibious (LHD/LPD/LPH/LSD)	4	–	–	3	2	2	–	7

France's existing fleet of escort vessels will largely be replaced by the new FREMM class of multi-mission frigates over the next decade, with the two remaining imposing but elderly members of the *Tourville* class (the class name ship is pictured here in March 2009) being amongst the first to go. *(Conrad Waters)*

D610

TABLE 2.4.2: FRENCH NAVY: PRINCIPAL UNITS AS AT MID-2009

TYPE	CLASS	NUMBER	TONNAGE	DIMENSIONS	PROPULSION	CREW	DATE
Aircraft Carriers							
Aircraft Carrier – CVN	CHARLES DE GAULLE	1	42,000 tons	262m x 33/64m x 9m	Nuclear, 27 knots	1,950	2001
Helicopter Carrier – CVH	JEANNE D'ARC	1	13,300 tons	182m x 24m x 7m	Steam, 27 knots	500	1964
Principal Surface Escorts							
Frigate – FFG	FORBIN	2	7,000 tons	153m x 20m x 8m	CODOG, 30+ knots	195	2008
Frigate – FFG	CASSARD (FAA-70)	2	5,000 tons	139m x 15m x 7m	CODAD, 30 knots	250	1988
Frigate – FFG	TOURVILLE (FASM-67)	2	6,100 tons	153m x 16m x 6m	Steam, 32 knots	300	1974
Frigate – FFG	GEORGES LEYGUES (FASM-70)	7	4,800 tons	139m x 15m x 6m	CODOG, 30 knots	245	1979
Frigate – FFG	LA FAYETTE	5	3,600 tons	125m x 15m x 5m	CODAD, 25 knots	150	1996
Frigate – FSG	FLORÉAL	6	3,000 tons	94m x 14m x 4m	CODAD, 20 knots	90	1992
Frigate – FS[1]	D'ESTIENNE D'ORVES (A-69)	9	1,300 tons	80m x 10m x 5m	Diesel, 24 knots	90	1976
Submarines							
Submarine – SSBN	LE TRIOMPHANT	3	14,400 tons	138m x 13m x 11m	Nuclear, 25 knots	110	1997
Submarine – SSN	RUBIS	6	2,700 tons	74m x 8m x 6m	Nuclear, 25+ knots	70	1983
Major Amphibious Units							
Helicopter Carrier – LHD	MISTRAL	2	21,500 tons	199m x 32m x 6m	Diesel-electric, 19 knots	160	2006
Landing Platform Dock – LPD	FOUDRE	2	12,000 tons	168m x 24m x 5m	Diesel, 20 knots	225	1990

1 Now officially reclassified as offshore patrol vessels.

eventually progress, it seems unlikely that the modified CVF design will survive the delay. Indeed, the French government has now announced further design studies, with a return to nuclear propulsion one option under consideration.[1]

The *Marine Nationale*'s future surface fleet will also be somewhat less potent than previously envisaged as a result of decisions taken in the White Paper. Planned orders for the new French *Aquitaine* variant of the Franco-Italian FREMM (*frégate multi-mission*) frigate will be reduced from seventeen to eleven as part of a broader plan to limit front-line surface escorts to a total of eighteen units. Whilst it was originally envisaged that the French vessels would be built to specialised anti-submarine and land-attack variants, the bulk of construction will now be focused on the former type. In effect, however, the class will be powerful general purpose-combatants displacing around 6,000 tons in full load condition and shipping an armament that will include Aster 15 surface-to-air, Exocet surface-to-surface and Scalp land-attack cruise missiles, as well as a 76mm gun and embarked helicopter. The last two units will be built to a modified anti-aircraft format with Aster 30 missiles to join the pair of existing *Forbin* 'Horizon' class ships in the air-defence role in replacement of the existing *Cassard*s. The balance of the 'first rate' surface fleet will comprise the five *La Fayette* stealth frigates commissioned in the late 1990s.

The truncation of the FREMM programme leaves the French Navy with the increasingly pressing problem of replacing its nine remaining A-69 *D'Estienne D'Orves* class frigates. These are now nearly thirty years old and have effectively been re-assigned to patrol duties. Given that the ten P-400 class offshore patrol ships that are used largely for presence missions in France's overseas territories are also falling due for replacement, a new class similar to the Spanish Navy's BAM type would seem to be called for. There have been reports that DCNS is attempting to interest the *Marine Nationale* in its revamped 'Gowind' family of oceanic patrol

A view of the French amphibious assault ship *Mistral* taken shortly after completion. A third vessel has been ordered under France's economic stimulus package. *(DCNS)*

vessels/light corvettes, which are being marketed in several different configurations.[2]

The revised defence strategy has not been entirely negative for France's maritime posture. The growing importance of amphibious shipping was reflected in a commitment to order two further 'BPC' type amphibious assault ships to join the existing *Mistral* and *Tonnerre* that were delivered in 2006 and 2007. A firm order for the first additional ship – reportedly valued at €400m (US$560m) – was subsequently placed with a consortium of DCNS and STX France (which has acquired the Saint-Nazaire Chantiers de l'Atlantique shipyard) on 16 April 2009 as part of France's economic recovery plan. France's under-water forces have also remained relatively unscathed as a result of the importance attached to ensuring the integrity of the submarine-based nuclear deterrent. As a result, the commitment to build six new 'Barracuda' nuclear-powered attack submarines (SSNs) remains intact. First of class *Suffren* was ordered in December 2006 under the first tranche of a series of agreements that eventually could amount to as much as €8bn (US$11.2bn). A second boat was contracted on 26 June 2009. Displacing 4,765 tons in submerged condition and with a length of 99m, the design is smaller than current-generation US and British designs but will still be able to deploy a mix of twenty torpedoes, Exocet anti-surface and Scalp land-attack cruise missiles. Propulsion will be provided by the same K-15 nuclear reactor installed in the *Le Triomphant* class nuclear-powered ballistic missile submarines (SSBNs), providing both a top speed in excess of 25 knots and a ten-year gap between refuellings.

Le Triomphant herself hit the headlines in February 2009 as a result of a collision with the Royal Navy's SSBN *Vanguard* in the North Atlantic whilst both were in the course of routine patrols. The freak accident was a clear demonstration of the effectiveness of the stealth technology employed on both submarines to ensure the integrity of their countries' respective nuclear deterrents but produced the inevitable negative reactions from anti-nuclear campaigners. The collision, which resulted in considerable damage to *Le Triomphant*'s bow-mounted sonar, came at a time when France's oceanic strategic force (FOST) had already been temporarily reduced to three boats. The last of the preceding *Le Redoutable.* class – *L'Inflexible* – concluded its final patrol on 15 January 2008 and the replacement *Le Terrible* is still undergoing trials.

With France also still without an operational aircraft carrier for much of the year due to the extension of *Charles de Gaulle*'s spell in dockyard hands due to problems with her propulsion system, fleet resources are more stretched than they have been for some time. Some respite has been provided by the new amphibious assault ships and by the first 'Horizon' air-defence frigate, *Forbin*, which was finally handed over to the navy on 19 December 2008. She subsequently undertook a lengthy deployment to the Americas during March and April, before being recalled early so as to participate in the formal inauguration of France's new naval facility in Abu Dhabi at the end of May.

MAJOR REGIONAL NAVAL POWERS – ITALY

Italy's *Marina Militare* has recently completed the renewal of the core components of its surface fleet with the delivery of the new aircraft carrier *Cavour* and its own pair of the Franco-Italian 'Horizon' class air-defence frigates. *Cavour* was handed over on 27 March 2008, with the frigates *Andrea Doria* and *Caio Duilio* being delivered on 22 December 2007 and 3 April 2009 respectively.[3] The latter are virtually identical to the two French ships of the class and have a similar role to the British Royal Navy's *Daring*, with which they share a common origin. The most significant difference is the use of the less advanced EMPAR multifunction radar in the 'Horizon' class ships, which offers reduced capabilities in the highest threat scenarios compared with the British Sampson.

Italy's attention is now turning to completion of its part of the follow-on FREMM programme, which is also being carried out in conjunction with France. The *Marina Militare* intends to acquire ten units of this multi-role frigate class as replacement for its existing *Maestrale* and *Artigliere* types in a project that is estimated to cost around €6bn (US$8.4bn). The first two ships – *Carlo Bergamini* and *Carlo Margottini* – were ordered in 2006, with contracts for a further four placed in January 2008. In contrast with the French approach, the Italians have elected to continue with original plans to build the ships in both anti-submarine and general-purpose configurations, with prototypes of each version included in the initial contract. Whilst much equipment is common to both variants, the general-purpose ship gains a larger 127mm gun compared with the standard 76mm fit on the ASW frigate but does not have the

An image of the Italian general purpose variant of the FREMM frigate. Note the differences with the French design pictured at the start of this chapter. *(Marina Militare)*

latter's towed-array sonar. The Italian ships also feature significant differences in appearance and specification compared with the French ships. This partly reflects Italy's wish to achieve a higher level of capability but could also have been driven by a desire to maximise local content. For example, all the Italian ships will feature the indigenously-manufactured EMPAR radar that is common to both *Cavour* and the 'Horizon' class.

The Italian sub-surface force has shrunk in recent years but quantity is being replaced with quality through the progressive introduction of licence-built patrol submarines of the German AIP-equipped Type 212A design. Italy is the only country other than Germany to operate the class following the delivery of its first two boats – *Salvatore Todaro* and *Scirè* – from shipbuilders Fincantieri during 2006–7. An order for a second pair was confirmed in 2008, with construction expected to commence in 2010 for a 2015–16 delivery. Meanwhile, *Todaro* undertook a lengthy deployment to the United States during much of the second half of 2008 for an extensive series of joint exercises with USN surface ships and nuclear-powered submarines. The mission, which was the first time since the Second World War that an Italian submarine had crossed the Atlantic, was considered successful by both parties and could become an ongoing arrangement.

The significant investment involved in constructing *Cavour* and upgrading the surface fleet has meant that the *Marina Militare* is arguably less advanced than some of its peers in developing a post-Cold War maritime structure. The need to replace the fleet's elderly amphibious ships is a particularly urgent requirement. The three current *San Giorgio* class LPD-type amphibious transport docks offer only limited capabilities on their 8,000

Table 2.4.3: ITALIAN NAVY: PRINCIPAL UNITS AS AT MID-2009

TYPE	CLASS	NUMBER	TONNAGE	DIMENSIONS	PROPULSION	CREW	DATE
Aircraft Carriers							
Aircraft Carrier – CV	CAVOUR	1	27,100 tons	244m x 30/39m x 9m	COGAG, 29 knots	800	2008
Aircraft Carrier – CVS	GIUSEPPE GARIBALDI	1	13,900 tons	180m x 23/31m x 7m	COGAG, 30 knots	825	1985
Principal Surface Escorts							
Frigate – FFG	ANDREA DORIA	2	7,100 tons	153m x 20m x 8m	CODOG, 30+ knots	190	2007
Destroyer – DDG	DE LA PENNE	2	5,400 tons	148m x 16m x 7m	CODOG, 31 knots	375	1993
Frigate – FFG	MAESTRALE	8	3,100 tons	123m x 13 x 5m	CODOG, 30+ knots	225	1982
Frigate – FFG	ARTIGLIERE	4	2,500 tons	114m x 12m x 5m	CODOG, 35 knots	185	1994
Frigate – FS	MINERVA	8	1,300 tons	87m x 11m x 3m	Diesel, 25 knots	120	1987
Submarines							
Submarine – SSK	TODARO (Type 212A)	2	1,800 tons	56m x 7m x 6m	AIP, 20+ knots	30	2006
Submarine – SSK	PELOSI	4	1,700 tons	64m x 7m x 6m	Diesel-electric, 20 knots	50	1988
Major Amphibious Units							
Landing Platform Dock – LPD	SAN GIORGIO	3	8,000 tons	133m x 21m x 5m	Diesel, 20 knots	165	1987

tons full-load displacement and the navy has long-held aspirations to replace them with more effective ships. Until recently, it appeared the most likely scenario was the construction of three new 16,000–20,000 ton ships in the 2018–28 time-frame. However, as in France, economic considerations might result in the project being pushed forward through use of industrial support funds. Italy also has a need for new offshore patrol vessels, with up to twelve ships envisaged to replace the *Minerva* class corvettes and *Cassiopea* class patrol ships. The role is of particular political significance given concerns over seaborne illegal immigration into Italy from the North African countries and could well be accorded a high priority.

Table 2.4.3 lists major fleet units.

MAJOR REGIONAL NAVAL POWERS – SPAIN

The *Armada Española* is probably the European navy that has achieved most progress in recent years. A key feature in the fleet's development has been the combination of an efficient local shipbuilding industry in the form of Navantia coupled with extensive use of acquired technology, largely of American origin, to keep costs down. Until the advent of the recent economic downturn, which has hit Spain particularly hard, budgetary support was also largely favourable. As a result, the Spanish navy of today is a modern and well-balanced force that has proved itself increasingly capable in a range of international stabilisation missions. Table 2.4.4 summarises the current fleet's principal ships.

The most important construction programme in recent years has been that for the five Aegis-equipped F-100 type frigates of the *Álvaro de Bazán* class. Designed as air-defence ships with a good range of general capabilities, an initial batch of four units was ordered in October 1996, with the resulting ships commissioned between 2002 and 2006. The intention to acquire the fifth vessel was first announced in May 2005 and, following the subsequent award of a formal contract, first steel was cut in June 2007 prior to formal keel-laying in

Left: The Italian Navy's 'Commandante' class patrol vessel *Sirio* and *Minerva* class corvette *Sfinge* on exercises with the Royal Australian Navy in the Mediterranean. New patrol vessels are planned. *(Royal Australian Navy)*

Below: Spain's LHD-type amphibious assault ship *Juan Carlos I* is nearing completion at Navantia's Ferrol shipyard. The type is known as a strategic projection ship under Spanish naval terminology. *(Navantia)*

Table 2.4.4: SPANISH NAVY: PRINCIPAL UNITS AS AT MID-2009

TYPE	CLASS	NUMBER	TONNAGE	DIMENSIONS	PROPULSION	CREW	DATE
Aircraft Carriers							
Aircraft Carrier – CVS	**PRINCIPE DE ASTURIAS**	1	16,700 tons	196m x 24/32m x 9m	COGAG, 25 knots	555	1988
Principal Surface Escorts							
Frigate – FFG	**ÁLVARO DE BAZÁN** (F-100)	4	6,250 tons	147m x 19m x 7m	CODAG, 28 knots	200	2002
Frigate – FFG	**SANTA MARIA** (FFG-7)	6	4,100 tons	138m x 14m x 8m	COGAG, 29 knots	225	1986
Submarines							
Submarine – SSK	**GALERNA** (S-70/AGOSTA)	4	1,800 tons	68m x 7m x 6m	Diesel-electric, 21 knots	60	1983
Major Amphibious Units							
Landing Platform Dock – LPD	**GALICIA**	2	13,000 tons	160m x 25m x 6m	Diesel, 20 knots	185	1998

February 2009. Completion of the new ship – to be named *Roger de Lauria* – is currently scheduled for 2012 and she will incorporate several detailed improvements over her sisters. Current unit cost of construction – at around €750m (US$1.05bn) – compares favourably with the specialist air-defence ships ordered for other European navies, largely reflecting the fact that development costs relating to the US-manufactured Aegis system – and associated Standard SM-2 surface-to-air missiles – have been spread over a large number of ships. Spain has also requested American authorisation to acquire Tomahawk land-attack cruise missiles to equip the class, marking the first non-USN use of this weapon on a surface ship.

Like many other European fleets, Spain is developing a two-tier structure for its surface fleet. Under this arrangement, the *Álvaro de Bazán* class and six older *Santa Maria* (FFG-7) type frigates will fill the higher end of the capability spectrum, with lower intensity operations conducted by a fleet of less expensive offshore patrol vessels. For the immediate

An artist's impression of a BAM class oceanic patrol vessel. Up to twelve of these ships are planned to recapitalise Spain's patrol forces. *(Navantia)*

future, these second-line duties largely fall to the reclassified corvettes of the *Descubierta* class and the four *Serviola* patrol ships, alongside a number of less capable vessels. However, in the medium term, the intention is to consolidate around the new BAM (buque de acción maritima) oceanic patrol vessels. An initial batch of four of these 2,500-ton, 94m-long vessels was ordered in 2006. A total of up to twelve is eventually planned. Intended for operation by a crew of just thirty-five, the ships will have a range of 8,000 miles and be capable of operations of up to forty days duration. Armament includes a 76mm gun and lighter weapons, whilst there is a hangar and flight deck for helicopter operations. The project is running a little behind schedule due to prioritisation of export work for Venezuela but the first vessel should have been launched by the end of September 2009.

Submarine forces are also being upgraded, albeit at the expense of overall numbers. The four 1970s-vintage *Daphné* class submarines were decommissioned between 2003 and 2006, leaving four S-70 *Galerna* (*Agosta*) class boats to be replaced by the new S-80 class in the early years of the coming decade. Although Spain has previously been closely associated with the French submarine-building industry through its alliance with DCNS in respect of the Scorpène type, the S-80 will be equipped with US-developed air-independent propulsion (AIP) and combat systems, whilst other equipment is being sourced from British firms. Displacing some 2,400 tons in dived condition and with a length of 71m, the new submarines will be large and capable boats that should be suitable for extended deployments and which could well be equipped with Tomahawk cruise missiles in due course.

The Spanish navy has always placed considerable

Opposite: The UK has significantly expanded its emphasis on amphibious operations since the end of the Cold War. Its capabilities in this area were demonstrated by the 2009 deployment of the TAURUS 09 task group, pictured here. *(MOD Navy)*

emphasis on amphibious operations. This specialisation is particularly advantageous in the post-Cold War era of expeditionary warfare and further investment is being made in developing the country's capabilities through construction of an LHD-type amphibious assault ship. Known as a strategic projection ship in Spanish terminology, *Juan Carlos I* was launched from Navantia's Ferrol shipyard on 10 March 2008 and is due to commence sea trials in the second half of 2009 prior to delivery around the year-end. Displacing around 27,000 tons in full load condition, the new ship is capable of deploying up to 1,200 troops by means of helicopters and landing craft and has a secondary role of acting as a substitute V/STOL carrier when *Principe de Asturias* is unavailable.

MAJOR REGIONAL NAVAL POWERS – UNITED KINGDOM

The British Royal Navy has been forced to undergo a significant change in emphasis since the end of the Cold War, as its previous focus on anti-submarine warfare has become much less relevant following the collapse of the Soviet threat. Ambitious plans set out as part of the UK's 1998 Strategic Defence Review (SDR) have resulted in a much greater emphasis on power projection and amphibious capabilities, in particular, have been significantly overhauled. A clear demonstration of the UK's increased effectiveness in this area was provided by the deployment of the TAURUS 09 task group, which saw an

Table 2.4.5: BRITISH ROYAL NAVY: PRINCIPAL UNITS AS AT MID-2009

TYPE	CLASS	NUMBER	TONNAGE	DIMENSIONS	PROPULSION	CREW	DATE
Aircraft Carriers							
Aircraft Carrier – CVS	INVINCIBLE	2 (1)	22,000 tons	210m x 31/36m x 8m	COGAG, 30 knots	1,100	1980
Principal Surface Escorts							
Destroyer – DDG	DARING (Type 45)	1	7,400 tons	152m x 21m x 5m	IEP, 30 knots	190	2008
Destroyer – DDG	MANCHESTER (Type 42-Batch 3)	4	5,200 tons	141m x 15m x 6m	COGOG, 30+ knots	290	1982
Destroyer – DDG	EXETER (Type 42 – Batch 2)	1 (1)	4,800 tons	125m x 14m x 6m	COGOG, 30 knots	290	1980
Frigate – FFG	CORNWALL (Type 22 – Batch 3)	4	5,300 tons	148m x 15m x 6m	COGOG, 30+ knots	250	1988
Frigate – FFG	NORFOLK (Type 23)	13	4,900 tons	133m x 16m x 7m	CODLAG, 30 knots	185	1990
Submarines							
Submarine – SSBN	VANGUARD	4	16,000 tons	150m x 13m x 12m	Nuclear, 25+ knots	135	1993
Submarine – SSN	TRAFALGAR	7	5,200 tons	85m x 10m x 10m	Nuclear, 30+knots	130	1983
Submarine – SSN	SWIFTSURE	1	4,900 tons	83m x 10n x 9m	Nuclear, 30+ knots	115	1973
Major Amphibious Units							
Helicopter Carrier – LPH	OCEAN	1	22,500 tons	203m x 35m x 7m	Diesel, 18 knots	490	1998
Landing Platform Dock – LPD	ALBION	2	18,500 tons	176m x 29m x 7m	IEP, 18 knots	325	2003
Landing Ship Dock – LSD (A)	LARGS BAY	4	16,200 tons	176m x 26m x 6m	Diesel-electric, 18 knots	60	2006

Note: Figures in brackets refer to ships in extended reserve.

amphibious force headed by the LPD *Bulwark* and including the helicopter carrier *Ocean*, two auxiliary dock landing ships of the 'Bay' class and a wide range of other assets embark on an extended deployment to the Mediterranean, Indian Ocean and Far East. Whilst the voyage provided an excellent opportunity to showcase the modern and potent vessels that now form the core of the Royal Navy's amphibious fleet, this progress has come at the expense of significant reductions in the rest of the fleet. Table 2.4.5 shows current numerical strength in terms of core units.

The two new *Queen Elizabeth* class CVF future aircraft carriers form the heart of an impressive forward construction programme that is set out in detail in Chapter 2.4A. Although likely reductions in an already over-stretched defence budget has resulted in ongoing speculation about their potential cancellation, the fact that much of the c.£4bn (US$6.4bn) project cost has already been committed makes it likely that their future is secure. There is, however, much more uncertainty about planned new construction that is less well advanced, with even the 'Successor' nuclear-powered ballistic missile submarines that are required to maintain the Trident nuclear deterrent not altogether safe from deferral. Any major decisions are unlikely to take place before a general election scheduled for 2010, with the probability of major cutbacks already resulting in unseemly squabbling amongst the service chiefs.

One area where there is already a greater degree of certainty is the nature of the Royal Navy's future support infrastructure, with decisions announced in May 2009 in respect of the Maritime Change Programme. The review has confirmed previous decisions to make Faslane in Scotland the sole operational base for all submarines, whilst Portsmouth will undertake a broadly similar role in respect of the principal components of the surface fleet. Meanwhile Devonport will become the focal point for amphibious ships and undertake most major refit work, as well as retaining its role as the basis for Flag Officer Sea Training. Probably as a result of political factors, the changes are being implemented over a number of years, with few major redeployments taking place prior to 2015.

Operationally, the surface fleet appears to be under greatest strain, with the need to find resources to support new commitments such as piracy operations resulting in previous core duties such as the

South Atlantic guardship role being partly undertaken by auxiliary vessels, most notably the hugely flexible 'Bay' class. The British military presence around the Falklands was also impacted by serious flood damage to the ice patrol ship *Endurance*'s engine room in December 2008, which resulted in her having to be transported back to Portsmouth by heavy-lift ship for significant repairs. The number of active surface escorts has now been reduced to twenty-two following the decommissioning of the veteran Type 42 destroyers *Southampton* and *Exeter*, with their sister-ship *Nottingham* laid up in extended readiness and the new Type 45 destroyer *Daring* still several months away from her official 'in service date'. A detailed description of this impressive new ship is contained in Chapter 3.2.

MID-SIZED REGIONAL FLEETS

Germany: Germany's *Deutsche Marine* has undergone a significant transformation over the last few years as it has embraced the benefits of adopting an increased international presence. Whilst a particular success was Germany's leadership of the maritime component of United Nation's UNIFIL peacekeeping force off the Lebanese coast, the navy has also been particularly active supporting anti-terrorism and anti-

piracy operations in the Indian Ocean. For example, it had taken command of the multinational coalition task force CTF-150 on no less than six occasions between 2002 and early 2009. The German Training Squadron has also been deployed increasingly widely. For example, exercises during 2008 with, inter alia, the South African and Indian Navies, were replicated in 2009 through participation in the US-sponsored UNITAS Gold that involved interaction with no less than ten fleets from the Americas. It is also worth noting that German maritime technology continues to enjoy widespread global demand, with ongoing sales of Type 214 submarines by Thyssen Krupp Marine Systems' HDW arguably making Germany the world leader in this particular field.

The fleet's composition is changing to reflect the different pattern of operations. Submarine numbers had fallen to just ten boats by the middle of 2009 as a result of progressive withdrawal of the Type 206/Type 206A coastal type, with just six of an original class of eighteen remaining operational. They have been joined by four of the larger, AIP-equipped Type 212A submarines, which are much more suited for extended operations. A further batch of two modified versions of this impressive design were ordered in 2006 and are currently under construc-

The German navy has been one of the more successful fleets in adapting to the new maritime environment. This has included orders for four new F-125 frigates that are specially designed for lengthy deployment on medium intensity operations. *(Thyssen Krupp Marine Systems/ARGE F125)*

tion for delivery during 2012/13. The *Deutsche Marine* would like to order a further batch in due course but this will be dependent on the availability of funding given a long list of other requirements.

The fleet of surface escorts currently comprises eight modernised F-122 *Bremen* class frigates that were built during the 1980s, four of the more recent F-123 *Brandenburg* class and three modern F-124 *Sachsen* type air-defence ships. At least some of the first mentioned class will be replaced by the new F-125 design, four of which were ordered from the ARGE F-125 consortium of Thyssen Krupp and Lürssen on 26 June 2007 under a contract reportedly valued at €2.2bn (US$3.1bn). Of around 7,000 tons full-load displacement, these new destroyer-size ships are intended for dispatch on potentially lengthy overseas medium-intensity operations. A system of crew rotation is intended to allow them to operate for as long as two years from their home base. This requirement for extended operations has influenced selection of a combined diesel-electric and gas (CODLAG) propulsion system. Considerable emphasis has also been placed on extensive duplication of equipment, not least through the implementation of a two-island arrangement by which important functions are divided between two distinctive pyramid-like deckhouses. The first ship should be in service by 2015. Expeditionary capabilities will also be bolstered by conclusion of a long-awaited order for a third Type 702 *Berlin* class combat support ship at the end of 2008. In the medium term, the navy has aspirations for a class of large joint support ships along the lines of those planned by Canada to improve military-lift capabilities. An embryonic concept for a multi-mission vessel, possibly similar to the Royal New Zealand Navy's *Canterbury*, has also been floated.

Coastal forces have been much reduced since the end of the Cold War, with only ten Type 134A *Gepard* class vessels remaining from a once extensive fleet. Their replacements are the much more flexible K-130 *Braunschweig* class corvettes, all five of which are now physically complete. Unfortunately, it appears that a manufacturing problem with the ships' gearboxes requires remedial work that is likely to delay their entry into full operational service for some time. However, the design concept behind these small but powerfully-armed ships, which are particularly well-suited for extended littoral operations, appears to be a sound one and a successor class is planned in due course.

Greece: The Hellenic Navy has traditionally been heavily reliant on Germany for its major surface and subsurface combatants, with Thyssen Krupp Marine Systems owning the local Hellenic Shipyards. However, a series of disputes in respect of submarine construction and refurbishment contracts have put this relationship under strain. Greece currently operates a homogeneous but ageing fleet of eight Type 209/1100 and Type 209/1200 boats built in two batches during the 1970s. It planned to renew this force through two separate deals with the German company. These involved construction of four new AIP-equipped submarines of the Type 214 class – three at Hellenic Shipyards – and refurbishment of three or four of the later batch of Type 209 boats at the local facility under the Neptune II project.

The first of the new Type 214 class, the Kiel-built *Papanikolis*, was launched as long ago as April 2004 but Greece has continuously refused to accept delivery on the grounds of alleged technical deficiencies, most notably poor surface stability. All the Greek-built boats have now undergone harbour tests but their own sea trials have been delayed pending resolution of the dispute. Meanwhile, the first refur-

bished Type 209, *Okeanos*, was re-launched by Hellenic Shipyards on 26 February 2009, after the insertion of a hull plug to accommodate AIP. However, the influential *Jane's Defence Weekly* has suggested that the rest of the project might be curtailed, with Greece reportedly requesting two newly-built Type 209 submarines instead.[4] There has been some speculation that a cash-strapped Greek military has been prolonging negotiations to ease payment difficulties, as several hundred million euros are reportedly due under the two contracts.

Whatever the reasons, the dispute looks set to impact Greek plans to modernise its surface fleet, where a new class of air-defence ships are a priority. Thyssen Krupp was one of a number of firms looking to win the contract, which is likely to involve the purchase of around six ships. However, Greece has recently announced that it is to pursue talks with France over the potential purchase of the air-defence version of the FREMM multi-mission frigate. In spite of this, Greek plans to cut equipment spending by 15 per cent from planned levels in 2009 and by 10 per cent p.a. thereafter suggests that a deal is by far from a foregone conclusion. In the interim, the Greek surface fleet comprises four MEKO 200

Modernisation of Greek underwater forces has been delayed by a lengthy dispute over acceptance of *Papanikolis*, the first of a four-boat order of Type 214 AIP-equipped submarines. *(Thyssen Krupp Marine Systems)*

Hydra class frigates and four *Elli* (*Kortenaer*) class frigates. Six of the latter have been subject to a mid-life modernisation package that should extend their service to around 2020.

Coastal forces, particularly fast attack craft, have always been an important constituent of the Hellenic Navy given local topography and the need to guard against Turkey as a potential enemy. As a result, there has been continued investment in this warship category in spite of the fact that it has increasingly fallen out of favour elsewhere. A two pronged modernisation approach has involved the progressive upgrade of the navy's fifteen 'La Combattante' II and III fast attack craft alongside a series of orders to the local Elefsis Shipyard for construction of VT Group (now BVT Surface Fleet) designed *Roussen* class vessels. A further two members of the class were ordered in September 2008 to take the class to a total of seven ships. The fast attack craft have been supplemented by a series of cheaper patrol vessels, most notably the HSY-55 and HSY-56 series that derived from the 600-ton 'Osprey' class.

The Netherlands: Once one of the more significant European maritime forces, the Royal Netherlands Navy has been progressively reduced in size and stature since the end of the Cold War until it barely ranks amongst Europe's second-tier fleets. By way of example, around seventeen fleet escorts have been decommissioned since 1995, whilst only four replacement frigates have joined the fleet. In spite of this, the navy has the support of a proficient local industry in the form of Thales Netherland and

Damen Schelde Naval Shipbuilding and continues to develop some innovative vessels.

Current fleet plans suggest the core surface flotilla will be composed of ten vessels by the middle of the coming decade. These will comprise four modern *De Zeven Provincien* air-defence frigates, two older *Karel Doorman* 'M' class general-purpose escorts – now all that remain in the Dutch inventory from an original class of eight – and four newly-built *Holland* class offshore patrol vessels. The last-mentioned are an extremely interesting 3,750-ton design intended for low-intensity operations in the North Sea and off the remaining Dutch colonies in the Caribbean. Designed to be operated by a core crew of just fifty, they are lightly armed with a 76mm gun but feature full helicopter facilities and a highly advanced set of sensors in the form of the new Thales integrated mast. This distinctive pyramidal structure features fixed, four-faced arrays for each of its two active phased-array radar systems (optimised for air and surface search) and also contains the ships' electro-optical and communications and antennae in its single structure. The aim is to speed construction and reduce future maintenance costs by concentrating relevant electronic systems in a single bolt-on structure. The ships were ordered in December 2007 under a contract worth €240m (US$340m) to the shipbuilder Schelde and a further €125m (US$175m) to Thales. The lead ship was laid down on 8 December 2008, with delivery scheduled for mid-2011.

Thales will also be involved in upgrading the two remaining 'M' type frigates with new surface surveil-

lance radar and infra-red sensors similar to those specified for the offshore patrol vessels. This enhancement might be extended to two further vessels transferred to Belgium. The four *Walrus* class patrol submarines are another class scheduled for modernisation, although funding constraints that are reported to have limited the programme to c.€100m (US$140m) suggest the focus will be on extending critical systems to a planned out of service date of c.2025 rather than any more significant upgrades.

The development of amphibious shipping is one area where the Netherlands Navy has made clear progress in recent years. The landing platform dock *Rotterdam* – first commissioned in 1998 – was joined by an enlarged half-sister, *Johan de Witt*, towards the end of 2007, providing a combined ability to transport and deploy two fully-equipped Royal Netherlands Marine Corps battalions. Expeditionary capabilities should be further enhanced by the planned construction of a new joint support ship in replacement of the existing replenishment vessel, *Zuiderkruis*, in yet another example of the attraction of these hybrid vessels to resource-limited fleets. Preliminary reports suggest that the Dutch version of the type will displace around 26,000 tons and be provided with extensive aviation and transportation facilities in addition to her core provisioning role.

Turkey: Operator of what is numerically the strongest of Europe's mid-sized naval forces, Turkey has managed to combine the creation of a modern and well-balanced fleet with a progressive increase in the

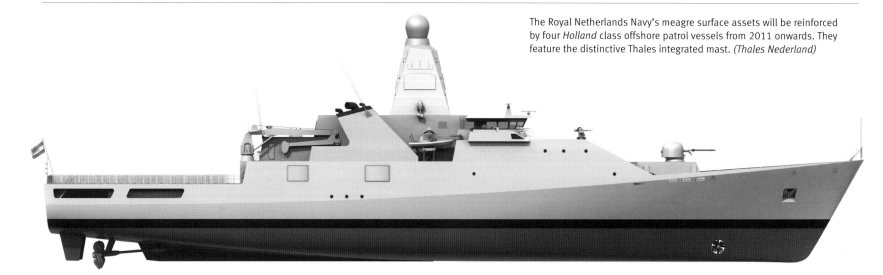

The Royal Netherlands Navy's meagre surface assets will be reinforced by four *Holland* class offshore patrol vessels from 2011 onwards. They feature the distinctive Thales integrated mast. *(Thales Nederland)*

involvement of indigenous industry in warship construction. Whilst most local fabrication has historically been of foreign, largely German, design, steady progress with the 'MilGem' national corvette programme suggests that Turkey will soon join the small group of countries able both to design and construct their own warships.

The Turkish navy has always placed considerable emphasis on underwater forces, with a current fleet of fourteen patrol submarines making it the largest European operator of this type. All of these are vari-ants of Germany's Type 209 design, with six Type 209/1200 boats of the *Atilay* class supplemented by eight of the larger Type 209/1400 *Preveze* and *Gür* subclasses. Plans to modernise the former vessels have been abandoned in favour of the acquisition of six of the new AIP-equipped Type 214 submarines, with a tentative €2.5bn (US$3.5bn) deal announced with Germany's HDW in July 2008. If the deal is confirmed, the new boats will be constructed at the local Gölcük shipyard that has built the majority of the submarines that are currently in service.

The front-line surface escort force is made up of new-build ships of German design, supplemented by second-hand US vessels. The former comprise eight MEKO 200 type frigates of the *Yavuz* and *Barbaros* types, whilst there are also eight former FFG-7 frigates of the *Gaziantep* class. Some of the latter may be fitted with the Mk41 vertical launch system (VLS) and improved fire control as a stopgap for the long-planned, but delayed, TF-2000 air-defence ships. With the former *Knox* class vessels being progressively withdrawn, second-line escort duties

The Royal Netherlands Navy's two remaining 'M' class frigates are also being refitted with some of the sensor technology incorporated in the integrated mast. These images show the *Van Speijk* and an impression of the improvements planned. *(Royal Netherlands Navy / Thales Nederland)*

are in the hands of the six ex-French A-69 *Burak* class patrol frigates delivered during 2001 and 2002. These are likely to be the first vessels replaced by the indigenous 2,000-ton MilGem corvettes, the prototype of which was launched on 27 September 2008. She is to enter service in 2011 and should be followed by eleven similar vessels, four of which might be upgraded to frigate status through the addition of a more sophisticated radar and VLS. The design is attracting considerable interest from overseas navies and could secure export success.

Turkey's core submarine and frigate fleets are supported by powerful coastal forces, as well as mine-countermeasures and amphibious assets. 2009 should see the last of the nine-strong Lürssen designed *Kiliç* class enter service. Delivery of the 'Aydin' class minehunters of similar origin is also almost complete. Amongst other capabilities under consideration is acquisition of at least one LPD to improve expeditionary posture. Turkey has been active supporting UNIFIL off Lebanon and the CTF-151 anti-piracy mission in the Indian Ocean, so this capability would fit well with evolving operational roles.

OTHER REGIONAL FLEETS

Black Sea and Mediterranean: The widespread restructuring of naval forces that has taken place across Europe has been of benefit to some of the minor fleets in southern Europe. In the Black Sea, **Romania** operates two former British Royal Navy Type 22 frigates, *Regele Ferdinand* (ex-*Coventry*) and *Regina Maria* (ex-*London*) as the core components of its surface fleet, whilst neighbouring **Bulgaria** has purchased three older *Wielingen* class frigates and a surplus 'Tripartite' type mine-countermeasures vessel from Belgium. More of the latter class might be acquired from France as it starts to decommission some of its own ships. In the longer term, Romania is reportedly looking to an alliance with Germany's Lürssen to support the construction of replacements for its Cold War-era corvettes, with Bulgaria considering a similar arrangement with France's DCNS. However, the latter's plans to co-produce 'Gowind' type ships with a local shipyard appear to have stalled on financial grounds. The **Ukraine** is another Black Sea country considering the local construction of new corvettes, although plans to start local construction of a new design during 2009 look optimistic given current economic conditions. Meanwhile, in the Adriatic, **Croatia** has taken delivery of two laid-

An image of the Portuguese Type 209 (PN) AIP-equipped submarine *Tridente* on sea trials in the first months of 2009. Whilst officially an extension of the long-running Type 209 design, the similarities with the later Type 214 design are clear. *(Thyssen Krupp Marine Systems)*

up *Helsinki* class fast attack craft from Finland under a €10m (US$14m) transaction intended to increase the navy's inter-operability with Western fleets.

North Sea and Atlantic: The most significant of the smaller Atlantic-facing European navies, **Portugal's** *Marinha Portuguesa* is currently in the middle of a major modernisation programme that will see a significant part of the fleet upgraded. Prominent amongst a series of new projects is the construction of two AIP-equipped, Type 209 (PN) submarines by Thyssen Krupp Marine Systems' HDW under a contract signed in 2004. The initial boat – *Tridente* – commenced sea trials in March 2009, whilst her sister was launched on 13 March 2009 before being formally named *Arpão* on 18 June. Although officially part of the Type 209 class, the Portuguese boats share significant similarities with the more recent Type 214 submarines, as published photographs show. Portugal is also in the course of receiving two surplus 'M' class frigates from the Netherlands. Together with the existing MEKO 200 type *Vasco da Gama* escorts, this will see the core of the surface fleet

consolidated around five modern ships. Meanwhile, elderly corvettes and patrol vessels will be replaced by the new locally built 1,600-ton *Viana do Castelo* oceanic patrol ships, whilst fabrication of a replacement class of inshore craft displacing around 700 tons is underway as well. Portugal is also one of an increasing number of countries looking to expand amphibious forces and future plans include local-build of a new LPD-type amphibious transport dock. **Belgium** is another country that has taken advantage of Dutch fleet reductions and two 'M' class frigates were transferred as *Leopold I* and *Louis-Marie* during 2007–8. These replace the three old *Wielingen* type frigates sold to Bulgaria. The new ships are being used quite intensively to support international stabilisation missions; for example, *Leopold I* served as flagship of UNIFIL's maritime component for three months during 2009. The six remaining 'Tripartite' minehunters have all completed upgrades, whilst a replacement for the support ship *Godetia* is planned in the medium term. **Ireland** is also looking for new ships to replace its older patrol ships, with two offshore and one multi-role vessel planned under a contract which is reportedly valued at €180m (US$250m). However, with Ireland's financial crisis so severe that all recruitment to the defence forces has been temporarily suspended, it must be doubtful whether a contract can be finalised with either of the two shortlisted bidders in the near term.

Scandinavia and The Baltic: Although overall force levels have shrunk significantly in recent years, the Scandinavian navies have all been taking delivery of powerful new units that make them amongst the most modern in the European region. The most substantial transformation has been that imple-

mented by **Norway**, with the key components of its surface fleet almost entirely overhauled by the progressive delivery of five Aegis-equipped *Fridtjof Nansen* class frigates and six *Skjold* class fast attack craft. The former vessels have been built by Navantia in Spain. They are effectively a cut-down, c.5,000-ton version of the *Armada Española*'s F-100 class, featuring lighter SPY-1F radar arrays and short-range Evolved Sea Sparrow missiles compared with the Spanish ships' Standard SM-2. Three of the five ships had entered service by mid-2009, with the fourth ship *Helge Ingstad* due for delivery in the autumn on completion of sea trials and the final unit, *Thor Heyerdahl*, launched on 11 February 2009. Largely

intended for blue-water operations, particularly in defence of Norway's far north, the frigates will be supplemented in the littoral by the fast and stealthy *Skjold* class, which should all be fully operational by the coming years of the next decade. Meanwhile, the six *Ula* class patrol submarines are all being progressively modernised to retain their effectiveness throughout the next decade, whilst naval aviation assets will be boosted by the introduction of the NH-90 helicopter in replacement of the older Lynx.

The Portuguese 'M' class frigate *Bartolomeu Dias* pictured during a Portsmouth port call whilst on her delivery voyage from the Netherlands in February 2009. *(Conrad Waters)*

Sweden's previously coastal-defence orientated fleet has suffered from reductions in defence funding in the post-Cold War environment as it has sought to find a more relevant role. Its existing fleet of small corvettes has, however, been increasingly deployed in international operations. Spells supporting the UNIFIL mission in the eastern Mediterranean have recently been supplemented by involvement in the growing security presence off the Horn of Africa through the dispatch of *Stockholm* and *Malmö* to the region by means of heavy-lift ship. The forthcoming introduction into operational service of the five new *Visby* class stealth corvettes in replacement for many

of the existing ships should assist such deployments in future. In addition, the Royal Swedish Navy is one of many forces interested in the concept of a multi-role support vessel, with *Jane's Defence Weekly* suggesting that a similar ship to New Zealand's *Canterbury* is the preferred option to meet the L10 support ship requirement. The five-strong AIP-equipped submarine fleet is also due for modernisation, with Sweden continuing to try to attract foreign participation, particularly from Norway and Singapore, in its A-26 design.

Denmark has already abandoned its submarine flotilla, with resources being focused on the two

Absalon class flexible support ships now in service and three associated 6,500-ton frigates of the *Ivar Huitfeldt* class currently under construction by Odense Steel for delivery between 2010 and 2012.[5] Amongst the Baltic countries, **Finland** has completed modernisation of its fast attack strike force with the delivery of the fourth *Hamina* class vessel. It will soon start to receive new mine-countermeasures vessels from Italy's Intermarine under the MCMV 2010 programme. The Baltic Republics have also been upgrading mine-warfare capabilities through acquisition of second-hand ships. **Lithuania** is to receive two former British Royal Navy 'Hunt' class minehunters to add to the three former Danish 'Stanflex' vessels it operates in patrol configuration, whilst the transfer of three *Sandown* class ships to **Estonia** is already complete following the delivery of *Ugandi* (ex-*Bridport*) at Rosyth on 22 January 2009.

The overhaul of Norway's surface fleet through acquisition of the new *Fridtjof Nansen* class of frigates is now close to completion. Derived from Spain's F-100 class and built in the same shipyard in Ferrol, the class is equipped with lightweight SPY-1F radars that effectively form a new variant of the Aegis combat system. Here fourth of the class *Helge Ingstad* is seen on sea trials. (*Navantia*)

Right: Sweden's diminutive corvettes are being increasingly deployed on international operations in advance of the imminent entry into service of the larger and more suitable *Visby* class. *Malmö* – pictured here – spent much of 2009 with her sister-ship *Stockholm* combating piracy off the Horn of Africa after being transported to the region by heavy-lift vessel. The planned acquisition of a new multi-role ship should also assist any such future deployments: a similar ship to the Royal New Zealand Navy's *Canterbury* is one possible option currently under consideration. *(Conrad Waters)*

Below: The Danish Stanflex design is now also seeing use in Lithuania's fleet following delivery of three surplus members of the class for use in patrol configuration. *Støren* – seen here entering Portsmouth Harbour in 2008 – remains in Danish service, where she is currently assigned a mine-countermeasures role. *(Conrad Waters)*

Although there is much publicity about revived Russian naval ambitions, the surface fleet is dominated by obsolescent Soviet-era designs. These images depict the *Udaloy* class destroyer *Admiral Vinogradov* (left) and the frigate *Neustrashimy* (below). *(US Navy)*

TABLE 2.4.6: RUSSIAN NAVY: SELECTED PRINCIPAL UNITS AS AT MID-2009

TYPE	CLASS	NUMBER[1]	TONNAGE	DIMENSIONS	PROPULSION	CREW	DATE
Aircraft carriers							
Aircraft Carrier – CV	Project 1143.5 **KUZNETSOV**	1	60,000 tons	306m x 35/73m x 10m	Steam, 32 knots	2,600	1991
Principal Surface Escorts							
Battlecruiser – BCGN	Project 1144.2 **KIROV**	1 (1)	25,000 tons	252m x 25m x 9m	CONAS, 32 knots	740	1980
Cruiser – CG	Project 1164 **MOSKVA** (Slava)	3	12,500 tons	186m x 21m x 9m	COGAG, 32 knots	530	1982
Destroyer – DDG	Project 956/956A **SOVREMENNY**	c. 5	8,000 tons	156m x 17m x 7m	Steam, 32 knots	300	1980
Destroyer – DDG	Project 1155.1 **CHABANENKO** (Udaloy II)	1	9,000 tons	163m x 19m x 8m	COGAG, 29 knots	250	1999
Destroyer – DDG	Project 1155 **UDALOY**	c.7	8.400 tons	163m x 19m x 8m	COGAG, 30 knots	300	1980
Frigate – FFG	Project 1154 **NEUSTRASHIMY**	2	4,400 tons	139m x 16m x 8m	COGAG, 30 knots	210	1993
Frigate – FFG	Project 1135 **BDITELNNY** ('Krivak I/II')	c.4	3,700 tons	123m x 14m x 7m	COGAG, 32 knots	180	1970
Frigate – FFG	Project 2038.0 **STERGUSHCHY**	1	2,200 tons	105m x 11m x 4m	CODAD, 27 knots[2]	100	2008
Frigate – FFG	Project 1161.1 **TATARSTAN**	2	2,000 tons	102m x 13m x 4m	CODOG, 27 knots	100	2002
Submarines							
Submarine – SSBN	Project 941 **DONSKOY** ('Typhoon')	1 (2)	33,000 tons	173m x 23m x 12m	Nuclear, 26 knots	150	1981
Submarine – SSBN	Project 677BDRM **VERKHOTURIE** ('Delta IV')	6	18,000 tons	167m x 12m x 9m	Nuclear, 24 knots	130	1985
Submarine – SSBN	Project 677BDR **ZVEZDA** ('Delta III')	5	12,000 tons	160m x 12m x 9m	Nuclear, 24 knots	130	1976
Submarine – SSGN	Project 949B ('Oscar II')	c.5	17,500 tons	154m x 8m x 9m	Nuclear, 30+ knots	100	1986
Submarine – SSN	Project 971 ('Akula I/II')	c.10	9,500 tons	110m x 14m x 10m	Nuclear, 30+ knots	60	1986
Submarine – SSK	Project 877/636 ('Kilo')	c.20	3,000 tons	73m x 10m x 7m	Diesel-electric, 20 knots	55	1981
Major Amphibious Units							
Landing Platform Dock – LPD	Project 1174 **IVAN ROGOV**	1	14,000 tons	157m x 24m x 7m	Gas, 19 knots	240	1978

Notes:

1 Table only includes main types & focuses on operational units: bracketed figures are ships being refurbished or in maintained reserve

2 Some sources state CODOG propulsion.

Neighbouring **Latvia** has turned to the Netherlands for its own fleet renewal with the acquisition of five 'Tripartite' vessels, the fourth of which was handed over in October 2008. However, there have been reports in the Latvian press that the new ships have proved expensive to maintain in service. Some might even be sold if a buyer can be found.

RUSSIA

Whilst it is clear that the Russian navy has started to recover from the nadir reached in the early years of the current millennium, it still has considerable challenges to overcome before it can be considered as having returned to its previous ranking as one of the world's leading fleets. Although the current naval force is impressive in purely numerical terms, the vast majority of ships date from the days of the Cold War and the operational status of many has to be considered as extremely uncertain. Indeed, published estimates of the present active fleet's strength vary significantly and the data set out in Table 2.4.6 therefore only attempts to detail of some of the more important classes. A significant programme of shipbuilding is needed to construct new designs relevant to the present era and this appears to be the official intention. However, the run-down and fragmented nature of current industrial infrastructure – some important facilities from the Soviet era are now out of Russian control – is making this task very difficult to achieve. To date, only two significant vessels designed after the end of the Cold War – the Project 677 'Lada' class patrol submarine *Saint Petersburg* and the Project 2038.0 light frigate *Steregushchy* – have been completed for the conventional forces, both in prototype form.

To some extent, this situation reflects the priority that Russia is placing on modernising its submarine-based nuclear deterrent. The strategic submarines that form this force all date from Soviet times and cannot be maintained in operational service indefinitely. A report carried by Russian News Agency *RIA Novosti* in June 2009 quoted Moscow defence analyst Mikhail Barabanov as stating that only around eight of the remaining vessels could be considered combat-ready, with overall force levels gradually declining as the 'Delta III' boats in Russia's Pacific Fleet are decommissioned. Russia plans to reverse this decline through the acquisition of new Project 955 'Borey' class, which will be equipped with the new SS-NX-30 'Bulava' ballistic missile. The first of these new SSBNs – *Yury Dolgoruky* – started long-delayed sea trials from the Sevmash facility at Severodvinsk on 19 June 2009 and a further two of a planned fleet of at least eight boats are under construction. In the meantime, the refurbished 'Typhoon' class submarine *Dimitry Donskoy* has been refitted to undertake a series of trials of the new missile, around half of which have ended in failure. As many as four or five further tests are planned from July 2009 onwards, demonstrating the importance that Russia attaches to being able to deploy a credible weapon in the new class.

The construction of non-strategic submarines is focused on the Project 885 'Yasen' class SSN

Severodvinsk and the Project 677 'Lada' class of SSK type patrol submarines. The former vessel was laid down as long ago as 1993. It has to be questionable whether such a dated design will be suitable for series production, although there are reports a second member of the class will be ordered soon. The Project 677 is a slightly later design intended to supersede the successful 'Kilo' type but has also suffered from a prolonged construction period before commencing sea trials at the end of 2005. The fact that these have been extended into 2009 suggests that these cannot have gone entirely smoothly, albeit recent reports suggest the boat will become operational in 2010. At least two additional units – *Kronstadt* and *Sevastopol* – are currently under construction out of a planned class total of eight.

The above-water equivalent of the 'Lada' design is the Project 2038.0 *Steregushchy* class of light stealth frigates. The first of this type hoisted the Russian flag on 27 February 2008. Displacing a little over 2,000 tons in full load conditions, they ship a powerful complement of sensors and weaponry in a 112m hull and benefit from substantial stealth features. Principally designed to operate in coastal waters, a key function will be to sweep the sea lanes transited by strategic submarines on their journeys to and from the open sea of surface and sub-surface threats. At least four additional members of the class are presently under construction, with the second ship expected to be ready by 2010. The Russian navy would like a total fleet of as many as twenty of these frigates but this seems optimistic.

Although Russia has announced ambitious plans to recapitalise 'blue water' forces with nuclear-powered aircraft carriers, the fact that only one modern surface vessel designed for such operations is currently under construction suggests that these ambitions will take time to realise. The Project 2235.0 frigate *Admiral Sergei Gorshkov*, scheduled for launch in 2011, is expected to be a general purpose escort of around 4,500 tons full load displacement with a balanced armament of surface-to-air and surface-to-surface missiles, a medium-calibre gun and an embarked helicopter. Although few details have been released on the new design, there has been some speculation that the ship could be derived from the Project 1135.6 *Talwar* class built for India and be fitted with the jointly developed BrahMos supersonic cruise missile. Meanwhile Russia has taken delivery of the second Project 1154.0 type frigate *Yaroslav Mudry* some sixteen years after *Neustrashimy*, the lead ship of the class, was commissioned. Her near twenty-year construction span must be a record in modern times and, in spite of claims that she has been totally rebuilt to incorporate the latest technology, it is difficult to see her as the equivalent of the latest ships in other major fleets.[6]

A file image of a Russian 'Typhoon' class submarine dating from 1985. Modernisation of the elderly flotilla of strategic missile submarines by new construction is Russia's top priority. *(US Department of Defense)*

Notes

1. The best English-language description available of the PA2 carrier project is contained on the Navy Matters website as an adjunct to its very comprehensive coverage of the British Royal Navy's CVF project. Please refer to http://navy-matters.beedall.com/pa2-1.htm and subsequent pages.

2. For French speakers, the informative *Mer et Marine* website is an excellent source of information on *Marine Nationale* and DCNS projects, including the 'Gowind' family. Please refer to www.meretmarine.com

3. Chapter 3.1 provides a full description of the origins and design of *Cavour*.

4. Janes's update on the current status of the Neptune II programme can be found in Tim Fish's 'Greece to scrap upgrades in favour of new Type 209s', *Jane's Defence Weekly* – 4 March 2009 (Coulsdon, HIS Jane's, 2009), p 33.

5. A more detailed overview of the current status of this project is contained in 'Danish Modern: Commercial shipbuilding cuts the cost of frigates', Joris Jansen Lok, *Defense Technology International* – July/August 2008 (Washington, DC, McGraw Hill Companies Inc, 2008), pp 28–9.

6. The best source of information on Russian naval developments is the Global Security website at www.globalsecurity.org

2.4A FLEET REVIEW

THE UNITED KINGDOM: THE ROYAL NAVY

The Royal Navy is in the midst of a revolution. Over the next ten years it will replace a fleet of ageing warships, submarines and auxiliary vessels – designed in the depths of the Cold War for North Atlantic operations – with a smaller number of much larger and more capable vessels optimised for global power projection. The relative scale and impact of this change exceeds anything since the decision in February 1966 to cancel the building of a new 55,000-ton aircraft carrier (CVA-01) and scrap the Royal Navy's existing aircraft carriers.

Author: **Richard Beedall**

Richard Beedall served for fourteen years in the Royal Naval Reserve, joining as a communications rating. He spent many years in the Arabian Gulf, often working with RN, USN and local naval forces. He left the RNR as a Lieutenant and now resides in Ireland; working as a writer and consultant. Founder of the influential 'Navy Matters' website on Royal Navy equipment projects, he is married with two young daughters.

OVERVIEW

The current naval construction programme can be traced back to the UK's 1998 'Strategic Defence Review' (SDR); this policy document set out the post-Cold War missions of the United Kingdom's armed forces. Its emphasis on world-wide expeditionary operations was a major shift from the previous defensive role in the European theatre and a triumph for the Royal Navy's new concept of a Maritime Contribution to Joint Operations (MCJO). The then First Sea Lord, Admiral Jock Slater, also successfully argued that such operations required 'versatile and deployable' forces, with a broadly 'balanced fleet' including two task groups for both littoral manoeuvre (operations close to the shore) and carrier strike. In a quirk of history, the centrepiece of SDR was a decision to replace the Royal Navy's three small aircraft carriers (20,600 tons, designated as 'command cruisers' when designed in the late 1960s) with two larger aircraft carriers which would 'have wide utility, particularly for power projection and rapid deployment operations'.

A naval construction programme was evolved to implement SDR and address the problem of ageing legacy platforms and systems. It was ambitious but got off to a good start as – during the period 2000 to 2002 – orders were placed for six destroyers, four

landing ships, six cargo ships for strategic sea lift and three patrol vessels.

The Ministry of Defence (MoD) became concerned that the United Kingdom's naval shipbuilding industrial base had insufficient capacity to cope with this 'feast' of orders, and delays in the construction of the new ships would thus result. This was a factor in the Ministry demanding consolidation of the UK's naval construction industry as a pre-requisite for ordering the two new aircraft carriers. This resulted in the establishment on 1 July 2008 of BVT Surface Fleet – bringing together the surface warship building and through-life support operations of BAE Systems and VT Group, as well as their existing joint venture, Fleet Support Limited. BVT Surface Fleet is now wholly owned by BAE Systems, which also owns BAE Systems Submarines Solutions – the sole remaining builder of submarines in the UK.

Concerns over naval construction capacity became superfluous as from 2002 the MoD prioritised the funding of operations in Afghanistan and Iraq, the Royal Navy suffering serious cuts as a result. The 'Defence Industrial Strategy' – published in December 2005 – promised a long term 'drumbeat' of producing one major surface ship every year, and one nuclear submarine every two years, but orders continued to be cancelled or deferred.

A revised procurement programme finally emerged in the middle of 2008 as the result of two decisions: firstly to sign contracts for the construction of the two new aircraft carriers (triggering the formation of BVT) and secondly the abandonment of plans for two more Type 45 destroyers in favour of progressing the Future Surface Combatant (FSC) project.

The UK's surface warship programme is now tightly focussed on executing three major projects in sequence. Up front is the completion of six Type 45 destroyers between 2009 and 2013; peak spending will then switch to the construction of the new aircraft carriers for completion between about 2015 and 2018; and finally priority will move to FSC, with the first of a new class of frigates expected to enter service in 2019. The MoD is expected to commit to this construction programme as the core workload in a fifteen-year Terms of Business agreement being negotiated with BVT Surface Fleet.

As regards the Royal Navy's submarine service, the initial priority is the completion of seven *Astute* class nuclear attack submarines (SSNs) between 2010 and about 2021. Three or four new ballistic missile nuclear submarines (SSBNs) will then start to succeed the current *Vanguard* class from 2024 onwards.

DARING CLASS TYPE 45 DESTROYER PROJECT

The Type 45 destroyers will replace the Type 42 anti-air warfare destroyers. At 7,350 tons full load and 152m long overall, they will be considerably larger than their predecessors.

Built by BVT Surface Fleet, the first of class (*Daring*) was delivered in December 2008. Construction of the remaining five units is proceeding well, with the launch of the sixth and last unit (*Duncan*) planned for October 2010. All six destroyers, built at total cost of £6.46bn (a 29 per cent increase from the original £5bn), should be in commission by 2013.

Please refer to Chapter 3.2: *HMS* Daring – *The Royal Navy's Type 45 Air Defence Destroyer* for more information on this programme.

QUEEN ELIZABETH CLASS, FUTURE AIRCRAFT CARRIER PROJECT

The Future Aircraft Carrier (CVF) project forms the core element of the MoD's Carrier Strike Programme, the other main elements being the Joint Combat Aircraft (JCA), the Maritime Airborne Surveillance and Control (MASC) platform and the Military Afloat Reach and Sustainability (MARS) support ships.

During the assessment and demonstration phases which ran from 1999 to 2007, an innovative and adaptable CVF design was evolved from a concept originally developed by Thales UK and BMT. The most unusual feature of the design is the twin island superstructure – the forward island being dedicated to ship control whilst the aft island manages flight deck operations. The ships will be built with a bow ramp and associated equipment for the operation of the short take-off and vertical landing (STOVL) capable Lockheed Martin F-35B Joint Strike Fighter (selected to meet the JCA requirement): however the design allows for the carriers to be modified to operate aircraft requiring catapult launch and arrested recovery.

Approval for the manufacture of two aircraft carriers (termed 'Main Gate') was announced by the government on 25 July 2007; contracts were finally signed by the MoD and industry on 3 July 2008. The carriers will be called *Queen Elizabeth* and *Prince of Wales*. With a displacement of 65,000 tons and an overall length of 284m they are the largest warships ever built for the Royal Navy, and also the most expensive, at £3.9bn for the two.

Responsibility for construction of the two new vessels has been given to the Aircraft Carrier Alliance (ACA) – a consortium of BVT Surface Fleet, Babcock Marine, Thales UK, BAE Systems and the MoD (which acts as both partner and client). No single UK shipyard has the facilities and capacity needed to build the carriers, so a strategy has been developed whereby they will be built in sections at shipyards around the UK:

- Lower Block 1 (bow section) – Babcock Marine's yards at Appledore and Rosyth
- Lower Block 2 (midships section) – BVT Surface Fleet in Portsmouth
- Lower Blocks 3 and 4 (stern section) – BVT on the Clyde
- Sponsons (overhanging upper hull structure) – Babcock

The Royal Navy is in the midst of a revolution. At its heart is the replacement of the fleet's existing small aircraft carriers with two new large CVF future carriers of the *Queen Elizabeth* class. *(BVT Surface Fleet)*

- Superstructure Islands – BVT in Portsmouth.
- Central upper blocks – A&P Tyne on Tyneside and Cammell Laird on Merseyside.

Steel working for the bow unit of *Queen Elizabeth* commenced at the Appledore shipyard in Devon in December 2008. Large scale manufacture will begin at other shipyards in summer 2009.

Final assembly and integration of the two ships will be undertaken at Rosyth. The first blocks for *Queen Elizabeth* will arrive there in summer 2011 for assembly in the No. 1 dock, which is being rebuilt for the task. Work will take two years before the hull is floated out and the assembly of *Prince of Wales* can begin.

In December 2008 the MoD sought a delay in the delivery of the ships and this was agreed with the ACA in March 2009. *Queen Elizabeth* is now expected to enter service in 2015 and *Prince of Wales* in 2018.

FUTURE SURFACE COMBATANT

The Future Surface Combatant (FSC) is the intended replacement for the Royal Navy's four Type 22 Batch 3 frigates (scheduled out of services dates of 2019 to 2022) and thirteen Type 23 frigates (2023 to 2036). Plans for FSC date back to the late 1990s but the latest iteration derives from the Sustained Surface Combatant Capability (S2C2) Pathfinder study of 2006/7.

S2C2 developed three flexible and adaptable concepts:

- **C1 – Task Group Enabled Surface Combatant:** A highly capable Anti-Submarine Warfare (ASW) and Land Attack optimised warship, designed for medium and large-scale war fighting operations but with wide utility.

- **C2 – Stabilisation Surface Combatant (General Purpose):** An escort able to contribute to:
  – Small-scale war fighting operations, providing a wide range of capabilities such as surveillance, maritime interdiction, ASW and surface warfare
  – Medium and large-scale operations through the protection of sea lines of communication

- **C3 – Ocean-Capable Patrol Vessel:** A modularised multi-role ship capable of acting as a patrol vessel, mine-countermeasures (MCM) vessel or a survey ship. C3 does not form part of the FSC programme.

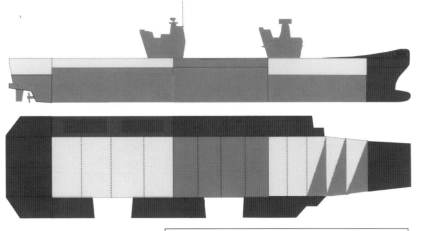

A graphic of the CVF build strategy. As no single UK facility has the capacity to build vessels of this size and complexity, they will be fabricated at shipyards around the country.
(Aircraft Carrier Alliance)

Nomenclature:

UB	- Upper Block (the 'Islands')
CB	- Centre Blocks (aka 'Central Upper Blocks')
SP	- Sponsons
LB	- Lower Block (main hull blocks)

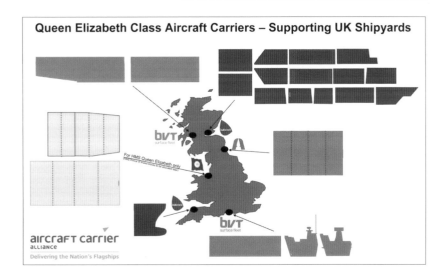

Queen Elizabeth Class Aircraft Carriers – Supporting UK Shipyards

An image of *Queen Elizabeth* and *Prince of Wales*. Due to delays in delivery times, it will be around the end of the decade before this sight becomes a reality.
(Aircraft Carrier Alliance)

Table 2.4A.1: UNITED KINGDOM, PROJECTED NAVAL CONSTRUCTION PROGRAMME (MID-2009)

PROJECT	MAIN GATE – ACTUAL (PLANNED)	NUMBER PLANNED	NUMBER ORDERED (BY 30 JUNE 2009)	IN SERVICE DATE	ESTIMATED COST
Daring class Type 45 Destroyer	2000	6	6	2010	£6.5bn
Queen Elizabeth class Future Aircraft Carrier (CVF)	2007	2	2	2015	£3.9bn
C1 Frigate Future Surface Combatant (FSC)	(2011)	10?	0	2019	Unknown
C3 Patrol Vessel Future Mine-Countermeasures	?	8 ?	0	2020	Unknown
Astute class Nuclear Attack Submarine	1997 (first 3 units)	7	4	2010	£3.65bn (first 3 units only)
'Successor'	(2012)	3 or 4	0	2024	£11.0bn

The Type 23 frigate *Kent* departing Portsmouth at the start of a deployment to the Persian Gulf in June 2009. Current plans envisage that she will be replaced by one of the future surface combatant FSC variants in around twenty-five years time. *(Conrad Waters)*

Little progress was being made on FSC until the decision in June 2008 to cancel plans for two further Type 45 destroyers in favour of advancing the FSC programme: in particular the C1 component which is needed by late next decade to replace Type 22 frigates.

In February 2009, BVT Surface Fleet was awarded a FSC concept phase contract and is now working in partnership with the Surface Combatants Directorate in the Defence Equipment and Support (DE&S) organisation to develop a costed assessment phase plan for FSC, and a cost model for the whole life of the programme. BVT will become the design lead during the assessment phase: the required approval being expected in mid-2009. BVT will also manufacture the ships and a Main Gate decision to order the first C1 is anticipated in late 2011, with an in-service date of 2019.

There has been considerable speculation as to possible FSC designs, with unofficial concepts appearing for 6,000-ton C1 frigates and 4,000-ton C2 escorts. The number of ships that will be built remains undecided – affordability is a critical factor – but for planning purposes a mix of ten C1 and eight C2 hulls has been used. The aspiration is to build one FSC per year, which given projected funding levels will mean a unit cost significantly below the £649m of the Type 45 destroyers. Difficult cost/capability trade-offs will need to be made.

It is hoped that the FSC designs will be attractive to foreign navies and export sales will result.

FUTURE MINE-COUNTERMEASURES

The Royal Navy currently operates sixteen mine-countermeasures (MCM) vessels, split equally between the 'Hunt' and *Sandown* classes. The first of these vessels is scheduled to retire in 2017 and the last by 2026.

A recently-completed joint MoD/industry Capability Investigation into the Future Mine Countermeasures capability considered a range of replacement options, including: mother ships controlling various unmanned surface and underwater vehicle options; traditional specialist vessels of under 1,000 tons; and larger, more versatile ships with modular equipment fits (including mine-hunting outfits). The last option, in the form of the C3 Ocean Patrol Vessel, has emerged as the favoured route forward.

The C3 concept is still evolving but the require-ments are likely to result in a ship of about 2,000 tons displacement. Eight C3s are needed to replace the existing MCM vessels but further hulls may be built to meet future hydrographical survey and offshore patrol vessel requirements. Current thinking is that the ships will be acquired through a part-nering arrangement with industry, in a similar manner to the 'River' class patrol vessels. The first vessels could enter service by 2020.

ASTUTE CLASS SUBMARINES

The *Astute* class of nuclear attack submarines will replace the current force of one *Swiftsure* class (*Sceptre*) and seven *Trafalgar* class boats. The new submarines will have a dived displacement of 7,400 tons and be 97m long.

A contract was placed in March 1997 with GEC-Marconi (now BAE Systems Submarine Solutions) for the design, build and in service support of the first three of the class. The first of class, *Astute*, was expected to enter service in June 2005.

Since then the project has faced significant delays and cost overruns – estimated costs for the three boats have escalated from £2.5bn to £3.8bn, whilst the project is running about five years late.

On 8 June 2007 *Astute* was finally rolled out from the Devonshire Dock Hall at Barrow-in-Furness for completion and trials. At the time BAE Systems was optimistic that *Astute* would be delivered in August 2008, however a series of accidents (including a fire in the sail in April 2009) and unconfirmed technical problems have resulted in further delays.

Astute is now expected to commence sea trials in autumn 2009, with delivery no earlier than spring 2010. It is hoped that second of class, *Ambush*, will roll-out by early 2010, with her delivery a year later. The third boat, *Artful*, should be delivered in 2012.

Since 2002 the MoD has been delaying orders for further *Astute*s because of the project's problems. A £200m order was finally placed on 21 May 2007 to start construction of the fourth *Astute* class subma-rine – *Audacious* – and her keel was ceremonially laid on 24 March 2009. The boat's full contract price is still being negotiated, but is likely to be around £940m.

Seven *Astute* class submarines are planned, deliv-ered at roughly 22-month intervals until 2020. Long lead items for boats five and six have been ordered; similar orders are expected in 2010 for the final boat.

An impression of an early VT Group multi-role ocean patrol vessel design concept for the Royal Navy's C3 MCMV replacement project. *(VT Group Plc)*

The modified 'River' class offshore patrol vessel *Clyde* (above) and 'Hunt' class mine-countermeasures vessel (MCMV) *Cattistock* (below). Both are candidates for replacement by the proposed C3 ocean patrol vessel. *(Conrad Waters)*

The lead *Astute* class submarine being rolled out of BAE's Barrow-in-Furness facility in June 2007. Ordered as long ago as March 1997, a series of technical problems means delivery will be delayed until spring 2010 at the earliest. *(BAE Systems)*

SUCCESSOR, FUTURE SUBMARINE PROJECT (FSM)

The future submarine project (FSM) will deliver a 'Successor' to the four *Vanguard* class nuclear-powered ballistic missile submarines.

On 14 March 2007 the British Parliament voted in favour of the renewal of Britain's nuclear deterrent at an estimated cost of £20bn, including up £14bn for new submarines. In May 2007 the DE&S established the Future Submarine (FSM) Integrated Project Team to manage the work. A team of 150 people at BAE Systems Submarine Solutions, Babcock Marine and Rolls-Royce Marine Power Solutions have already spent two years developing a concept design for the Successor submarine. Work is due to complete in September 2009, followed by an initial gate submission seeking approval to progress the project.

No details of the Successor design have been revealed, but likely starting points are an evolution of the current *Vanguard* class submarines, or a version of the *Astute* class with a missile compartment inserted behind the sail. A key factor affecting the design is the missiles. The new submarines will initially carry American-manufactured, life-extended Trident II (D5) missiles. The US Navy plans to replace Trident by 2042 and Successor will need to be able to carry the new missile – whose size and design is still uncertain. The MoD has commissioned General Dynamics Electric Boat to design a new missile compartment for Successor, with tubes for missiles larger than the 83in (2.1m) diameter Trident II. It is possible that the new compartment will contain twelve missiles, rather than the sixteen fitted in the *Vanguard* class. Another key decision is whether for propulsion Successor will use a development of the Rolls-Royce core H PWR2 reactor that is fitted to the *Astute* class, or whether a new design will be developed.

Main Gate approval for ordering the first Successor is expected in 2012. The class will be built by BAE Systems Submarine Solutions at its Barrow-in-Furness shipyard, with the first boat entering service in 2024. Three or four boats will be built – the MoD is studying whether a continuous patrol could be maintained with just three.

AMPHIBIOUS SHIPPING

In 2003 the Royal Navy considered options for the replacement of the landing platform helicopter (LPH) *Ocean*, which was due to leave service in 2018. This went no further and *Ocean* has been refitted to allow her to remain in service until 2022. Studies have now resumed, but with the intent of also replacing the two landing platform docks (LPD) – *Albion* and *Bulwark* – that are scheduled to leave service in 2033 and 2034. The construction of two relatively low-cost, medium displacement (perhaps 25,000–30,000 ton) amphibious assault ships of the LHD type is seen as the likeliest recommendation.

MILITARY AFLOAT REACH AND SUSTAINABILITY (MARS) PROGRAMME

The Royal Fleet Auxiliary (RFA) provides afloat support to the Royal Navy and joint operations – a fundamental requirement for world-wide deployment and sustainment. Many of the RFA's ships are old and since 2002 the Military Afloat Reach and Sustainability (MARS) programme has been studying their replacement. By 2005 the MARS team had developed a solution based on the procurement of eleven ships in three types to enter service between 2011 and 2021:

- **Fleet Tanker (FT):** For the delivery of bulk fluids (petroleum products and potable water) and the provision of forward aviation support (the logistical maintenance and support of aircraft and helicopters). Has a limited non-bulk consumables capacity to support small naval deployments.
- **Fleet Solid Support Ship (FSS):** For the delivery of consumables (stores, ammunition and food) and the provision of forward aviation support. Optimised for supporting the Carrier Strike Group and the *Queen Elizabeth* class carriers.
- **Joint Sea-Based Logistics Ship (JSBL):** For the delivery of consumables and forward aviation support. Optimised for supporting the Littoral Manoeuvre group, amphibious operations and the delivery of logistical support to forces ashore.

In 2007 the project prioritised the procurement of double-hulled fleet tankers to replace the existing 'Leaf' and 'Rover' class single-hulled tankers, which no longer comply with internal maritime pollution regulations.

On 10 December 2007 the MoD issued an 'Invitation to Participate in Dialogue' to industry for six fleet tankers capable of a speed of 15 knots and carrying 18,000 cubic metres of fuel. In May 2008 four companies were short-listed, none of whom proposed to build the tankers in the United Kingdom. The award of a contract worth up to £800m was expected in April 2009, with the first tanker being accepted off contract in 2012. However, after a review of its equipment programme, the MoD decided in December 2008 not to proceed with the fleet tanker order. It is now examining alternative approaches for their procurement and a three-year delay to the whole MARS programme is likely.

CONCLUDING REMARKS

BAE Systems, through its subsidiaries BVT Surface Fleet and BAE Systems Submarine Solutions has emerged as the primary supplier of warships in the UK – famous names such as Vickers, Vosper Thornycroft and Swan Hunter have all left the stage in recent years, whilst the reborn companies of Cammell Laird and Harland and Wolff are still barely recognisable from their shipbuilding glory days, and the Aircraft Carrier Alliance is an oddity unlikely to be repeated.

The future of the BAE Systems shipyards at Govan, Scotstoun, Portsmouth and Barrow-in-Furness seems to be secure if the Ministry of Defence continues to progress current core naval programmes and finally signs the Terms of Business Agreement that commits it to this. However, there will be a UK general election by May 2010 with the high expectation that the new government will conduct a defence review in order to match the MoD's equipment programme with allocated funding. The failure to progress the high priority MARS Fleet Tanker is already a serious concern, and potential casualties of a budget-driven defence review include the cancellation of the aircraft carrier *Prince of Wales* and the deferment or even cancellation of the Trident Successor Future Submarine. The RN's near-term focus is also on gaining approval for FSC in order to prevent the number of its destroyers and frigates falling below twenty, and advancing Future MCM so as to preserve a vital but often unsung capability.

Decisions will be made over the next twelve months which, by the end of 2010, could well determine both the shape of the UK's naval industry and the size and constitution of the Royal Navy well into the middle of this century.

Notes

This article has utilised information from a wide variety of official and commercial sources; a few of these are both readily accessible and deserve highlighting for further reading:

1. Although old, the starting point for understanding the UK's naval procurement plans remains the *Strategic Defence Review CM 3999* (London, The Stationary Office, 1998). An electronic version is accessible on the Ministry of Defence's website at www.mod.uk. A new strategic review is likely in the next Parliament.

2. Another important policy document that can be found on the MoD website is the *Defence Industrial Strategy: Defence White Paper CM 6697* (London, The Stationary Office, 2005), large elements of which relate to the maritime sector. Well received when published in December 2005, the implementation of DIS has suffered from under-funding. A second version (DIS v2.0) was expected to be issued in December 2007, but had still not appeared by June 2009.

3. The reference library section on the official Royal Navy website – www.royalnavy.mod.uk – includes pertinent policy documents on the future Royal Navy; information on naval developments; and the informative *Broadsheet* magazine (published annually).

4. In 2003 the RAND Corporation – www.rand.org – was requested by the MoD to conduct a study which led to Mark V Arena, Hans Pung, Cynthia R Cook, Jefferson P Marquis, Jessie Riposo and Gordon T Lee, *The United Kingdom's Naval Shipbuilding Industrial Base: The Next Fifteen Years* (Santa Monica, CA, RAND Corporation, 2005). This work contains a mass of detailed information which whilst now rather dated, is still often the best in the public domain.

5. The annual *MoD Major Projects Report* from the UK's National Audit Office – www.nao.uk – provides a rare insight in to the progress and cost of RN equipment programmes.

6. For news and articles on naval procurement with a UK slant, the magazines *Warship World* (Liskeard, Cornwall, Maritime Books) and *Warships International Fleet Review* (St Leonards-on-Sea, Sussex, HPC Publishing) are unrivalled sources.

3.1 SIGNIFICANT SHIPS

THE AIRCRAFT CARRIER CAVOUR

Doctrine and Sea Power in the Italian Navy

Italy's navy, the *Marina Militare*, has passed several substantial milestones over the past decade during a steady return to its historical position as one of the world's premier fleets. The 2003 launching of the AIP submarine *Salvatore Todaro* was one such marker, but more significant is the 2008 delivery of Italy's first major aircraft carrier, *Cavour*.

As a nation with an extensive coastline and major islands, the ability to control the surrounding seas has always been an imperative for Italy's security and economy. While *Cavour* is the largest warship to be commissioned by the post-war *Marina Militare*, it is a logical expression of the Italian way of asserting sea power. In modern times, because it has faced potential foes with stronger economies or greater military potential, Italy has always embraced innovation and strived to obtain the best available ships within the economic and geographic constraints that have historically confronted its navy. These limitations have led to a tendency to sacrifice range and protection for speed and punch, and a quest to square the circle between displacement and seaworthiness: sometimes successfully, sometimes not.

Italy's innovative tendencies can be traced to the 1814 order of a pair of American-style 48-gun heavy frigates (the *Commercio di Genova* and *Cristina*) by the Sardinian navy. During the modern period the Italian Navy has a history of commissioning the smallest capital ships or the most powerful cruisers world-wide, happily mixing categories, like the 2,682-ton broadside ironclads of the *Formidabile* class ordered by the Sardinian Premier (and Navy Minister) – Conte di Cavour – in 1859, or the small,

fast battleships of the *Saint Bon* class of 1892 and the *Regina Elena* of 1900. Being faster than the warships of the same category and more powerful than anyone else's armoured cruisers, they were the forerunners of the 'pocket battleships' conceived long before the more famous German *Deutschland* of the 1930s.

Italy's was the largest navy of the Second World War that did not operate an aircraft carrier. However, this did not represent a lack of 'air-mindedness' in navy circles. Italy's first flattop study dated back to 1919 with a proposal to convert the uncompleted battleship *Caracciolo* to a fast carrier. As early as 1924 it seemed a 9,000-ton design – inspired by the United States' *Langley* (CV-1) – would be ordered, with preparations underway, such as testing fighters and torpedo-bombers on a simulated wooden deck. However, budget cuts forced its cancellation. The next year, another innovative approach to the problem of exerting sea power – a hybrid carrier-cruiser with a floating dock for launching MAS boats – likewise could not clear the monetary hurdles. The same held true for carrier proposals in 1931, 1932, 1936 and 1937. In 1941 the hard experiences of war finally led to the conversion of the liner *Roma* into what would have been Italy's first carrier. Unfortunately, *Aquila* was only 80 per cent complete

by the time construction stopped in June 1943 to concentrate resources on more immediate needs like destroyers, torpedo boats, submarines and MTBs.

However, money was not the only problem, not even the main problem, delaying the navy's acquisition of a carrier. If the wartime relationship between sea and air was ideal in the United States and Japan, where the navies operated their own, full-capability air force (and even the US Marines and Coast Guard had their own air forces) and if it was barely acceptable in Great Britain, where the navy at least controlled its carrier aircraft and enjoyed a good deal of co-operation with RAF Coastal Command, in Italy it was miserable. The navy only possessed direct control over cruiser- and battleship-carried floatplanes and flying boats dedicated to reconnaissance and ASW duties. Air force co-operation was always half-hearted and stingy. This troubled relationship continued to haunt Italy's military after the war. The ridiculous and self-destructive lengths to which this sibling rivalry went was demonstrated by an event in December 1952. In view of the planned delivery to Italy of a war-surplus escort carrier and a *Independence* class light carrier, the US Navy agreed to provide Helldiver dive bombers for antisubmarine purposes and to train Italian navy pilots. When the first two, painted in *Marina Militare* colours and manned by navy personnel, landed in Naples, an air force officer dispatched the police to arrest the pilots for breaking Mussolini's old law restricting fixed-wing aircraft to the air force.[1]

In the early 1950s the *Marina Militare* began contemplating its first significant post-war growth phase. In light of the air force's continuing control over all fixed-wing aircraft, a minority of younger officers believed that the best path for the *Marina Militare* would be to become a destroyer navy like the new Japanese and German services, with a force much greater than the ragbag squadron of eight vessels – old ships laid down before the war or former USN units – then in commission. The naval staff rejected this idea and, instead, continued Italy's tradition of producing innovative warships and building as big as possible until better times would permit the construction of better ships. In 1957 the navy ordered two 'helicopter cruisers' of the *Doria* class (each at the price equivalent of four *Impetuoso* class destroyers, ordered in 1950 and completed in 1958).

The delivery of Italy's new aircraft carrier *Cavour* in 2008 marked a major step towards the *Marina Militare*'s return to its historical position as one of the world's premier fleets. *(Italian Navy)*

These vessels, which displaced 6,500 tons full load, proved too small to excel in the role envisaged for them. Therefore, in 1965, the navy ordered *Vittorio Veneto*, which had a full-load displacement of 8,850 tons and was capable of operating up to nine helicopters. Besides providing valuable combatants, the *Dorias* and *Vittorio Veneto* also allowed the *Marina Miltare* to conceive and develop, by experience, an original air doctrine – limited at first to helicopters – that led to Italy being the first of the Western navies to arm her helicopters with missiles.

The long budgetary crisis that lasted from 1962 to

Authors

Enrico Cernuschi and Vincent P O' Hara have co-authored articles for British and American publications including *Warship*, *World War II Quarterly* and *World War II*. Mr O'Hara is the author of three books published by Naval Institute Press, including *Struggle for the Middle Sea: The Great Navies at War in the Mediterranean Theater, 1940-1945*. He resides outside San Diego, California. Mr Cernuschi, based in Pavia, Italy, is a frequent contributor to *Storia Militare* and *Rivista Marittima* and has nearly 200 articles as well a dozen books to his credit, including, with E Bagnasco, the definitive *Le navi da guerra italiane 1940-1945*.

Above: Laid down in 1981, the mini-carrier *Garibaldi* was the first Italian flattop to see operational service. She is pictured here in company with the USN's giant *Nimitz* class strike carrier *Harry S Truman* (CVN-75). *(US Navy via Maurizio Brescia)*

Left: The amphibious transport dock *San Giorgio* pictured at Venice in 1988. Italy's experience with the three ships of this class had a significant impact on *Cavour*'s design. *(Aureliano Molinari via Maurizio Brescia)*

1973 scuttled the order for a *Vittorio Veneto* follow-up named *Italia* and a later 1965 design for a 'through-deck cruiser' named *Trieste*. This induced some critics to propose – during the early 1970s – the sale of the helicopter cruisers to a South American navy.[2] The money gained could buy an appreciable force of the new and handsome *Audace* class destroyers (laid down 1968, completed 1972 and displacing 4,400 tons full load). This suggestion thrived in the pages of the vivacious Italian naval and

Above: The launch of *Cavour*'s middle and aft sections took place from Fincantieri's Riva Trigoso facility on 20 July 2004. She was subsequently towed to the company's Mugiano yard near La Spezia for mating with the bow section and final fitting out. *(Maurizio Brescia)*

defence magazines but did not find favour with the naval staff. In 1975 they confirmed the classic *Marina Militare* line by proposing a slightly larger development of the *Trieste* project which became the *incrociatore tuttoponte* (through-deck cruiser) *Garibaldi*, laid down in 1981 and commissioned four years later. This 10,000-ton mini-carrier (13,500 tons full load displacement) marked the Italian Navy's first major milestone in its return to exerting significant influence in the Mediterranean, as it had before the Second World War.

Nonetheless – even as it neared completion – the purpose behind *Garibaldi* seemed likely to be still-born. The Italian Communist Party claimed in parliament that the construction of a carrier violated the 1947 peace treaty. Next, a newspaper storm erupted when someone noted that the ship on the slip, even if still rated as a helicopter carrier, had suddenly developed a growing protuberance forward on the deck which was very similar to a ski-jump.[3] The air force, meanwhile, strengthened its maritime presence and began publishing pictures of F-104s buzzing warships, as if to demonstrate that the navy did not need a carrier. The momentum, however, proved too great for the reactionaries to overcome. On 26 January 1989 the Italian Parliament, ignoring pressure from both the left and the air force lobby, ratified the vessel's true intention by enacting a law that abolished, after almost sixty-six years, Mussolini's legislation that had granted the air force a controlling monopoly over everything that flew.

The first Italian Navy AV-8B Harrier, purchased from McDonald Douglas, finally embarked on 23 August 1991.

Garibaldi has repaid Parliament's trust in her mission and vindicated the navy's vision. In her combat career in the Adriatic during the Kosovo crisis, in the Indian Ocean off Somalia and operating her AV-8B aircraft even in Afghan skies, she has provided the *Marina Militare* with reliable and efficient air cover despite being much smaller than the British *Invincible*, not to mention the French *Charles de Gaulle*. This is a tribute both to the ship's design and the skill of her personnel.

DESIGN HISTORY:
A TROUBLED CONCEPTION

Far from being a happy ending, Italy's never-ending carrier saga began a new, uneasy chapter in 1989 when the naval staff started to debate a successor to *Vittorio Veneto*, which was due to retire in the next decade. The logic behind *Garibaldi*'s design – and its evolution – argued, of course, for a new, enlarged *Garibaldi*. The design, labelled – Soviet style – Project 148, was for a 15,000-ton light carrier. This soon increased to 16,000 tons.

After a further design update (Project 156), a new budget crisis erupted in 1993 that delayed both *Vittorio Veneto*'s retirement (she remained in commission until 2003) and the laying-down of her replacement. This lapse of time allowed a further increase in the displacement of the planned carrier (20,000 tons as Project 160) but also jeopardised the ship. Since 1967, some writers in the *Rivista Marittima* (the Italian Navy's monthly staff journal) had supported the ideal of a dock landing ship for the Italian Navy. As the *Marina Militare*'s main task from around this time onwards was to counter, in conjunction with

the US 6th Fleet, the dramatically increased Soviet squadron in the Mediterranean, these pundits even claimed such a warship could operate against surface vessels by acting as a mother ship for small PHMs (Patrol Combatant Hydrofoil-Missile). These could be launched from her dock: an idea that went back to the torpedo-armed steam launches deployed from cruisers of the late nineteenth century but had not proved practical then either.[4] This movement to convert the *Marina Militare* into a brown-water navy centred on a dock landing ship was endorsed by the American lobby, which would have appreciated adding an additional *Iwo Jima* type LPH to the NATO inventory – especially as it would not cost its own citizens a penny. This idea was renewed, for the same purposes, during the first half of the 1970s, this time for a *Tarawa* LHA clone.

The third wave in this tenacious endeavour to make the *Marina Militare*'s major warship a brown-water vessel crested in the mid-1990s. It was supported, this time, by the recent experiences off Lebanon, Albania, Yugoslavia, Somalia and in the Persian Gulf, all trouble spots where the Italian Navy had supported the army there by ferrying rapid deployment units and their supplies. In spite of the availability, since 1988, of the three 5,000-ton helicopter-capable amphibious transport dock ships (LPDs) of the *San Giorgio* class,[5] experience soon confirmed that, as always, the bigger the better. Project 160 was therefore given the capacity to transport a 180-man raiding force from the San Marco Regiment and to land them with her own helicopters. Between 1996 and 1998 the ability to insert ground troops became the dominant attraction of this design and the new Projects 163 and 168 included a dock and a capacity to transport 620 personnel. The ship's acronym, NUMA (*Nuova*

Below and right: *Cavour*'s maiden sea trials were carried out in December 2006. She is pictured here on 19 December. *(Italian Navy)*

Opposite: Following delivery to the Italian Navy in March 2008, *Cavour* has been subject to a series of trials and enhancements as she works up to full operational capability. Although designed to be flexible, the defeat of attempts to give priority to amphibious capabilities means that she is first and foremost an aircraft carrier well equipped to operate a mixed group of fast jets and helicopters *(Italian Navy)*

Unità Maggiore: new main ship) soon became NUMPA (*Nuova Unità Maggiore Polifunzionale Anfibia*: new main multi-use landing ship).

Even if the choice finally seemed mature, an uproar in the navy's ranks – and a flaming debate that raged on the pages of *Rivista Marittima* – froze implementation of the revised design. The arguments against the planned NUMPA noted, for example, that experience showed how multi-capability approaches seldom lived up to their promise and that personnel always gave a ship a single soul, paying at best lip-service to the other

tasks planners expected the hull to perform. The final nail in NUMPA's coffin was a critical article that stated the new ship would be only a very expensive, less-than-useful auxiliary vessel and not a flagship. In early 1999, the Italian Navy's new Chief of Staff, Admiral Umberto Guarnieri, ordered the project altered again. This time the ship returned to her true carrier nature giving up the dock (considered inevitably by many of the naval staff to be a hole in the hull), thereby recovering space for – and giving priority to – aircraft operations. The ability to ferry troops was reduced to a total force of c.450 men to

be landed by helicopter, while two ramps gave a RO-RO capacity for transporting main battle tanks and other vehicles. The new ship, whose name suffered vicissitudes similar to those of the whole design process, went from *Giuseppe Mazzini* to *Luigi Einaudi* to *Andrea Doria* and finally to *Cavour*.[6] Ordered from Fincantieri on 22 November 2000, construction of the new ship began in July 2001 at the company's yards in Riva Trigoso and Mugiano. She was launched on 20 July 2004, handed over to the Italian Navy on 27 March 2008 and entered operational service the following year.

Cavour at sea. She has a standard displacement of 22,290 tons and at full load weighs 27,100 tons. *(Italian Navy)*

FUNCTION AND DESIGN

Cavour is designed to be flexible. Although first and foremost an aircraft carrier, she is one with enhanced amphibious and flag capabilities. She has a standard displacement of 22,290 tons and at full load weighs in at 27,100 tons. Her overall dimensions are 244m x 39m x 8.7m, while her flight deck is 232.6m x 34.5m. The runway is 183m long with a 12-degree ski jump. The ship's crew numbers 451, the air group 203, the command group 140, and she can lift over 400 troops in austerity conditions. Total accommodation of c.1,300 berths is provided.

Above: An interior view of *Cavour*'s hangar. Measuring 134.2m x 21m x 7.2m it can hold either eight fixed-wing aircraft or twelve helicopters. *(Maurizio Brescia)*

Right: *Cavour* has a secondary role as an amphibious assault ship. One of two roll-on/roll-off ramps can be seen in this stern view. *(Italian Navy via Maurizio Brescia)*

Above: A *Marina Militare* AV-8B Harrier II Plus pictured during initial trials on *Cavour*. The type will provide the new aircraft carrier's principal strike force during its early years in service. *(Italian Navy via Maurizio Brescia)*

Right: The forward end of *Cavour*'s island structure. The big radar dome for the SPY-790 EMPAR multifunction radar that controls the SAAM-IT air-defence system and its associated Aster 15 missiles is clearly visible. *(Maurizio Brescia)*

Cavour is powered by four General Electric/Avio LM2500 gas turbines producing a total of 88 MW. These drive two gear units that provide 60,000shp each and turn five bladed shafts giving the vessel a maximum speed of more than 28 knots. Her capacity of 2,500 tons of fuel provides a range of 7,000 nautical miles at 16 knots and a sustained autonomy of 18 days. Unlike her namesake – and many other Italian warships of the Second World War – she is an economic steamer, consuming just 3 tons of fuel per hour at cruising speed, compared to 25 tons at full speed. Her six Wärtsilä CW 12V200 diesel generators provide a total output of 13.2 MW. She has twin rudders, together with bow and stern thrusters.

As a carrier, *Cavour* can accommodate Vertical/Short Take-Off and Landing (V/STOL) aircraft such as AV-8B+ Harriers and/or helicopters, such as the EH-101, NH-90, or SH-3D. She will also operate the F-35B Joint Strike Fighter (JSF) STOVL variant when it comes on line. Her flight deck can accommodate up to a dozen fixed-wing aircraft and six helicopters. Her 2,500m² hanger/garage space measures 134m x 21m x 7.2m

Right: The new fifth-generation Lockheed Martin F-35 Lightning II Joint Strike Fighter will be *Cavour*'s sword from the middle of the next decade. *(US Navy)*

and can hold either eight fixed-wing aircraft or twelve helicopters. She has a pair of 30-ton aircraft elevators, two 15-ton armament elevators and two smaller elevators. Her design, which includes two pairs of active stabilising fins, will permit flight operations in up to sea state 6. She can sail with a mixed group of up to twenty-four aircraft, depending on her mission.

As an amphibious platform, *Cavour* can lift different mixes of vehicles, including 100 light vehicles or 50 amphibious assault vehicles or 24 main battle tanks. Two roll-on/roll-off ramps provide access. Accommodation is provided for 325 marines of the San Marco Regiment, plus a further 91 in overload condition. She is fitted with more than 150 workstations and, as a flagship, can manage the navy's air and amphibious operations. She also contains extensive medical facilities, including three operating theatres, a dental surgery, a laboratory and a radiology department, as well as a full hospital ward.

Cavour carries a powerful weapons suite and capable sensors. Principal anti-air armament is the Franco-Italian Eurosam SAAM-IT missile system. This comprises the Selix Sistemi Integrati SPY-790 EMPAR multifunction radar and four Sylver eight-cell vertical launchers for the Aster 15 missile, controlled by a CMS-Italia combat system ultimately derived from the SENIT-8 system installed in *Charles de Gaulle*. The highly manoeuvrable Aster, which also equips the two *Andrea Doria* 'Horizon' class frigates and the forthcoming FREMM escorts, carries a 13kg warhead at a speed of Mach 3 to a maximum range of 30km in its short range version. Guidance is by telemetry uplink provided by the EMPAR radar, with active terminal homing taking over in the final stages of an engagement. At least twelve aircraft or missile targets can be engaged simultaneously. There will also be two Oto Melara 76mm/62 Super Rapid Fire guns, rated at 120 rounds per minute and firing a 12.34kg round at a muzzle velocity of 925m/s to a range of 30km, and three 25mm Oerlikon Contraves KBA anti-aircraft guns. Other sensors include a SPS-798 RAN 40L 3D

Right: The *Marina Militare* will operate the STOVL F-35B variant of the Lightning II. This picture shows the type's first flight on 11 June 2008. *(Lockheed Martin)*

D-band long range air search radar, SPS-791 RASS RAN 30X/I surface-search radar plus navigation and air-control arrays, whilst a SIR-R interrogation friend or foe (IFF) system is also shipped. *Cavour's* countermeasures suite includes two 20-barrel Oto Melara/Selex SCLAR-H decoy launchers for 105mm or 118mm multipurpose rockets. She also carries two SLAT torpedo defence systems and a bow-mounted WASS mine avoidance sonar. Electronic counter-measures and electronic support measures include the Elettronica SpA integrated ESM/Elint/ECM (see further below).

Cavour is divided into seven zones for security and damage control with computerised monitoring systems. Her habitability is high: personal space allotments are generous and built to civilian standards of comfort. Public spaces include bars, a cinema and a gym. She adheres to modern environmental standards with respect to emissions control and waste management.

CAPABILITIES:
THE SWORD AND THE SHIELD

With her air component – and hence her 'soul' – apparently assured by the 1989 repeal of the air force's fixed-wing monopoly, *Cavour* can look forward to a future based on operating the new JSF. This will strengthen her core capability and, there-fore, her justification. If this article had been written three quarters of a century previously, the new Italian flagship would have been, like everywhere, a battle-ship and her punch would have been formed by her guns. Being a carrier, her 21st-century offensive weapon will, instead, be the new fifth- generation fighter, the F-35B Lightning II JSF. The Italian Navy plans to acquire at least twenty-two of the F-35B STOVL version to equip *Cavour's* strike group. This supersonic, multi-role stealth aircraft is currently undergoing a rocky development process due to cost overruns. However, the first STOVL variant began test flights in 2008 and its engine, a Pratt & Whitney F135, received a Statement of Qualification for full

Table 3.1.1.

CAVOUR PRINCIPAL PARTICULARS

Building Information:

Fabrication Commenced:	17 July 2001
Launched:	20 July 2004
Delivered:	27 March 2008
Builders:	Fincantieri – Cantieri Navali Italiani SpA at its Riva Trigoso and Mugiano facilities.

Dimensions:

Displacement:	22,290 tons standard displacement, 27,100 tons full load displacement.
Overall Hull Dimensions:	244.0m x 39.0m x 8.7m. Length between perpendiculars is 215.6m.
Flight Deck Dimensions:	232.6m x 34.5m. The ski jump has 12° elevation. There are 2 x 30-ton aircraft lifts, 2 x 15-ton ammunition lifts and 2 service lifts.
Hangar Dimensions:	134.2m x 21.0m x 7.2m.

Weapons Systems:

Aircraft:	A mixed air group of c.24 aircraft can be accommodated. Typical initial air group: 8 AV-8B Harriers and 12 EH- 101 Merlins.
Missiles:	4 x Sylver A43 8 cell VLS modules (arranged in two pairs) for Aster 15 surface-to-air missiles.
Guns:	2 x Oto Melara 76mm Super Rapid (initially fitted for but not with), 3 x 25mm anti-aircraft guns.
Countermeasures:	Elettronica SpA integrated ESM/Elint/ECM system, 2 x SCLAR-H decoy launchers, 2 x SLAT torpedo defence systems.
Principal Sensors:	1 x EMPAR multifunction radar, 1 x RAN-40L air search radar, 1 x RAN-30X/I surface search radar, navigation and air control arrays. 1 x SNA-2000 mine avoidance sonar, SLAT towed-array as part of torpedo defence system.
Combat System:	CMS-Italia combat system. Communications include Links 11 and 16 with provision for Link 22.

Propulsion Systems:

Machinery:	COGAG machinery arrangement. 4 x GE/Avio LM2500 gas turbines rated at 88MW total produce 118,000shp through two shafts. 6 x 2.2MW diesel generators.
Speed and Range:	Maximum speed 28/29 knots. Range is 7,000 nautical miles at 16 knots.

Other Details:

Complement:	Accommodation provided for c.1,300 personnel.
Military Lift:	Up to 100 light vehicles, 50 medium vehicles or 24 main battle tanks can be shipped. Two 60-ton RO/RO ramps are fitted. There is provision for up to four light landing craft of the LCVP type.

powered lift operations in February 2009. The plane, when finally deployed in the first half of the next decade, will give the *Marina Militare* unprecedented hitting power and protection. US military spokesmen have claimed that the F-35 will be four times more capable than any fourth-generation fighter. It can carry more air to air and air to ground weapons than its predecessors and its stealth capability and electronics will guarantee that its only credible threat, at least for the near term, will be either the US Air Force's F-22 'Raptor' or another F-35.

Continuing with the battleship analogy, defensive strength would previously have been provided by armour. But in the case of *Cavour*, although she does have some sensitive areas protected by Kevlar, her true defense is her electronics. Between 1941 and 1943 the Italian navy learned the hard way about the increasing role of radar in 'sea denial' naval night fighting. By the spring of 1944, it was also well aware that electronics would soon become the dominant factor in the exercise of 'sea power' as well. Beginning in the late 1940s the *Marina Militare* and private enterprise therefore began a revolutionary programme to achieve future excellence in the field of electronic warfare. The goal was ambitious – but not impossible. The shared conclusion was that battles had been lost due to the lack of an adequate industrial base, not through a deficit in knowledge.

Italy's expert scientists therefore had to make an evolutionary leap from the phase of producing handcrafted prototypes to working on an industrial scale. This required enterprises dedicated to defence purposes because such a task needed, in the long term, the development of an intellectual doctrine that was incompatible with purely commercial goals.

Although it was a difficult vision to realise, this transformation started to take shape in the 1940s with foundation of SMA by Eng. Nello Carrara. This was followed in 1951 by the formation of Elettronica SpA by Eng. Filippo Fratalocchi. Always exploring the boundaries of technology, their philosophy was not to limit their imagination to raw mate-

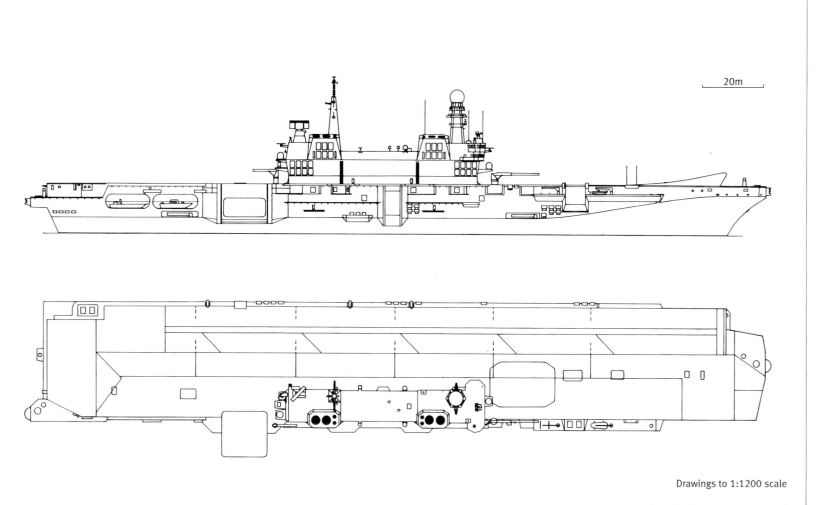

20m

Drawings to 1:1200 scale

(Drawings by Ian Sturton, 2009)

A Sylver eight-cell vertical launch module for *Cavour*'s Aster 15 anti-air missiles. These are installed in pairs in sponsons located just below flight-deck level towards the starboard fore and port aft ends of the ship. *(Maurizio Brescia)*

rials alone. Being confident that the right path in any future confrontation at sea would be dominance of the radio and ultraviolet spectrum – thereby denying an adversary the opportunity to detect friendly electronic signals and collect related intelligence whilst disrupting the opponent's own – Elettronica SpA gained its first success in the 1973 Yom Kippur war between Israel, Egypt and Syria. In this conflict its Electronic Counter Measures (ECM) range gate pull-off allowed the Israeli Navy to deflect and cover the sea bed with fifty-two Soviet-made Styx missiles (a burst of machine gun fire destroyed a 53rd).[7] From the early 1970s, Italian warships had a defensive anti-missile capacity better than that of the USN, which was still in its infancy compared to Italy's twenty years of experience. The Falklands conflict, in which the British task force employed

helicopters as missile decoys, likewise demonstrated Italian strengths compared with the Royal Navy – another electronic warfare leader. Today over 2,000 ship-borne defence systems sold to nearly two dozen European, Middle Eastern, Latin American and Far East navies confirm Elettronica's leading place in electronic warfare capabilities.

Cavour's 'armour' is based on Elettronica's Nettuno 4100 ECM system. The Nettuno 4100 consists of two Jamming Antenna Sub Systems (JASS) featuring an antenna front-end and a Jammer Antenna Unit (JAU) with a Jammer Source Unit

The aging Italian frigate *Maestrale*. Some suggest that investment in *Cavour* has delayed renewal of the surface fleet. *(Italian Navy)*

(JSU) RF and control, a Transformer Rectifier Unit (TRU) and a cooling system. The new *Doria* class destroyers also carry this system. It provides these platforms with active electronic defence using ECM tactics equally effective against both terminal missile attacks and long-range designation radar systems, exploiting a wide range of ECM techniques against surface search and tracking radars in support of anti-surface engagements. The frequency range extends from H to J bands and sensitivity is adequate for side-lobe jamming, while the ECM response has a multi-threat jamming capability. The ECM system gives a complete set of programmes also effective against coded emitters exploiting DRMF-generated jamming signals. Its high level of readiness (no warm-up needed) is combined, according to the Italian Navy's extensive experience of previous systems, with high reliability and maintainability and easy onboard integration and installation.

Compared to the earlier Nettuno radome system mounted on the *Garibaldi* and the Spanish *Principe*

de Asturias light carriers, the Nettuno 4100 is a new generation development whose main feature is its full solid-state design, ensuring high Effective Radiated Power (ERP). Such a solution avoids the significant cooling problems caused by mobile antennas. A further Italian novelty is the fact that the same system is used by the Eurofighter (twelve 'boxes' compared to hundreds on *Cavour*), confirming its new generation, modularised nature.

CONCLUSION: AFTER *CAVOUR*?

The story of *Cavour*'s design confirms that the Italian Navy's doctrine of sea power is not bound by a pure faith in the maxims of Mahan but that is has evolved on the basis of hard experience. Italian doctrine demonstrates – above all – flexibility. In this sense it shows alignment with the particular nature of naval warfare that has been practised in the Mediterranean during any given period.[8] Since the sudden summer 1979 mission in the South China Sea to rescue Vietnamese boat people – decided with

Above and below: *Cavour* combines sophisticated aviation facilities and combat systems with high standards of habitability – the internal fittings in the senior officers' wardroom pictured have been built to civilian standards of comfort. However, whilst undoubtedly an impressive ship, she has drawn many tenacious opponents, particularly from amongst the ranks of the Italian Air Force. *(Italian Navy via Maurizio Brescia / Maurizio Brescia)*

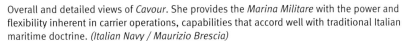

Overall and detailed views of *Cavour*. She provides the *Marina Militare* with the power and flexibility inherent in carrier operations, capabilities that accord well with traditional Italian maritime doctrine. *(Italian Navy / Maurizio Brescia)*

seventy-two hours notice by the government in Rome – navy doctrine has likewise demonstrated a pragmatism which refuses to be limited by past experiences or textbook applications.[9] Given that the navy's operations in war and peace during the following decades confirmed – if additional confirmation was necessary – that there is no practical substitute for size in ensuring operational flexibility, *Cavour*'s design characteristics can be seen in the light of these factors. In short, Italy's decision to bend, if not break, the previous pattern of commissioning the smallest capital ships of any given cate-

gory by building a true aircraft carrier is based not on prestige but on need.

The development of the material and intellectual capability to operate carriers requires the elapse of dozens of years, even in the most favourable circumstances. Moreover, as shown by the Dutch, Australian and Argentine experiences, this same capability can be lost – often forever – in just a few months. In spite of the tension between this fact and public parsimony, the continuing tendency of many navies to commission carriers, even if sometimes disguised from their own peoples and governments

in the most ingenuous and brazen ways, is far from over. The superstructure of the new Japanese 13,500-ton *Hyuga* class helicopter destroyers, for example, has a curious resemblance to *Cavour*'s island, itself dominated by a forebridge which is the trademark of the new generation of Italian warships.[10] Equally, however, the voices of opponents of maritime aviation – often found amongst the ranks of the air force – continue to make themselves heard.

Notwithstanding its prolonged evolution, its capability and its critical role in the Italian Navy's future evolution, *Cavour* is therefore still considered by many as the wrong ship at the wrong time, or at best, as the right ship at the wrong time.

Part of this argument relates to a perceived weakness in the Italian navy's surface fleet. The general world-wide economic crisis delayed for too long the order for ten new, long-awaited frigates of the *Bergamini* FREMM type and today's frontline (the backbone of the 'true' everyday navy patrolling the Mediterranean and the Indian Ocean) is still based on the eight *Maestrale* class frigates of the 1980s. Thus, many critics consider the new carrier to be a 'monster' consuming too many sailors in a sacrifice to prestige; in their view it is a millstone that handicaps the navy in fulfilling its day-to-day duties imposed by its demanding anti-terrorism and anti-piracy missions. Other critics debate the utility of a lone carrier (the old nickname 'white elephant' used during the late 1960s to label the modernised Second World War missile cruiser *Giuseppe Garibaldi* has been dusted off recently with reference to *Cavour*), as the current *Garibaldi* is not getting younger and will dedicate herself more and more to amphibious duties. This – as is the case for France – will effectively reduce Italy to a single carrier for the next decade. For the longer term, whispers can be heard in the navy ministry along the banks of the Tiber River about a further, slightly enlarged *Cavour*. Some have even dared to suggest a name, *Cesare*, but this is still, in any event, in the lap of the gods.

The most insidious menace to the new ship, however, is again the usual rival, the Italian air force. Still thrashing about in the industrial, economic and military swamp that the Eurofighter nightmare has turned out to be, the *Aeronautica Militare* is, according to some recently published articles, planning to launch an initiative, similar to that proposed by the British Royal Air Force (RAF), to regain – 'for economic reasons' – control of the Fleet Air Arm. This move would seem to have the dual goals of pocketing, at zero cost, the new STOVL F-35B fighters, whilst eliminating the Italian Air Force's illegitimate naval cousin at the same time. The RAF's similar attempt has already cast doubts on the future Royal Navy carriers *Queen Elizabeth* and *Prince of Wales*, so this strategy could menace *Cavour*'s future as well. In fact, some journalists, traditionally very close to the Italian air force, have already suggested it would be a good bargain to sell the ship, maybe to India, to buy 'more ships or, better, planes.' Even if such a proposal has no real support among politicians or in the military, it provides confirmation that

the Italian carriers still have many pertinacious enemies impervious both to the lessons of history and to more recent demonstrations of the power and flexibility that carriers bestow on the navies fortunate enough to possess them.

Whichever way the Italian carrier line evolves, one of the more interesting products of the long history behind *Cavour* is, in any event, an intellectual one. The whole origin and development of her design confirms the enduring freedom that the Italian Navy enjoys to debate its doctrine and future openly and loudly, at any rank – of itself an historic heritage

which even fascism was never able to trample. The result has often been the conception and materialisation of new and innovative solutions. At the same time it also confirms the leadership system which gives the Chief of Staff advice from the *Comitato degli Ammiragli* (Committee of the Admirals) but which ultimately leaves him the final choice as to the appropriate way forward. Thus survives a tradition that has seen a steady evolution from the sailing ships and galleys of yesteryear to Italy's present day carrier force and which, one day, will witness their inevitable successors on the seas.

Notes

1. For further reading, see Enrico Cernuschi and Vincent O'Hara, 'Search for a Flattop: the Italian Navy and the Aircraft Carrier 1907-2007', *Warship* 2007 (London, Conway, 2007), pp 61–81.

2. Archivio Ufficio Storico della Marina Militare, Rome, Fondo Disegni e monografie di unità, Nave *Trieste*, Maricominav, Aug. 1965 – Dec. 1965.

3. S. Rissotto, 'La funzione del trampolino sulla portaeromobili', *Rivista Marittima* (May 1989).

4. This concept had been conceived and dismissed by the Italian navy between 1870 and 1880 with the new and revolutionary battleships of the *Duilio* class. It was rejected again in 1926, as noted above.

5. Nicknamed *Qui*, *Quo* and *Qua* (the Italian names of the Disney characters Huey, Dewey and Louie) for their ability to operate together and overcome difficult situations. The first two will be replaced, probably in the next budget, by a 20,000-ton Dock Landing Ship whose name could be *San Martino*.

6. Giuseppe Mazzini was the father of the Italian Republicans and one of the main figures of the Risorgimento, Italy's nineteenth-century reunification. Luigi Einaudi was the Italian Republic's first president, an illustrious economist, the ideal *trait d'union* of Italy's steady economical development from the beginning of the last century until the 'economical miracle' of the 1950s and 1960s, and the Liberal Party's most eminent twentieth-century representative. Both names were sponsored by their respective parties. The name Andrea Doria was, instead, chosen by the navy's incumbent chief of staff, according to a traditional privilege which permitted him to name new ships ordered during his command. The cruiser *Andrea Doria*, which paid off on 1992, had been his last sea command. The name Cavour also caused some problems for the traditionalists, as the

previous battleship's name had been *Conte di Cavour* and the same full name had been used by a former steamship employed by the Italian navy during the second half of the nineteenth century both as a transport and a training ship.

7. See Andrea Tani, 'Guerra fredda sui sette mari', *Supplemento alla Rivista Marittima* (July 2001), pp 241–4.

8. For an interesting survey about the lack of application of Mahan's theories in the Mediterranean setting over the centuries see, John Francis Guilmartin, *Gunpowder and Galleys* (London, Conway Maritime Press, 2003).

9. The origin of this remarkable and unexpected forty-six day, 15,000-mile mission was never explained. The Italian people's reaction to the Vietnamese tragedy – brought home by television – was indeed sympathetic. However, the traditionally cool Premier Andreotti was not motivated by humanitarian considerations alone. The most common explanation for the gesture was that the time had come – according to an agreement between the political class and the navy staff – for a more visible Italian participation in world affairs, maybe not in the first rank but certainly no longer in the third row. The Second World War was long over and, considering the new (and final) stage of the Cold War, the drab but effective low-profile-policy which had paid Rome so many dividends since 1949 (including founder status in NATO) had to be replaced by something more assertive. This obtained some benefits for Italy within the Alliance over the much more important but still politically tainted Germany. The Italian Navy, being arguably the most efficient of the three Italian services, was therefore in the most effective position to carry out this role.

10. In a similar fashion, the funnel cap was characteristic of the Italian ships of the 1970s and 1980s, from the test bed prototype survey ship *Ammiraglio Magnaghi* to the *Lupo* class frigates sold world-wide.

3.2 SIGNIFICANT SHIPS

HMS DARING

The Royal Navy's Type 45 Air-Defence Destroyer

The British Royal Navy received the most significant reinforcement to its depleted ranks for many years at the end of 2008 when the first of its new Type 45 destroyers, HMS *Daring*, was formally handed over to the UK Ministry of Defence. A ceremony at BVT's Scotstoun shipyard on the River Clyde on 10 December 2008 saw *Daring*'s commanding officer, Captain Paul Bennett OBE, raise her White Ensign for the first time as the new ship's company marched onboard. Planned to become fully operational during 2010, *Daring* and her subsequent sister-ships will be amongst the most potent air-defence ships in service anywhere in the world and a quantum leap forward from the remaining obsolescent Type 42 class escorts that currently form the backbone of the Royal Navy's anti-air capability. However, the enhanced capacity that *Daring* represents has been a long time coming, with the origins of the class being traced back over a quarter of a century to the lessons learned from the 1982 Falklands War.

Author: Conrad Waters

See page 12

TYPE 45 CLASS ORIGINS

The Falklands War clearly demonstrated the Royal Navy's vulnerability to saturation aircraft and missile attack. Whilst the GWS 30 Sea Dart missile system that formed the mainstay of the fleet's air defences was largely successful in combating high-level air assault, performance against low-flying aircraft and the Argentine Navy's modest inventory of air-launched Exocet missiles was less impressive. The losses of the Sea Dart-equipped Type 42 destroyers *Sheffield* and *Coventry* to, respectively, missile and aircraft strikes were particularly embarrassing examples of limited air-defence capability against even a second-rank power operating at maximum endurance from its bases. Particular weaknesses identified were the Type 42 destroyer's inability to illuminate – and therefore engage – more than two targets simultaneously from its pair of Type 909 guidance radars, lengthy missile reaction times and limited capabilities against low-level or short-range attack.[1] The immediate solution was implementation of a programme of upgrades for the remaining Type 42

vessels. These encompassed a series of improvements to the capabilities of the Sea Dart system and the installation of the Vulcan Phalanx close-in weapons system (CIWS) for last ditch defence. However, in the longer term, a more comprehensive response was required, particularly given ongoing improvements in anti-surface missile technology being achieved by the Soviet Union, the principal Cold War enemy. This involved both a replacement design for the cramped Type 42 hull and a new missile/radar combination.

It was initially hoped that the replacement air-defence ship would be based on the international NFR-90 programme, which was intended to produce a common frigate design for the main NATO navies in the 1990s. A collaborative project involving the common procurement of around fifty surface escorts for the navies of Canada, France, Germany, Italy, the Netherlands, Spain, the United Kingdom and the United States, NFR-90 design studies moved slowly forward throughout the 1980s before collapsing at the end of the decade as the differing needs of the partner countries proved impossible to reconcile. A

Opposite: The new Type 45 destroyer class represents a significant reinforcement to the Royal Navy's depleted ranks, with the new Sea Viper missile system providing world-leading air defence capabilities. Here first of class *Daring* is seen on sea trials during April 2008 prior to delivery at the end of that year. *(BVT Surface Fleet)*

Type 45 Design Evolution

Whilst initially drawing on preparatory work carried out for the trilateral Project Horizon, the Type 45 design steadily evolved after re-establishment as a national project. This is demonstrated by computer-generated images A to C, which illustrate changes to the design between 1999 and 2001. *(BAE Systems)*

period followed during which the various European participants attempted to form revised alliances, the UK eventually joining with France and Italy to design a Common New Generation Frigate (CNGF) under Project Horizon following signature of a tri-national staff requirement in December 1992. At first it was hoped that construction of three initial ships (one for each nation) would commence in 1997 and that they would enter service around 2002.

Unfortunately, the new alliance was also beset with problems. An early point of difficulty was the choice of multi-function radar for the PAAMS principal anti-air missile system, which was to combine surveillance, target indication/tracking and missile guidance roles in a single unit. Whilst the French and Italian navies supported selection of the EMPAR (European Multi-function Phased Array Radar) system, the UK preferred the more advanced technology offered by the Sampson active phased array derived from the MESAR (Multi-function Electronically Scanned Adaptive Radar) demonstrator programme. This solution was felt to offer a far superior area-defence capability against saturation attack, a key Royal Navy requirement given the Falklands' experience touched upon above. In the end, it proved possible to design PAAMS in such a way that it could interface with both radars and the three partners agreed to proceed

The Type 42 destroyer *Exeter* leaving Portsmouth in April 2007. The Type 45 is a long overdue replacement for this cramped and somewhat limited air defence design, which suffered badly during the Falklands War. *(Conrad Waters)*

with the air-defence system on that basis. However, other disputes focusing on Project Horizon's industrial and management structure – not least a perception that France and Italy were seeking an unreasonably large work-share compared with the number of ships they required – ultimately proved insurmountable in spite of political support for the programme at the highest levels. As a result, it was announced in April 1999 that the UK would abandon participation in Project Horizon – but not PAAMS – in favour of the development of a new national design, the Type 45 destroyer. The Type 45 designation continued the post-war sequence adopted for Royal Navy anti-aircraft escorts, with Type 41 being the *Leopard* class frigates of the 1950s and Type 43 and Type 44 abandoned studies for enhanced Sea Dart-armed ships following on from the Type 42.

PROGRAMME REQUIREMENTS

Although principally designed as high-specification anti-air warfare ships for local area fleet defence, *Daring* and her sisters were configured from the outset to be versatile warships capable of carrying out a range of tasks on a world-wide basis. Whilst budgetary constraints meant that not all desired equipment could be fitted immediately, a significant amount of flexibility to upgrade the class to meet evolving requirements through an incremental acquisition plan (IAP) was also built into the design. This desire to balance specialised and more general purpose functions was clearly demonstrated by the nine key user requirements (KURs) established at the time the Type 45 programme was authorised, as set out in full below:

■ **KUR 1: Principal Anti-Air Missile System:** The Type 45 shall be able to protect with a Probability of Escaping Hit of (x?) all units operating within a radius of 6.5km against up to eight supersonic sea skimming missiles arriving randomly within (y?) seconds. (? = Classified Information.)
■ **KUR 2: Force Anti-Air Warfare Situational Awareness:** The Type 45 shall be able to assess the Air Warfare Tactical Situation of 1,000 air real world objects against a total arrival and/or departure rate of 500 air real world objects per hour.
■ **KUR 3: Aircraft Control:** The Type 45 shall be able to provide close tactical control to at least four fixed-wing aircraft or four groups of aircraft in single speaking units assigned to the force.
■ **KUR 4: Aircraft Operation:** The Type 45 shall be able to operate both one organic Merlin (Anti-Submarine Warfare and Utility variants) and one organic Lynx Mk8 helicopter, although not simultaneously.
■ **KUR 5: Embarked Military Force:** The Type 45 shall be able to operate an Embarked Military Force of at least thirty deployable troops.
■ **KUR 6: Naval Diplomacy:** The Type 45 shall be able to coerce potential adversaries into compliance with the wishes of Her Majesty's Government or the wider international community through the presence of a Medium Calibre Gun System of at least 114mm.
■ **KUR 7: Range:** The Type 45 shall be able to transit at least 3,000 nautical miles to its assigned mission, operate for three days and return to point of origin, unsupported throughout, within twenty days.
■ **KUR 8: Growth Potential:** The Type 45 capability shall be able to be upgraded to incorporate new capabilities or to enhance extant capabilities through displacement Margins of at least 11.5 per cent.
■ **KUR 9: Availability:** The Type 45 shall have a 70 per cent availability to contribute to Maritime Operations over a period of at least twenty-five years, of which at least 35 per cent shall be spent at sea.

This demanding set of requirements – translating into over 700 functional performance specifications – inevitably required a large, expensive ship more akin to the imposing – if flawed – 'County' class of the 1960s than recent Royal Navy surface escorts. Whilst initially drawing heavily on the preparatory work carried out on Project Horizon, these national requirements also resulted in a steady divergence from the French and Italian warships that emerged from the remaining partners' decision to continue with the project. This is evident in the various computerised images released as design-work progressed. Although still bearing a broad resemblance to the Franco-Italian ships, variations in propulsion and combat systems – when added to the different multi-function radar selection – provide the Type 45 destroyers with arguably significantly enhanced characteristics over their European half-sisters.

BUILD AND DESIGN RESPONSIBILITIES

Preparations for construction of the new Type 45 design moved forward relatively quickly following the decision to pursue a national programme, with BAE Systems appointed as prime contractor on the project in November 1999. This was followed by confirmation of initial approval for the first three members of a class of up to twelve ships on 11 July 2000 after so-called 'Main Gate' approval. An actual contract for their design and manufacture was signed in December that year. At this stage it was anticipated that the destroyers would be constructed from competitively-bid modules, with final assembly being shared between BAE Systems' Clyde facilities at Govan and Scotstoun and VT Group's shipyard on the south coast. However, subsequent BAE Systems' attempts to secure all assembly work upset these arrangements, leading the UK Government to appoint the independent RAND Corporation to assess the merits of various construction approaches.[2] The result was a decision to construct the class in pre-allocated blocks shared between BAE and VT, final assembly of ships being assigned to BAE. A contract for a further three destroyers was placed in February 2002 to facilitate this strategy. The debate surrounding this process was subject to controversy at the time and inevitably delayed the entire project. However, the revised arrangements have ultimately worked well in practice, facilitating the subsequent merger of BAE Systems' and VT's shipbuilding assets into BVT Surface Fleet.

Responsibility for the design of the Type 45 was placed in the hands of BAE Systems, as both prime contractor and design authority. Actual design work was carried out by BAE Systems' Naval Ships teams at Scotstoun and Filton (Bristol), working closely both with the Defence Procurement Agency's Type 45 Integrated Project Team and a small group of principal suppliers. In addition to VT, these included Rolls-Royce and Alstom/Converteam in respect of propulsion equipment, BAE's Insyte Integrated System Technologies subsidiary (radar and combat management system), Thales (integrated communications) and the Europaams consortium (anti-air missile system).

CONSTRUCTION

Fabrication of *Daring* commenced with the first cutting of steel at BAE Systems' Govan yard in Glasgow on 28 March 2003. In accordance with the agreed build strategy, construction was divided into six main modules. Modules A to D, stretching from the stern to the bridge, were allocated to BAE's Clyde facilities at Govan and Scotstoun. VT's

Portsmouth yard was responsible for the two forward modules, as well as the masts and funnels. Govan-built Block A was the first to be moved onto the building berth at Scotstoun in December 2004, with hull assembly being completed in November 2005 following the arrival of VT's blocks from the south coast in June.

Daring was launched from Scotstoun's covered building hall on 1 February 2006 under Yard No. 311060. HRH, The Countess of Wessex officiated at the naming and launching ceremony. With a launch weight of 5,222 tonnes, she was reportedly the largest ship to be launched from what was previously the famous Yarrow shipyard and the first Royal Navy vessel to be dispatched into the Clyde for six years. She was subsequently berthed in Scotstoun's dry dock for installation of funnels, masts and remaining superstructure followed by installation and integration of her various weapons systems. The process was facilitated by significant pre-installation testing of many of the most significant items of equipment. As a result, outfitting progressed very much to target and initial sea trials were commenced as planned on 18 July 2007.

Build strategy was slightly revised for the five subsequent class members, with hull assembly and launch taking place at Govan before transfer to Scotstoun for final outfitting. At the time of writing, a further three ships of the class have been launched, with the final vessel – *Duncan* – due to go down the slipway during 2010. It was originally hoped that a total class of twelve Type 45 destroyers would ultimately be built. However, demands on a stretched UK defence budget emanating from the need to support operations in Afghanistan and Iraq, when combined with ongoing cost overruns across a range of defence equipment projects, has meant that this hope will not be realised. Class numbers were reduced to eight as a result of the New Chapter to the Strategic Defence Review published in July 2004, with a further reduction to the six already on order confirmed in June 2008.

Opposite: A series of images of *Daring* taken during sea trials in April 2008 (top) and July/August 2007 (below). Although the Type 45 design produced by prime contractor BAE Systems following the decision to pursue a national programme betrays considerable French influence as a carry over from the UK's initial involvement in Project Horizon, overall layout is more traditionally British and therefore quite similar to that of the previous Type 23 frigate. *(BVT Surface Fleet / BAE Systems)*

Above: *Daring* was built in modules at different yards. Here the stern 'A' Module is pictured being moved onto the building berth at Scotstoun in December 2004 following fabrication further up the River Clyde at Govan. *(BAE Systems)*

Below: *Daring*'s hull structure was finally completed with the arrival of the forward hull blocks from VT's Portsmouth shipyard in summer 2005. *(BAE Systems)*

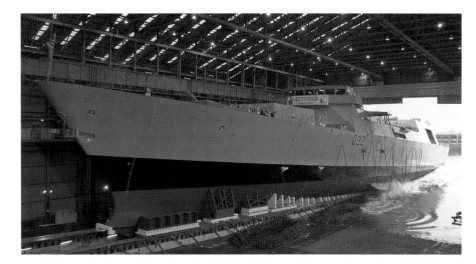

GENERAL DESIGN FEATURES

At around 7,350 tons full load displacement and with an overall length of 152.4m or approximately 500ft, *Daring* is the largest Royal Navy surface escort to be completed since the *Tiger* class cruisers of the 1950s. She is also broadly comparable with the original United States Navy (USN) *Arleigh Burke* (DDG-51) class destroyers in overall size. The main factor determining her dimensions has been the desirability of placing her Sampson multi-function radar as high above the waterline as possible so as to increase radar horizon, requiring a comparatively large and beamy hull to ensure stability. The bulk – and particularly depth – of the 48-cell Sylver silo for the Aster surface-to-air missiles that form another key component of PAAMS, as well as the considerable space requirements of the design's innovative integrated electrical propulsion (IEP) systems, were also important influences. Other considerations have been the requirement to allow incremental insertion of additional equipment and capabilities throughout the class's service life without the need to resort to major reconstruction, as well as increased importance given to upgrading crew living conditions.

In general appearance, *Daring* betrays much of the French influence in the Horizon project from which many of her initial design features originated. In particular, considerable attention has been given to reducing radar cross section through careful superstructure design and the concealment of external equipment. She consequently carries more than a passing resemblance to the *La Fayette* class stealth frigates. Overall layout is, however, more reminiscent of previous Royal Navy designs, with the concentration of all principal armament (viz. medium-calibre gun, PAAMS missile silo and positions for Harpoon surface-to-surface missiles) forward of the bridge similar to the arrangement seen in the previous Type 23 frigate class. An interesting feature is the incorporation of three masts. The Sampson multi-function radar is housed in a goldfish-bowl like dome on the top of the prominent foremast, whilst the complementary S1850M long-range search array is located towards the aft of the main superstructure. The intermediate mainmast is reserved for communications functions associated with the ship's fully integrated communications system.

Internally, the greatest impression is one of space, with compartments and walkways considerably larger than those seen in previous post-war Royal Navy escorts. This impression is reinforced by a significant reduction in crew size compared with previous destroyers, a significant level of automation meaning that a Type 45 destroyer can operate with just over 190 personnel as compared with the 287 nominal complement of the preceding – and much smaller – Type 42. Accommodation is in the form of ninety-four modularised cabins, which were prefabricated off-site by Vinci Services before being slotted into position at the shipyard. Officers are generally housed in single cabins, Senior Rates in single or double-berth cabins and Junior Ratings in cabins with no more than six berths. Additional accommodation is provided to facilitate the transportation of specialist teams: for example, up to sixty Royal Marines can be embarked under austerity conditions. All ranks have their own dedicated recreational spaces. It is therefore not surprising that living conditions are claimed to be the best in the fleet.

WEAPONRY AND COMBAT SYSTEMS

Given their core role as fleet air-defence ships, the heart of the Type 45 destroyer class' combat capabilities is inevitably built around the PAAMS principal anti-air missile system. The PAAMS (S) version used by the Royal Navy in *Daring* and her sisters comprises a number of building blocks, the principal elements of which are:

- A BAE Systems Insyte Sampson multi-function active phased-array radar.
- A DCNS Sylver (*système de lancement vertical*) silo with – initially – forty-eight missile cells.
- MBDA Aster 15 and Aster 30 surface-to-air missiles.
- A MBDA PAAMS command and control (C2) system.

Whilst not formally part of PAAMS, the BAE Systems Insyte/Thales S1850M long-range search radar also installed in the class works in close conjunction with the system. The Royal Navy announced that the new combination was to be given the designation Sea Viper during the ceremonies marking the first arrival of *Daring* at her homeport of Portsmouth on 28 January 2009. This follows a chain of nomenclature starting with the Sea Slug and Sea Cat missiles of the 1960s leading onto Sea Dart of the 1970s and the Sea Wolf system introduced at the end of that decade.

The key distinguishing feature of Sea Viper is clearly its use of the Sampson radar. One of the new generation of multi-function, active electronically scanned array (AESA) radars, Sampson combines the roles of surveillance, target tracking and missile guidance in a single system. In contrast to traditional mechanical radars, electronically scanned arrays such as Sampson use state of the art electronics to form and direct their radar beams, thereby allowing

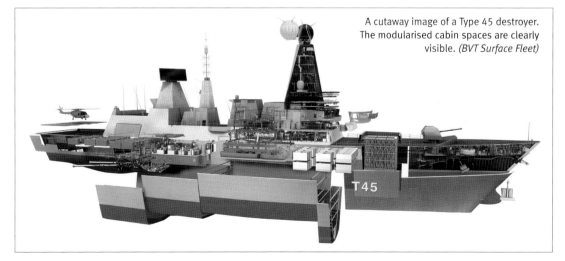

A cutaway image of a Type 45 destroyer. The modularised cabin spaces are clearly visible. *(BVT Surface Fleet)*

Opposite and above: The Type 45 destroyers' core combat capability is provided by the PAAMS (S) Sea Viper anti-air missile system, of which a core component is the BAE Systems Insyte Sampson multi-function radar. One of the new generation of active electronically-scanned array (AESA) radars, Sampson is installed at masthead height to provide maximum search radius for its two rotating back-to-back arrays. The goldfish-bowl like dome that houses the radar assembly is prominent in these three images, which were taken at the time of *Daring*'s initial sea trials between 18 July and 14 August 2007. *(BAE Systems / Conrad Waters / Conrad Waters)*

simultaneous tracking and engagement of larger numbers of targets at greater ranges than hitherto. The 'active' part of the system relates to the nature of the array's radio frequency (RF) source, with each of the radar's numerous receiving and transmitting elements being individually energised. This differs from earlier 'passive' electronically phased array (PESA) radars – such as the AN/SPY-1 associated with the US Aegis combat system – that use a single energy source to send energy into the radar's elements. Although AESA radars are typically more complicated and expensive to fabricate than PESA systems, the greater level of redundancy inherent in their construction makes them less prone to failure. Energy requirements are also less. Sampson has no high-voltage, high-power microwave parts or associated water cooling systems, thereby easing both installation and ongoing maintenance.

As installed in *Daring*, Sampson features two back-to-back arrays – each with over 2,000 individual radiating elements – installed in a masthead assembly that rotates at 30rpm and weighs a little more than 5 tons. Whilst involving greater mechanical complexity than systems that use four fixed arrays to produce 360-degree coverage such as AN/SPY-1 Aegis or Thales' APAR, this solution extends radar horizon by allowing installation at a greater height in the ship and reduces overall cost. Operating in the 2,000–4,000 MHz frequency E/F bands (USN S-band) as a compromise between the greater surveillance range obtainable from lower frequency systems and the enhanced tracking abilities of radars operating in the higher frequency bands, Sampson is claimed to have a search range of over 400km. This search capability is supplemented by the more specialised S1850M array, a modified version of the Thales SMART-L long range volume search radar working on a 1,000–2,000 MHz D (L) band frequency. The S1850M mounts Thales interrogator IFF equipment, which is supplemented by a Raytheon IFF system.

The second key element of Sea Viper is the MBDA Aster missile and the associated Sylver vertical launch system (VLS). Each Type 45 destroyer is equipped with six Sylver A-50 eight-cell launcher modules, with space and weight reserved for two further modules should circumstances so require. This provides capacity for up to forty-eight Aster missiles in either the shorter-range Aster 15 or longer-range Aster 30 variant, with the time between missile launches being less than half a second if ripple firing is required. Whilst the Sylver VLS is capable of being developed to launch a range of other weapons – not least the proposed Fireshadow loitering munition – this does not include the TLAM Tomahawk land-attack cruise missile. As such, it is possible that modules from the competing US Mk41 VLS will be installed if a decision is made to use the surplus space available to increase fighting potential.

The combination of Sampson and Aster is intended to provide multi-layered air defence – ship self defence, local area defence for ships in company and long-range fleet area defence – in the most hostile environments. Potential targets identified will be tracked by Sampson and co-ordinated with the overall air picture compiled by the ship's combat management system in conjunction with other surveillance equipment. If an anti-air engagement is required, Sampson will provide uplink information to the Aster missiles in flight on the latest position of the targets. At least ten missiles are capable of being controlled simultaneously. The Aster's active radar seeker then takes over for the final stages of the 'kill', with the patented PIF-PAF system combining conventional aerodynamic controls with direct thrust vectoring in the terminal phase being particularly potent in ensuring success against the new breed of 'corkscrewing' anti-ship missiles. A range of up to 120km is claimed for the longer-range Aster 30 missile, which employs a larger booster section than the shorter-range Aster 15. The latter has a claimed interception range of between 1.7km and 30km for self and localised defence missions.

The command and control sub-system that regulates PAAMS' operation interfaces with *Daring's* overall CMS-1 combat management system, which provides the command team the functionality required to deploy the ship's weaponry to best advantage. Designed by BAE Systems Insyte, CMS-1 is a scalable, fully-distributed system based on a dual redundant local area network that serves a series of

Table 3.2.1.

HMS DARING PRINCIPAL PARTICULARS

Building Information:

Fabrication Commenced:	28 March 2003
Launched:	1 February 2006
Delivered:	10 December 2008
Builders:	BVT Surface Fleet at its Scotstoun, Govan and Portsmouth facilities.

Dimensions:

Displacement:	5,800 tons standard displacement, 7,350 tons full load displacement.
Overall Hull Dimensions:	152.4m x 21.2m x 5.4m. Length between perpendiculars is 143.5m.

Weapons Systems:

Missiles:	6 x Sylver A50 8-cell VLS modules for Aster 30 and Aster 15 surface-to-air missiles as part of the Sea Viper air defence system.
	Provision for 2 x quad Harpoon surface-to-surface missiles.
Guns:	1 x 4.5in (114mm) Mk8, Mod 1, 2 x 30mm, 2 x 20mm Vulcan Phalanx CIWS (initially fitted for but not with).
Torpedoes:	Provision for 2 x twin fixed 324mm anti-submarine torpedo tubes.
Aircraft:	1 EH-101 Merlin or 2 Lynx helicopters.
Countermeasures:	Thales radar electronic support measures (RESM) system complementing IFF system mounted on S1850M radar.
	RN Outfit DLF and RN Outfit DLH Sea Gnat decoy systems. Provision for Type 2170 surface ship torpedo defence (SSTD) system.
Principal Sensors:	1 x Sampson multifunction radar, 1 x S1850M long-range search radar, surface search and navigation arrays.
	1 x Type 2091 MFS-7000 bow-mounted sonar. Provision for towed-array as part of the SSTD system.
Combat System:	BAE Systems Insyte CMS-1 combat system. Communications include links 11, 16 and 22.

Propulsion Systems:

Machinery:	IEP. 2 x WR-21 gas turbines rated at 42MW total. 2 x Wärtsilä 12V200 diesel generators rated at 4MW total.
	Propulsion through 2 x Converteam advanced induction motors rated at 40MW total producing 54,000shp through 2 shafts.
Speed and Range:	Designed maximum speed 29 knots (over 30 knots was achieved on trials). Range is 7,000 nautical miles at 18 knots.

Other Details:

Complement:	A typical crew comprises c. 190 personnel, including 20 officers. Accommodation is provided for c.235.
Class:	Six ships have been ordered: *Daring* (D32), *Dauntless* (D33), *Diamond* (D44), *Dragon* (D35), *Defender* (D36) and *Duncan* (D37).

multi-function consoles from tactical data servers linked by an ethernet data transfer system (DTS) to the ship's sensors and weapons. Specifically developed for the Type 45 destroyer programme on the basis of experience gained from the previous Type 23 frigates, it can be configured for ships of all sizes from patrol vessels to aircraft carriers. For example, the offshore patrol vessel *Clyde* is fitted with a single console compared with the more than twenty-five installed in *Daring*. Incorporating gun fire control and data link capabilities, CMS-1 supports tasks such as tactical picture compilation, threat evaluation, weapons assignment and kill assessment, with

tactical data links – links 11, 16 and 22 are or will be installed – allowing information to be shared widely with other allied platforms. The US developed Co-operative Engagement Capability (CEC) will also be fitted to all six ships of the class from 2014 onwards.

Focus on the Type 45's air-defence role has resulted in the remaining weapons fit being somewhat sparse for a ship of *Daring*'s size. However, additional capabilities are likely to be acquired over time as part of the incremental acquisition plan. Initial weaponry includes a 4.5in (114mm) Mk8 Mod 1 medium calibre gun, two smaller 30mm guns for the destruction of close-range threats and facili-

ties to embark and sustain either one Merlin HM Mk1 or two Lynx HMA Mk8 helicopters. Countermeasures include RN Outfit DLF Siren and Outfit DLH Sea Gnat decoys, whilst a comprehensive radar electronic support measures package is provided by Thales Aerospace. Underwater threats such as submarines and mines can be detected by an Ultra Electronics MFS-7000 bow-mounted sonar developed from a design supplied by EDO Corporation to the Brazilian Navy. In addition to possible upgrades already mentioned, potential future enhancements include installation of an upgraded 6in (152mm) main gun, Phalanx CIWS,

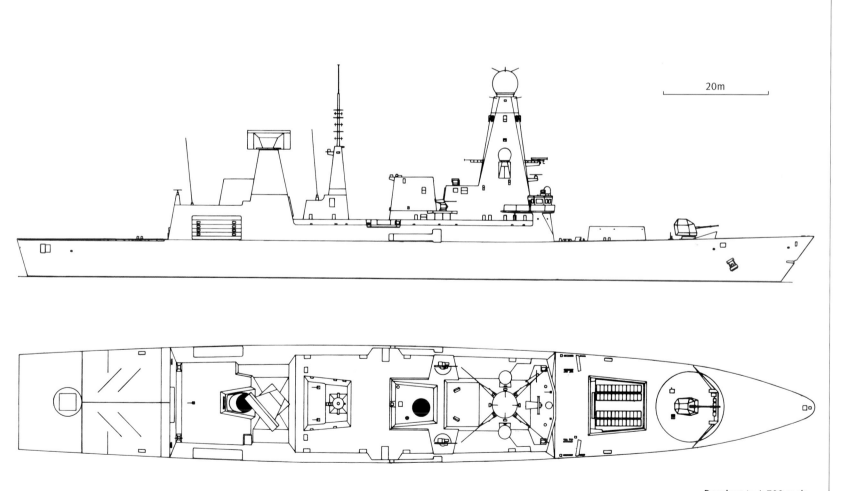

20m

Drawings to 1:700 scale

(Drawings by Ian Sturton, 2009)

Daring departing Portsmouth under the White Ensign in March 2009 whilst conducting an ongoing programme of post-delivery trials prior to commissioning in the summer. Focus on her primary air defence role means that the remaining weapons fit is somewhat sparse but additional capabilities should be obtained under an incremental acquisitions programme. *(Conrad Waters)*

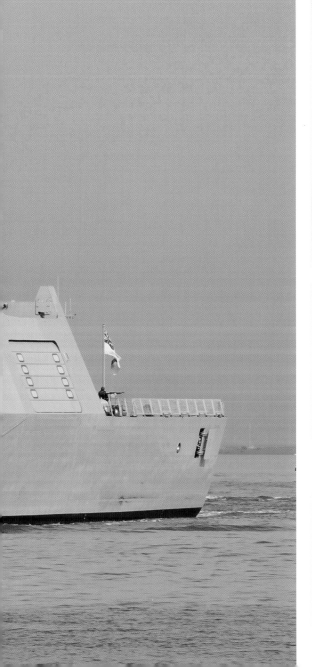

Daring's new propulsion system performed well during sea trials, comfortably exceeding the ship's 28-knot design target with a speed of over 30 knots. *(BAE Systems)*

As well as being fast and manoeuvrable, *Daring*'s propulsion system provides her with a considerable radius of action. For example, a range of 7,000 miles at 18 knots allows her to travel from the UK to the Falkland Islands with fuel to spare. *(BVT Surface Fleet)*

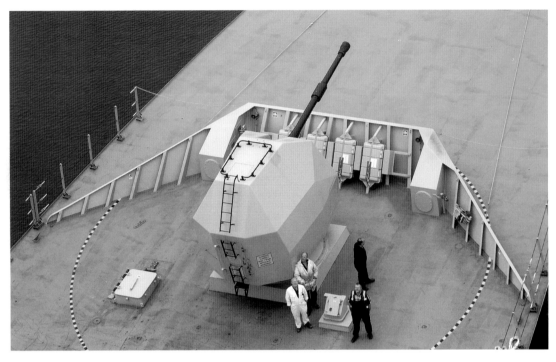

Above: *Daring* is equipped with a CMS-1 combat management system supplied by BAE Systems Insyte. Featuring Windows-based software, the user interface is through multifunction consoles that are distributed around the ship to assist local tasks by means of a dual redundant local area network. The ship's networks also support access to the integrated platform management system used for ship and damage control functions. *(BVT Surface Fleet)*

Above: In addition to Sea Viper, *Daring*'s initial armament includes a 4.5in (114mm) Mk 8 Mod 1 medium-calibre gun. *(Conrad Waters)*

Below: The Type 45 destroyer can embark and sustain one AW-101 Merlin or two Lynx helicopters. Here a Merlin is pictured on *Daring*'s flight deck. *(John Jordan)*

anti-submarine torpedo launchers and the Surface Ship Torpedo Defence (SSTD) system.

PROPULSION

In addition to having what is possibly the world's leading air-defence capability, *Daring* is also innovative in that she is the first major surface combatant with military standard integrated electric propulsion (IEP). Previously confined to passenger ships and auxiliaries, IEP employs electric motors to transmit power from generation systems to the propeller shafts. This avoids the complexity of mechanical transmission. Under IEP, all propulsion and auxiliary electrical (e.g. weapons systems and 'hotel' services) requirements are met by common generation units, greatly increasing flexibility.[3]

The generation plant in *Daring* comprises two 25MW (down-rated to 21.5MW) Rolls-Royce WR-21 intercooled recuperated (ICR) gas turbines and two 2MW Wärtsilä 12V200 diesel generators. These feed two high-voltage switchboards that distribute power both to the ship's systems via high-voltage transformers and, through two propulsion converters, to the 20MW Converteam advanced induction motors that actually drive the twin shafts. Design speed was set at 28 knots, although well in excess of 30 knots was achieved during the first set of sea trials. A Converteam-designed electric power system controls and monitors the overall network,

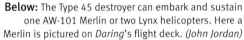

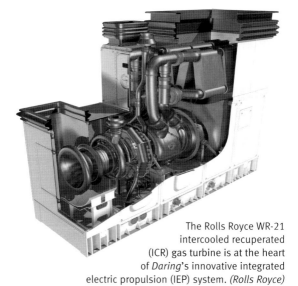

The Rolls Royce WR-21 intercooled recuperated (ICR) gas turbine is at the heart of *Daring*'s innovative integrated electric propulsion (IEP) system. *(Rolls Royce)*

integrating with the ship's wider platform management system designed by Northrop Grumman Marine Systems and Rockwell Automation. In addition to the normal machinery control room, this latter system is accessible from a ship-wide network of plug-in points. This facilitates surveillance and damage control in a combat scenario.

Whilst IEP is the main innovation in *Daring*'s propulsion system, the WR-21 gas turbines also represent a significant technological step forward. Developed under what was originally a US Navy project by a consortium of Northrop Grumman, Rolls Royce and DCNS, the turbines' ability to recycle hot gases reduces fuel consumption across the entire power range and produces a lower heat signature. Although not widely adopted – possibly due to its initial high capital cost – WR-21 appears to have worked well during *Daring*'s initial sea trials. The system should be invaluable in reducing overall life cycle expenses and is a key feature behind the class' lengthy 7,000 nautical mile operating range.

DAMAGE CONTROL

Effective damage control has been afforded a high priority in the Royal Navy since the painful lessons of the Falklands War. This is clearly evident in *Daring*'s design. The ship is divided into four principal zones for damage-control purposes, each of which is equipped with colour-coded lockers housing equipment needed to deal with fire, water, electrical and other damage. All major facilities such as the opera-

tions room, machinery control centre and even the galley are duplicated, whilst the extensive network of plug-in points referenced above allows effective control actions to be directed from undamaged zones. Access between zones is facilitated by the use of curtains to create smoke-free pockets between compartments. Little has been revealed in public about incorporation of physical protection in the design, although use of Kevlar composite armour to safeguard sensitive areas such as the operations room – located in a relatively exposed position at main deck level beneath the bridge and forward mast – would seem likely. Other protective features include the incorporation of technical galleries for cabling and other services alongside most of the ship's length – effectively providing a double skin – as well as extensive measures to reduce shock damage.

COST

The maximum acceptable cost of the first six ships of the Type 45 destroyer programme at the time of main gate approval in December was set at £5,475m, although a somewhat lower total cost of £5,000m was targeted. This figure was in addition to a further £232m that had already been spent in the assessment phase of the design. The unit cost of each ship was expected to be £582m, suggesting development costs of a little over £1.5bn.

Unfortunately, in common with many major defence projects, the Type 45 programme has suffered from significant cost overruns. According to subsequent oversight by the UK National Audit Office, the UK Ministry of Defence (MOD) and its industrial partners were initially over-optimistic about the resources and time required to procure the required ships and did not establish the project on a suitable basis given the immaturity of both the Type 45 and associated PAAMS missile system design.[4] For example, the original contract was signed before the commercial alliance required to build the ships has been formed and – in spite of agreement of a fixed price contract for the first threes ships – the MOD retained considerable financial exposure if key equipment such as PAAMS was delivered late. These initial failings were exacerbated by poor project management and supervision. As a result, the total cost of the project had risen to £6,464m (plus the initial £232m assessment phase expenses) by 2007, of which unit costs amounted to £649m for each ship. In addition, delays associated with agreeing the original build strategy were a key factor behind

cumulative delays of as much as thirty-six months in *Daring*'s targeted 'in service' date by this time.

More positively, considerable effort devoted to put the programme on a firmer footing – most notably renegotiation of the contract for the six ships then under construction in 2007 – have been broadly successful. As of mid-2009, no additional costs or delivery slippage had been reported since that date. In addition, whilst *Daring*'s official in service date of November 2010 remains three years late, the current trials programme is being managed with the aim of bringing this process forward by between six and twelve months. The National Audit Office has also commissioned independent analysis that suggests the revised unit cost of £649m is broadly in line with the costs associated with similar types of vessel, albeit the comparison is not so favourable when development charges are taken into account.

TRIALS AND ENTRY INTO SERVICE

As an entirely new design featuring a significant amount of innovative equipment – not to say the first Royal Navy frontline surface combatant built to Lloyd's Register's 1999 Rules and Regulations for the Classification of Naval Ships – *Daring* has undergone a significant programme of trials. To a great extent, these were already well underway prior to her maiden voyage on 18 July 2007, as key elements of her equipment were tested on land before being trialled at sea. The most visible of these test arrangements was the construction of a Maritime Integration and Support Centre (MISC) overlooking Portsmouth Harbour on Portsdown, which was commissioned in 2004. Encompassing both the combat management system and key elements of PAAMS – including both Sampson and S1850M radars – MISC allowed acceptance of key elements of the ship's combat system before installation in the ship.

The actual programme of sea trials has been split into two main stages, with Stage 1 being conducted by shipbuilder BVT and Stage 2 by the Royal Navy. Stage 1 trials were divided into three separate phases of broadly one month each between July 2007 and September 2008, allowing structural, propulsion, radar and communications systems to be fully tested. Key user requirements 7, 8 and 9 had been fully met by the time this process was completed. Following acceptance off contract in December 2008, *Daring* departed the River Clyde under the White Ensign for the first time on 16 January 2009 and arrived at her new home port of Portsmouth on the 28th of that month. Stage 2 trials – intended to ensure full demonstration of all outstanding key user requirements – commenced almost immediately and were still continuing at the time of writing. Whilst formal commissioning was scheduled for the summer of 2009, it is unlikely to be before the start of 2011 that *Daring* is operationally deployed.

Daring's trials have run in parallel with testing of the Sea Viper PAAMS (S) missile system, for which the trials barge *Longbow* has been fitted out with a full replica of a Type 45 destroyer air-defence outfit. A first firing of the system – that deployed an Aster

30 missile against a simulated aircraft target – was completed to plan on 4 June 2008. This was followed by a second trial, utilising an Aster 15 missile to destroy a short-range target simulating an anti-ship missile, on 4 February 2009. A further test from *Longbow* is scheduled for later in 2009. The first firing of Sea Viper from an actual Type 45 vessel is not expected until 2010, with second of class *Dauntless* likely to claim this honour.

COMPARISONS AND CONCLUSION

Whilst the course of *Daring*'s design development and acquisition have proved to be far from straightforward, the ultimate result appears to have been successful. Even though she incorporates a significant amount of new technology, the progress so far achieved with ongoing sea trials suggests that the extensive programme of de-risking that was carried out in advance of and during construction has served

its purpose. It appears likely, therefore, that *Daring* will more than satisfy the demanding set of key user objectives established when the programme was authorised.

Whilst comparisons with other warship designs are always fraught with danger given wide variations in the strategic and tactical objectives influencing shipbuilders in different nations, it is perhaps inevitable that *Daring* will be measured against the alternate European air-defence vessels that emerged from the ashes of the original NFR-90 project. These can be broadly divided into three categories, viz. the two pairs of Franco-Italian *Forbin/Andrea Doria* escorts that were the fruits of those countries continued involvement in Project Horizon, the Thales APAR-equipped Dutch and German ships and the Spanish F-100 class frigates that feature the Aegis combat system and associated AN/SPY-1 radar.

Daring departing the River Clyde for first-phase sea trials on 18 July 2007. Implementation of an extensive programme of de-risking through advanced testing of major items of equipment has meant that the trials programme has progressed well in spite of the introduction of a significant amount of new technology. (*Conrad Waters*)

Right: It appears likely that *Daring* will more than satisfy the demanding objectives set when the Type 45 project was established. She is pictured here in September 2008 towards the end of the Stage 1 trials programme. *(BVT Surface Fleet)*

Of these ships, the Project Horizon vessels inevitably share the closest design antecedents with *Daring* and have significant similarities. However, the decision to accept the less capable EMPAR to meet the multi-function radar requirement makes them less potent warships in the area defence role, whilst other equipment choices appear to have been influenced more by national industrial priorities than purely military factors. Short production runs also suggest that little has been gained in cost terms, albeit EMPAR will also be used to equip Italian versions of the new FREMM type frigates. Meanwhile, the collaboration between Germany and the Netherlands has produced a series of well-balanced if comparatively shorter-ranged ships that combine the excellent tracking and control capabilities of the APAR 8,000–12,000 MHz I/J (X) band multi-function radar with a SMART-L volume search array optimised for longer range surveillance. Whilst the selection of US Standard and ESSM missiles possibly suggests lower absolute performance in the anti-missile role than that provided by Aster, this is counterbalanced by the possibilities of utilising existing US missile development work as a shortcut to developing a theatre ballistic missile defence (TBMD) capability. Finally, the Spanish F-100 class frigates have followed the low-risk route of purchasing the well-established US Aegis system. This might have fewer advantages for the national high-end industrial base and could also be seen as adopting less than cutting-edge technology. However, it allows Spain to take full benefit from ongoing upgrade work being carried out to Aegis on the basis of USN and – increasingly – other fleets' operating experience. It has also allowed the lucrative sale of spin-offs of the design to Australia and Norway.

In conclusion, *Daring* and her sisters represent extremely potent additions to the Royal Navy. They already compare well with other recent designs and will benefit from further upgrades as the incremental acquisition plan is implemented. Whilst defence economies have halved class numbers, when considered together with the new CVF aircraft carriers and *Astute* class submarines, they will leave the Royal Navy in the forefront of today's fleets.

Notes

1. For a more detailed description of the Type 42 destroyer design process and the abortive Type 43 and Type 44 successor projects, see Norman Friedman, *British Destroyers & Frigates – the Second World War and After* (London, Chatham Publishing, 2006), Chapter 14, pp 274–313.

2. RAND Corporation's influential report has been published and provides an interesting overview of the benefits and demerits of competitive procurement. See John Birkler, John F Schank, Mark V Arena, Giles Smith and Gordon Lee, *The Royal Navy's New Generation Type 45 Destroyer – Acquisition Options and Implications* (Santa Monica, CA, RAND Corporation, 2002).

3. A good summary of recent developments in integrated electric propulsion is provided in 'IES primed for warship propulsion', Editor: David Foxwell, *Warship Technology – March 2008* (London, RINA, 2008), pp 28–30.

4. The UK National Audit Office's (NAO) annual reports on MOD Major Projects provide a clear and independent analysis of the extent to which a range of major British new equipment programmes have managed to achieve both the operational and cost targets required when the relevant project was first approved. Whilst there appears to be some improvement arising from implementation of the more commercially realistic UK Defence Industrial Strategy (DIS), the underlying picture of over-optimism and poor management continues to make fairly depressing reading. In addition, for a specific NAO analysis of the Type 45 project, see Report by the Comptroller and Auditor General, *Providing Anti-Air Warfare Capability: the Type 45 Destroyer* (London, The Stationery Office, 2009).

General Note on Sources and Further Reading:
This chapter has inevitably relied heavily on press releases and other public relations material issued by the UK MOD and by its commercial partners in the Type 45 project, most notably BVT and its constituent companies. For those wanting to read more on the class, in addition to the various publications referenced above, the Type 45 section of the Navy Matters website – http://navy-matters.beedall. com/t45main.htm – provides an interesting and contemporaneous view of the project's progression.

3.3 SIGNIFICANT SHIPS

USS FREEDOM

Littoral Combat Ship – 'Seaframe' for the Future US Fleet

'The Navy's most transformational effort and my number-one budget priority,' was how then-US Navy Chief of Naval Operations (CNO) Admiral Vernon E Clark described the Littoral Combat Ship (LCS) in a March 2003 interview. He was quite enthusiastic about the little warship – at roughly 3,500 tons, the LCS is just one-third the displacement of a *Ticonderoga* (CG-47) class Aegis cruiser. 'The LCS is key to enhancing our ability to establish sea superiority not just for our carrier strike groups and expeditionary strike groups,' Clark explained, 'but for future joint logistics, command and control, and prepositioned ships moving to support forces ashore.'

Author: **Scott Truver**

See page 27

US Navy materials describe the LCS as a small, fast, relatively inexpensive, optimally-manned surface combatant equipped with modular 'plug-and-fight' mission packages, including a variety of unmanned aerial, surface and subsurface vehicles. A core crew of about forty will be augmented by focused-mission package and aviation detachments, for a total of seventy-five crew members. The LCS 'truck' – without any mission packages – is referred to as the 'seaframe'. Rather than being a multi-mission warship like the navy's Aegis cruisers and destroyers, the LCS is a 'focused-mission' ship tailored to perform one primary mission at any one time. The programme's current primary missions are: mine warfare/countermeasures (MIW/MCM); anti-submarine warfare (ASW); and surface warfare (SUW). To enhance operational flexibility and agility, according to navy plans, the ship's mission capabilities can be quickly refocused by changing its mission packages, with some estimates saying only about 24 hours or so will be needed for swapping out and in. The navy might acquire as many as fifty-five LCS units to provide the 'quantity' if not 'focused-quality' elements for the 313-ship fleet (see the author's companion USN Fleet Review in Chapter 2.1A for more detail).

Speaking at the Surface Navy Association's annual symposium in January 2009, Admiral Gary Roughead, the current CNO, underscored the navy's commitment to its newest warship: '... at the end of the day, I will always look at what makes the biggest difference in the fight and LCS, to me, is an example of that. LCS has the right capabilities for the times. Its modularity, its open architecture and its minimal manning will give us more flexibility and its speed and draft will take us to places where we must be. It is a ship ready for many different missions.'

This overview focuses on the LCS programme generally, and on LCS-1 *Freedom* specifically. A future edition of the *Seaforth World Naval Review* will examine the *Independence* (LCS-2) design.

PROGRAMME OVERVIEW: FROM FIRST CONTRACTS TO TODAY

After what was a 'lightning-fast' process initially involving five industry groups, on 17 July 2003 the USN awarded fixed-price contracts to teams headed by General Dynamics (GD), Lockheed Martin Naval Electronics & Surveillance Systems–Surface Systems and Raytheon Integrated Defense Systems to develop preliminary designs for the Flight 0 LCS. These incorporated the basic hull, mechanical and electrical

Opposite: *Freedom* (LCS-1) in the course of highly successful builder's trials on Lake Michigan during August 2008. The littoral combat ship (LCS) programme has been described as the USN's most transformational effort and is key to providing the 'quantity' element of the targeted 313-ship fleet. *(Lockheed Martin via US Navy)*

Left and above: As these images show, the two LCS designs are very different. Lockheed Martin's LCS-1 features a semi-planing all steel monohull with aluminium superstructure whilst General Dynamic's *Independence* (LCS-2) uses an all-aluminium trimaran hull. A future edition of the *Seaforth Word Naval Review* will consider the LCS-2 design. *(Lockheed Martin via US Navy/US Navy)*

Right: Another in a series of images taken of *Freedom* (LCS-1) on initial sea trials on Lake Michigan during August 2008. Operating close to land, the new littoral combat ships will complement capabilities provided by current 'blue water' surface escorts such as the *Arleigh Burke* (DDG-51) Aegis-equipped destroyers, as well as planned next-generation ships such as the DDG-1000 *Zumwalt* class. *(Lockheed Martin via US Navy)*

(HM&E) seaframe – with reconfigurable and inter-changeable mission modules to come later. 'LCS will be a high-speed ship designed for fighting in littoral or coastal areas,' the navy announcement noted. 'LCS will feature an advanced hull form and a shallow draft and will be capable of quickly moving through the littoral at speeds of up to 40 to 50 knots… Operating close to land, LCS will enhance the capabilities of the navy's larger multi-mission surface ships such as the planned next-generation [DDG-1000 *Zumwalt*] destroyer and [CGX] cruiser and today's fleet of Aegis warships.'

On 27 May 2004, the navy awarded contracts to two industry teams – one led by Lockheed Martin,

Contracts for the design and construction of up to two littoral combat ships each were awarded to teams headed by Lockheed Martin and General Dynamics on 27 May 2004. These are artist's concepts of the two different designs that date from around this time. Whilst project delivery has been relatively rapid considering the LCS was an entirely new concept, construction costs have been much higher than envisaged, causing a degree of controversy. (Lockheed Martin via US Navy / General Dynamics via US Navy)

the other by General Dynamics – to construct two versions of the LCS, with options for each team to build up to two LCSs each. The two LCS designs are very different: Lockheed's features a semi-planing all-steel monohull with aluminium superstructure, while GD's uses an all-aluminium trimaran hull and superstructure. The Lockheed team was assigned LCS-1 and LCS-3 (subsequently cancelled, see below), while the GD team was assigned LCS-2 and LCS-4 (also subsequently cancelled). Lockheed built LCS-1 at Marinette Marine Corporation in Marinette, Wisconsin, with the possibility of team-mate Bollinger Shipyards in Lockport, Louisiana, also getting business once production ramps up. On 23 March 2009, the navy awarded Lockheed Martin a fixed-price incentive fee contract for a revived

LCS-3 – Marinette Marine will construct the ship – under a contract including options for another three *Freedom* class LCS. Meanwhile, GD is building its own variants of the LCS at the Austal USA shipyard in Mobile, Alabama.

But the programme has not been without controversy and concern, particularly in terms of costs. According to Ronald O'Rourke, the US Congressional Research Service's naval analyst, the US Congress originally funded a total of seven LCS sea frames in the FY2005–FY2008 defence budgets. However, the navy substantially restructured the LCS programme in 2007 in response to significant cost growth and construction delays, cancelling four of those ships. In 2008, it cancelled another ship – the single LCS funded in FY2008 – following

Congress' action in respect of the FY2009 defence budget to rescind the funding for that ship. Of the seven LCSs originally funded in the FY2005–FY2008 defence budgets, therefore, a total of five were later cancelled.

The USN originally estimated that the end-cost of LCS seaframes would be about US$220m each in constant FY2005 dollars. ('End-cost' is the figure often reported as the total procurement cost of a USN warship. It is a fairly comprehensive figure for a ship's procurement cost but does exclude certain post-shakedown cost elements.) O'Rourke reports that estimated LCS seaframe procurement costs for both designs have increased substantially. The end-cost estimate for LCS-1 had grown from US$215.5m in the FY2005 budget to US$531m in the FY2009 budget; estimated end-cost for LCS-2 had increased from US$213.7m in the FY2005 budget to US$507m in 2009. The USN's FY2010 budget request notes that, when additional costs for outfitting and post delivery and for 'final system design/mission systems and ship integration team' are included, the total estimated procurement costs of LCS-1 will be approximately US$631m and for LCS-2, US$636m. These are still moving targets.

This flies in the face of the US Congress' imposition of a US$460m 'cost cap' for the FY2010 ships, a ceiling that might yet have to be modified. During a June 2009 Senate Armed Services Committee hearing, for example, the new Secretary of the Navy, Raymond Mabus, said 'there's a realistic prospect that we can drive toward that goal'. However, he also stated that the cost cap, as written, makes reaching that price 'less realistic'. Secretary Mabus estimated the navy would have a better idea of the cost of the FY2010 and follow-on ships in 'the early fall'.

With or without the cost cap, moreover, this does not include additional outlays for the mission packages. O'Rourke has noted that the navy wants to procure twenty-four mine warfare mission packages at an average cost of US$68m each, sixteen anti-submarine warfare mission packages at an average cost of US$42.3m each, and twenty-four surface warfare packages at an average cost of US$16.7m each.

In October 2008, John Young, the US Under-Secretary of Defense for Acquisition, Technology and Logistics, approved a revised acquisition strategy to cover procurement of the FY2009 and FY2010 ships. The updated acquisition strategy combines the FY 2009 procurement and FY 2010 options (the navy

Left: A large flight deck for helicopters and unmanned aerial vehicles provides *Freedom* (LCS-1) with increased operational flexibility. *(Lockheed Martin)*

Above: The LCS-1 design's fixed but steerable waterjets are a key feature supporting its high manoeuvrability. *(Lockheed Martin)*

Below: A broadside view of *Freedom* (LCS-1). Optimised to defeat anti-access threats in the littoral, she is essentially a 'seaframe' intended to carry out a range of single-focus missions through the installation of various mission packages. The initial packages will focus on anti-submarine, anti-surface and anti-mine warfare. *(Lockheed Martin)*

has requested funds for three LCSs in FY2010) to maximise competitive pressure on shipyard pricing as a key element of cost control. As of mid-2009, acquisition strategies for FY 2011 and out-year ships remain under development. Indeed, a major question concerning future acquisition strategy is whether the navy will 'neck-down' to just one of the two competing LCS designs. Apparently hedging his bets during a roundtable interview with reporters on 18 April 2009, Under-Secretary Young said the service could end up buying large numbers of each LCS design.

Freedom (LCS-1) was commissioned in November 2008 and has now completed post-delivery tests and trials. In mid-2009 some navy officials were looking to the possibility of a much-accelerated initial deployment. GD's all-aluminium trimaran, *Independence*, was still under construction in mid-2009, with an expected completion later in the year.

Ultimately, the initial LCSs will be home-ported in San Diego, California.

LCS PROGRAMME – CONCEPT PROVENANCE

An element of the USN's future surface combatant family of ships, the LCS has been optimised to defeat anti-access threats in the littoral. It uses an open-systems architecture design, modular weapons and sensor systems, and a variety of manned and unmanned vehicles to expand the battle space and project naval power in critical regions. Focused-mission LCS mission packages are being developed and deployed, which will provide capabilities vital to forcible entry, open-ocean/littoral superiority, and homeland-defence missions. The operational concept calls for the ability to swap-out/in mission modules in forward areas – as well as homeports – to reconfigure the ship for changing mission needs.

Regardless of the mission package installed, *Freedom* and her sisters are designed and engineered with inherent capabilities to conduct missions supporting intelligence, surveillance and reconnaissance (ISR); special operations; and maritime interception. 'Fully self-deployable and capable of sustained underway operations from homeports to any part of the world,' the 2009 edition of the CNO's *Navy Program Guide* explains, 'the LCS will

Below and opposite: Further views of *Freedom* (LCS-1) during the course of initial sea trials on Lake Michigan that commenced on 28 July 2008. Tracing its origins from studies into small, fast warships that dated from the time of the Cold War and which were developed during the 1990s, *Freedom* is intended to be capable of sustained, unsupported deployment to any part of the world regardless of the specific mission package embarked. *(Lockheed Martin via US Navy / US Navy)*

have the speed, endurance, and underway replenishment capabilities to transit and operate independently or with carrier strike groups, surface action groups and expeditionary strike groups.'

Freedom's provenance extends to the mid-1980s. Even at the height of the Cold War, with billions of dollars allocated to nuclear aircraft carriers and submarines and to 9,800-ton Aegis guided-missile cruisers, the USN examined the contributions that small, fast warships could make in increasingly numerous and frequent forward-presence and crisis-response missions world-wide. In 1985, the navy established a top-level operational requirement for a small, fast ship, the PXM, and later carried out a three-year study of a small, fast, stealthy deployable ship called the 'Scout Fighter' that could be acquired in different variants for specific missions. Vice-Admiral Arthur K Cebrowski's 'Streetfighter' and other advanced small warship concepts of the 1990s also stimulated the navy's 'next-gen' warship thinking. 'Streetfighter' was an element of the June 1999 Global War Game at the Naval War College, which underscored the value of a reconfigurable warship focused on defeating littoral threats. Research and analysis continued during the next eighteen months. This culminated in the Navy Warfare Development Command and the Defence Advanced Research Projects Agency 'Capabilities for the Navy After Next' wargame, which played a small, fast, reconfigurable/modular warship linked to off-board systems against anti-access littoral threats.

In the early 2000s, a series of navy campaign analyses, exercises, and experiments indicated a compelling need for a small, stealthy and fast surface warship that could be focused on specific littoral warfare missions. In January 2001, the navy concluded that there were critical gaps in ASW, MIW and SUW capabilities that challenged navy assumptions about assured access in the littoral. In 2002, the navy began a series of studies, analyses, wargames and experiments that identified technologies that could address the gap, and sought to identify an optimal platform to employ these systems, which ultimately led to the LCS. In addition to identifying a required force structure of approximately 375 warships (since then whittled down to the 313-ship fleet), the iterative analyses were the analytical framework for the concepts of thirty-seven independent carrier and expeditionary strike groups articulated in the navy's *Sea Power 21* strategic white paper. A total of fifty-five LCS and as many as 112 modern cruisers and

destroyers would be required to carry out the *Sea Power 21* global concept of operations.

The LCS programme formally commenced on 1 November 2001, when the navy stated that it was launching a 'Future Surface Combatant Program' aimed at acquiring a family of next-generation surface warships. In May 2002 the US Defence Planning Guidance specifically called for the navy to introduce the LCS into near-term plans and programmes and to articulate LCS operational concepts and needs. The Flight 0 LCS seaframe – focusing on HM&E elements – built upon lessons learned from several experimental navy ships, such as the HSV *Joint Venture*, the Office of Naval Research X-Craft, and others, as well as small combatants of foreign navies and coastguards, as risk-reduction measures in the areas of hull form, propulsion system, and materials.

During their testimony before the US Congress on the status of the LCS programme in March 2009, navy surface and littoral warfare officials explained that the LCS programme is structured in flights of 'seaframes' and 'spirals' of mission packages, which will enable relatively rapid, continuous and economical responses to change in technologies and threats, taking full advantage of the open-architecture, 'plug-and-fight' environment. The spiral design philosophy was mandated in an October 2002 US Department of Defense memo, which noted that 'Evolutionary acquisition is DoD's preferred strategy for acquisition of mature technology for the user. An evolutionary approach delivers capability in increments, recognizing, up front, the need for future capability improvements.' In the spiral development process, a desired capability is identified, but the end-state requirements are not known at programme initiation. Those requirements are refined through demonstration and risk management; there is continuous user feedback; and each increment must provide the user the best possible – and affordable – capability.

LCS PROGRAMME – KEY DESIGN REQUIREMENTS

The anti-access threats challenging US naval forces in the littorals include quiet submarines armed with

---

Table 3.3.1.

USS FREEDOM PRINCIPAL PARTICULARS

Building Information:

Fabrication Commenced:	1 February 2005
Launched:	23 September 2006
Delivered:	18 September 2008
Builders:	Lockheed Martin Corporation – systems integrator and prime contractor.
	Marinette Marine Corporation (now part of Fincantieri – Cantieri Navali Italiani SpA), Marinette, Wisconsin – shipbuilder.

Dimensions:

Displacement:	3,089 tons full load displacement.
Overall Hull Dimensions:	115.3m x 17.4m x 4.1m.

Weapons Systems:

Missiles:	1x RAM Mk49 21-cell launcher for RIM-116 rolling airframe missiles.
Guns:	1 x 57mm Mk110, machine guns.
Aircraft:	2 x MH-60R/S Seahawk helicopters (alternatively 1 x MH-60 and 3 x Fire Scout VTUAVs)
Countermeasures:	WBR-3000ESM/Elint system, 2 x SKWS/SRBOC decoy launching systems.
Principal Sensors:	1 x EADS TRS-3D air/surface search/target acquisition radar, navigation arrays.
Combat System:	COMBATSS-21 combat management system. Open architecture arrangement interfacing with interchangeable mission modules.
	Fully integrated communication suite.

Propulsion Systems:

Machinery:	CODAG. 2 x RR MT-30 gas turbines rated at 72MW. 2 x Fairbanks Morse Colt-Pielstick 16PA6B diesels rated at 12.8MW.
	Machinery arrangement produces a maximum of 113,710hp, directed through 4 steerable RR Kamewa 153SII waterjets.
Speed and Range:	Designed maximum speed in excess of 40 knots (over 47 knots was achieved on trials). Range is 3,500 nautical miles at 18 knots.

Other Details:

Complement:	Accommodation provided for 75 crew members. The core crew is less than 50, supplemented by 25 – 30 mission-related personnel.
Class:	One additional ship, *Fort Worth* (LCS-3), has been ordered. Further vessels are planned.

a variety of anti-ship weapons, mines that can be deployed from virtually any platform, and attacks by small surface craft. Diesel and advanced air-independent subs are quiet and can remain on the bottom for relatively long periods, in essence 'smart' mobile mines. Even highly sophisticated mines are cheap to acquire and easy to deploy from a variety of platforms, as the 1984 mining of the Red Sea and Gulf of Suez by Libya proved. While not a significant factor in the 2003 Gulf War, Iraqi mines clearly had a dramatic impact on coalition operations in 1991, with two US warships taken out of action by mine strikes and a planned amphibious assault frustrated. Attacks from small, fast surface warships and craft armed with missiles, guns or high explosives

likewise pose significant threats, and have great potential to be used effectively by many countries and even non-state actors – witness the October 2002 attack on *Cole* – to prevent US 'assured access' to littoral areas.

The USN has thus identified three principal warfare areas in which the *Freedom* will play major roles: the means to detect, avoid, and if necessary neutralise naval mines; the ability to defeat attacks by small surface warships and craft; and enhanced capabilities to counter the littoral submarine threat.

With an objective to be completely self-deployable and capable of sustained underway operations from homeports to any part of the world, *Freedom* must have the speed, endurance and underway

replenishment capabilities to transit with carrier strike groups, expeditionary strike groups and expeditionary strike forces. Initial requirements that included sprint speeds of some 50 knots, endurance of 3,500–4,300 miles, good seakeeping and low-speed stability, stealth and signature management, and the capability to accommodate manned and unmanned aviation, surface and undersea vehicles have challenged engineers.

The USN's concept of operations calls for the *Freedom* and its follow-on LCSs to serve as 'complementary force multipliers' to existing and planned littoral capabilities, and to exploit maturing networks, off board systems, and advances in platform technology. The LCS force will be:

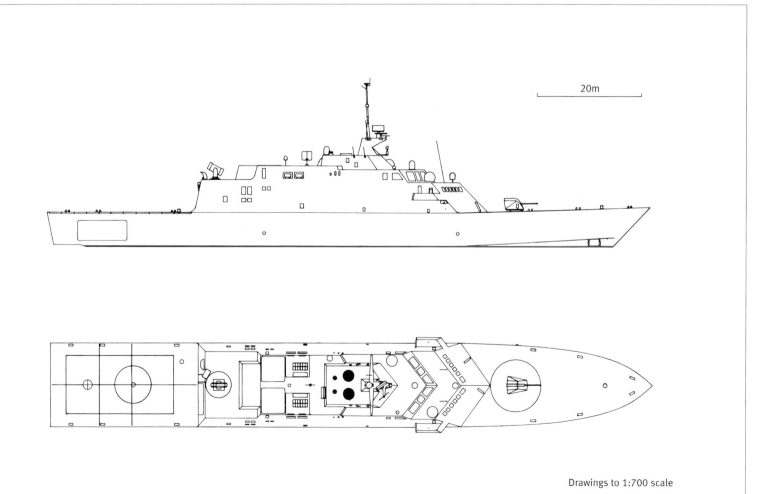

20m

Drawings to 1:700 scale

(Drawings by Ian Sturton, 2009)

Top left: Although built around a modularised mission-package concept, *Freedom* (LCS-1) ships a number of core self-defence systems, not least a 57mm Mk 110 gun. The gun can fire 220 rounds per minute with a range of up to nine miles. *(Lockheed Martin)*

Top right: An interesting feature of the LCS-1 design is a stern ramp for the launching and recovery of small boats. This is particularly useful for special operations forces. *(Lockheed Martin)*

Bottom: In addition to core defence systems and embarked mission packages, speed and manoeuvrability are regarded as key littoral combat ship capabilities, particularly in the anti-surface role. Attention has also been provided to incorporating appropriate signature reduction and soft kill capabilities into the design. *(Lockheed Martin via US Navy)*

- A distributed force deployed in groups, as compared to single, multi-mission capable ships.
- Modular in design, mission flexibility, and with innovative crew optimal manning.
- Designed around open architecture.
- Interwoven, both tactically and operationally, with traditional power-projection forces.
- Able to integrate with and to leverage all-service information gathering and targeting capabilities.

In addition, *Freedom* is intended to enable more efficient conduct of frequently conducted missions such as special operations force support, maritime interception operations, force protection, humanitarian assistance and disaster response, logistics, medical support, and non-combatant evacuation operations. The navy characterises these as 'long burn' missions that need platforms with endurance, speed, payload capacity, seakeeping and tailored-mission reconfigurability. The LCS force will thus help free up scarce multi-mission platforms to prepare for potential power-projection operations. The image of multi-billion-dollar Aegis cruisers and destroyers on anti-piracy patrols comes to mind: send, instead, a mission-focused LCS like *Freedom*. As Defense Under-Secretary John Young noted in an April 2008 interview, 'I need to stop boarding small ships in a terrorist world with billion-dollar destroyers.'

Freedom's operations in the littoral will be characterised by speed, agility, integration with off-board systems, survivability and signature control. Self-deployability and blue-water endurance are needed to allow the LCS to get to the operating areas without the need for open-ocean replenishment or the support of a mothership. That said, while range and endurance are dependent upon the type of operations being conducted, the navy intends that the LCS self-deployment range of at least 3,500 nautical miles will ensure a quick repositioning from one theatre to another.

The *Freedom*'s operational requirements are focused on three primary mission areas: MIW, SUW and ASW. Specific mission requirements may dictate employing different mission package configurations on multiple LCSs in the same area of operations. The USN and US Marine Corps are – as of 2009 – also investigating other primary mission-sets, including special operations and naval surface fire support. In all mission configurations the LCS will have core systems that provide the capability to conduct multi-sensor search, detection, classification, localisation and tracking of surface contacts in its assigned area of responsibility. The LCS will also have the core capability to protect itself against small-boat attacks, including the use of speed and manoeuvrability, and to conduct warning and disabling fire. Currently, however, the navy is fielding primary mission capabilities in just the three, albeit critically important, primary mission areas.

LCS PROGRAMME – MODULARISED MISSION PACKAGE CONCEPT

In all of these three areas, the modular mission packages are a central feature of both the *Freedom* and *Independence* designs and provide the principal warfighting capabilities and functionalities for specific mission areas. These mission packages can be further defined as follows:

- **LCS Mission Package:** Mission Module Crew + Support Aircraft + Mission Modules.
- **Mission Modules:** Mission Systems + Support Equipment.

The **MIW mission package** will enable *Freedom* to conduct MCM missions using onboard and off-board systems, from deep water up to the very-shallow MCM region near the beach. It allows her to:

- Detect classify and identify surface, moored and bottom mines to permit manoeuvre or use of selected sea areas.
- Co-ordinate/support mission planning and execution with joint and combined assets in the absence of dedicated MIW command and control plat-

forms. MIW mission planning will include the use of organic and remotely operated sensors. The LCS will exchange MIW tactical information including mine danger areas, mine locations, mine types, environmental data, bottom maps, off-board system locations, planned search areas and confidence factors.

- Conduct mine reconnaissance.
- Perform bottom mapping.
- Perform minefield break through/punch through operations using off-board systems.
- Perform minesweeping using off-board mission systems.
- Conduct precise location and reporting of a full range of mine countermeasures (MCM) contact data, for example, identified mines and non-mine bottom objects.
- Perform mine neutralisation.
- Employ, reconfigure, and support MH-60S helicopters for MCM operations.
- Embark an explosive ordnance disposal detachment.
- Deploy, control, and recover off-board systems, and process data from off-board systems.

The **SUW mission package** will provide *Freedom* with the capability to engage surface threats, particularly small fast boats, and to minimise threats to friendly units. It will enable her to:

- Conduct integrated surface surveillance using onboard and off-board sensors.
- Discriminate and identify friendly and neutral surface vessels from surface threats in high-density shipping environments.
- Conduct co-ordinated SUW mission planning, contribute to and receive a common tactical picture, and initiate engagement of surface threats. It will also allow her to maintain and share situational awareness and tactical control in a co-ordinated SUW environment. When operating in company with other SUW assets, such as fixed-wing and helicopter attack aircraft and maritime patrol aircraft, the LCS must be capable of planning and co-ordinating the SUW mission.
- Engage surface threats independently, as part of a LCS group, and in co-ordination with other friendly forces. This includes threats in the line-of-sight and over-the-horizon. In addition to hard kill capabilities, the LCS will use agility and speed, signature management and soft kill measures to

disrupt the threat's detect-to-engage sequence and conduct offensive operations against surface threats.

■ Deploy, control and recover off-board systems, and process data from off-board systems.

■ Employ, reconfigure and support MH-60 helicopters and smaller rotary-wing aircraft for SUW operations.

■ Conduct SUW battle damage assessment after engagements against surface threats.

Finally *Freedom*'s **ASW missions** include multi-sensor detection, classification, localisation, tracking and engagement of submarines throughout the water column in the littoral operating environment. The LCS will have the capability to embark ASW/multi-mission helicopters and unmanned vehicles and will employ undersea surveillance systems, environmental models and databases. The ASW mission package will enable the *Freedom* to:

■ Conduct offensive ASW operations. The LCS must achieve a mission abort or sink a threat submarine, if the submarine contact of interest is

Initial LCS Mission Modules

LCS Mine Warfare 'Spiral Alpha' Module

Unmanned Surface Vehicle	1
Unmanned Surface Sweep System	1
Remote Multi Mission Vehicle	2
Organic Air and Surface Influence System	1
Airborne Mine Neutralization System	1
Airborne Laser Mine Detection System	1
AQS-20 Mine Hunting Sonar	3
Rapid Airborne Mine Clearance System	1
Coastal Battlefield Reconnaissance and Analysis system	1

LCS Surface Warfare 'Spiral Alpha' Module

Non-Line-of-Sight missile Launching System	4
30mm Bushmaster Gun System	2

LCS Anti-Submarine Warfare 'Spiral Alpha' Module

Unmanned Surface Vehicle	1
Remote Multi Mission Vehicle	2
USV Towed Array System	1
USV Dipping Sonar	1
Multi-Static Off-Board Source	1
Multi-Function Towed Array	1
Remote Towed Active Source	1

transiting through a designated key choke point or operating (e.g., patrolling) in a designated search/surveillance area.

■ Conduct defensive ASW operations. The LCS must defeat threat submarine attacks against units operating in company with carrier or expeditionary strike groups or LCS squadrons. The LCS must achieve a mission abort or sink a threat submarine that poses a threat to any friendly units.

■ Conduct co-ordinated ASW, contribute to the common undersea picture, maintain and share situational awareness and tactical control in a co-ordinated ASW environment.

■ Maintain the surface picture while conducting ASW in a high-density shipping environment.

■ Detect, classify, localise, track and attack diesel submarines operating on batteries in a shallow-water environment to include submarines resting on the sea floor.

■ Perform acoustic range prediction and ASW search planning.

■ Conduct integrated undersea surveillance employing onboard and off-board systems.

■ Achieve a mission kill of ASW threats through engagement with hard kill weapons from onboard and off-board systems.

■ Employ signature management and soft kill systems to counter and disrupt the threat's detect-to-engage sequence in the littoral environment.

■ Deploy, control, recover, and conduct day and night operations with towed and off-board systems, and process data from off-board systems.

■ Employ, reconfigure, and support MH-60R helicopters in ASW operations.

■ Conduct ASW battle damage assessment after engagements against undersea threats.

Two aviation systems and detachments will round out the LCS capabilities. The MH-60 Seahawk helicopter – in the '60S' configuration for MCM operations and the '60R' armed variant for SUW and ASW tasks – and the MQ-8B Vertical Takeoff Unmanned Air Vehicle, with its organic electro-optical/infra-red (EO/IR) sensor, will extend the 'reach' of the LCS.

LCS-1 *FREEDOM*: INDUSTRY TEAM AND DESIGN CHARACTERISTICS

The Lockheed Martin team tasked with designing and building *Freedom* includes Gibbs & Cox,

Marinette Marine and Bollinger Shipyards, Donald L Blount and Associates, IZAR, Fincantieri, NAVATEK, Blohm + Voss, Angle, American Bureau of Shipping, BBN Technologies, Charters Technical Services, DRS Technologies, and Micro Analysis & Design. Using what Lockheed Martin describes as a competitive open business model to identify 'best-of-industry' technologies and practices, the core partners are supported by key US and international companies including:

■ Angle Incorporated
■ ArgonST
■ Data Links Solutions
■ DRS Technologies
■ EADS
■ Fairbanks Morse Engine
■ Jere
■ L3 Communications
■ MAAG Gear AG
■ MacTaggart Scott
■ MAS Industries
■ Navantia
■ Raytheon
■ Rolls Royce
■ Sperry
■ Terma
■ United Defense

The Lockheed Martin *Freedom* Seaframe Flight 0 design incorporates large reconfigurable spaces; an integrated launch, recovery and handling system; a large flight deck; and provides mission flexibility through rapid change-out of mission modules and support equipment. The all-steel semi-planing monohull combines high speed, sufficient payload and range to provide flexibility across all LCS missions. Optimised for watercraft launch and recovery, the design includes stern and side launch capability near the waterline and an integrated command and control system to support mission module operation. The design also integrates non-developmental sensors and weapons systems, building on proven technologies for combat power and mission flexibility, as well as a layered self-defence system. The LCS design is the first surface warship to be classed under the new Naval Vessel Rules by the American Bureau of Shipping. Core features are set out in Table 3.1.on page 158.

Freedom's shallow draft of less than 14ft (4.25m) and water-jet propulsion give the ship access to thou-

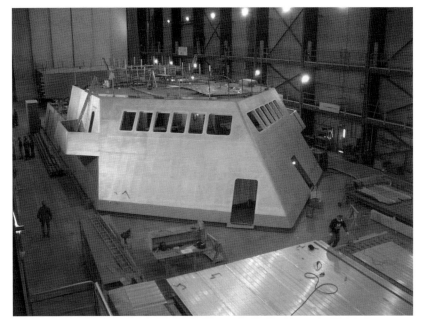

Two views of *Freedom*'s (LCS-1) distinctive aluminium deckhouse taken whilst under construction and then being lowered into position. *(Lockheed Martin)*

sands of more ports and littoral waters world-wide than other USN surface warships. Although more than a football (or rugby) pitch in length, the ship can turn 360 degrees in less than eight boat lengths at its rated sprint speed, and can accelerate from a standing-start to full speed in about two minutes. The design combines high-speed manoeuvrability with seakeeping that support launch and recovery, combat operations, and optimal human performance from the crew.

The Lockheed Martin team has leveraged the navy's investment in open architecture and common command-and-control (C^2) systems to deliver required littoral warfighting capability and to enhance commonality if not interoperability across numerous navy surface ships and US Coast Guard cutters. For example, more than 95 per cent of the COMBATSS-21 software was built from proven USN open-architecture programmes. The open architecture will enable rapid and cost effective technology insertion and spiral development throughout the ship's service life. The Combat Management System uses 'boundary components' – i.e. software interfaces – for rapid integration of new capabilities such as sensors, communications and weapons. In addition, the LCS and the Coast Guard's National Security Cutter also share the same primary gun weapon system. *Freedom*'s fully

Integrated Communications Suite introduces the submarine common radio room into the surface fleet for commonality within the USN. The ship's Integrated Bridge System and fully digital nautical charts are interfaced to ship sensors to support safe ship operation.

The ship's stern ramp provides the capability of launching and recovering large hard-bottomed vehicles, such as 11m rigid-hull inflatable boats or the special operations forces' high-speed boats while *Freedom* is underway. The unique side door provides a second launch and recovery point for smaller vehicles and can also be used for replenishment and refuelling at-sea of mission packages. The Universal Three-Axis Overhead Crane System serves both access points and provides positive control movement of mission modules and off-board vehicles for safe and efficient launch, recovery and handling.

LCS-1 *FREEDOM*:
CONSTRUCTION & DELIVERY

On 2 June 2005, the *Freedom*'s keel was laid at Marinette Marine. Other milestones since then have included:

- **23 September 2006:** LCS-1 launched and christened.
- **11 October 2007:** Successful demonstration of

the operation of *Freedom*'s automated stern doors, articulated stern ramp and the side launch doors, thereby 'proving' key elements of the launch and recovery system.

- **17 March 2008:** Electric plant 'light off' and test of the ship's four 750-kilowatt Fincantieri Isotta Fraschini diesel generators and the ship's three-megawatt electrical power plant. The testing of the generators involved loading each generator to its full-power capacity. Following successful completion of this step, additional testing included synchronising – or 'paralleling' in shipbuilding terms – the generators to attain the power levels required to support operations at sea. This marked a significant milestone for *Freedom*, as it ensured its electric plant was completely functional and able to support all tests, evaluations and operations at sea.

- **4 June 2008:** *Freedom* successfully completed the 'light off' of the twin gas turbine propulsion engines in final preparation for sea trials. The two Rolls-Royce MT30 gas turbines are the largest and most powerful ever installed on a USM ship – rated at 36MW or 48,000hp each – and drive steerable water-jet propulsor, allowing LCS-1 to reach sprint speeds approaching 50 knots.

- **16 June 2008:** Successful integration of key combat system components – radar, gun weapon

system, missile launcher, decoy launcher and electronic warfare system – with COMBATSS-21, the ship's core combat management system. During the integration testing, targets of opportunity were detected and tracked to demonstrate operability.

- **10 July 2008:** *Freedom*'s propulsion plant completed testing in preparation for dock trials: the final stage of testing before underway trials. Dock trials include a series of demonstrations of propulsion, navigation, communication and other systems conducted to ensure the ship is ready for sea trials.
- **28 July 2008:** *Freedom* first put to 'sea' in Lake Michigan. This marked the start of Builder's Sea Trials.
- **18 September 2008:** Lockheed Martin delivered LCS-1 to the navy, marking preliminary acceptance of the ship and clearing the way for the ship's crew to prepare for commission and service.
- **8 November 2008:** *Freedom* commissioned and commenced sea trials. The ship's 'speed-of-heat' construction and delivery – only forty-one months from keel laying to commissioning – was a significant accomplishment, in itself.

In light of recent USN troubles with lead ships, particularly the ill-starred *San Antonio* (LPD-17), which has been plagued with poor workmanship and roundly criticised for cost overruns and delays, the positive early experience of *Freedom* is something of a sea change for the navy. In August 2008, the navy's Board of Inspection and Survey (INSURV) conducted Acceptance Trial 1 and found the ship to be 'capable, well-built, and inspection-ready', and recommended that the CNO authorise delivery of the ship following correction or waiver of material deficiencies. INSURV identified only twenty-one 'starred' deficiencies on *Freedom*, a relatively low number that compares very favourably with other first-of-class ships. Twelve were closed prior to delivery, five more were closed during the ship's industrial post-delivery availability, and the final four will be closed during post-shakedown availability in FY2010. After commissioning, the crew conducted a vigorous shakedown of the ship during her transit from the building yard in Wisconsin to Norfolk. The ship will be temporarily based there

Freedom (LCS-1) was subject to a spectacular sideways launch into the Menominee River on 23 September 2006. *(Lockheed Martin)*

whilst the crew carries out additional tests and trials to complete certifications and mission package integration testing.

In late May 2009, the navy completed the final acceptance trials for *Freedom*, operating out of Norfolk Naval Base. These were designed to measure the ship's propulsion, communications and navigation systems, as well as other technologies. A navy news release noted that the tests included a successful 'four-hour, full-power run and both surface and air detect-to-engagement demonstrations of the ship's combat management system'. Indeed, the tests were so successful that, in June 2009, USN officials began studying the possibility that LCS-1 could make a short deployment earlier than the initial operational mission that was originally planned for FY2012. The CNO has certainly become 'bullish' about employing the first LCS as soon as possible. However, this possibility will have to take into consideration the milestones associated with a first-of-class warship – in this case additional tests at Naval Station Norfolk and experiments with its focused-mission modules at Naval Surface Warfare Centre Panama City, Florida – that will need to be completed before *Freedom* heads to its homeport at Naval Base San Diego. Although a Pacific Rim deployment had been envisaged initially, the CNO reportedly wants *Freedom* to join the warships in Combined Task Force (CTF) 151 patrolling in response to the pirate threat off the coast of Somalia. This is, perhaps, mindful of Under-Secretary John Young's comment: 'I need to stop boarding small ships in a terrorist world with billion-dollar destroyers.'

OPERATING CONCEPT: *FREEDOM*'S 'HYBRID' SAILOR

As the USN was pushing the operational and design envelopes for *Freedom*, a similar sea change was needed in how the LCS type is to be manned and maintained. As a result, the navy has identified the need for a new 'breed' of sailors for *Freedom* and other next-generation warships. New technologies are at the root of the new designs, resulting in a need for increased capabilities in young sailors to multitask and work with leading-edge electronic systems. Experience has also taught the navy that it cannot just throw advanced technologies into ships and aircraft without first understanding their impact on the people who will have to use them. In the LCS design studies – and even more so in the *Zumwalt*

A lot of attention has been paid to developing efficient operating concepts for the LCS-1 *Freedom* design, including development of a fully integrated shore-based trainer: the Future Surface Combatant - Scalable Shore Based Trainer (FSC-SSBT). These images show bridge and combat system simulators. *(Lockheed Martin)*

(DDG-1000) destroyer design – the navy and industry have embraced more fully the concept of human systems integration. This involves taking account of human performance standards and providing the technologies, systems policies, processes and training to enable the right skills, in the right people, at the right time.

Cost has also come into the equation. As the service has examined its requirements to ensure critical war-fighting capabilities are achieved while reducing total ownership costs of today's – and especially tomorrow's – operating forces, study after study has concluded that some 70 per cent of the costs of designing and engineering, acquiring, operating and maintaining, and disposing warships are directly related to their crews. Looking to achieve 'optimal' manning levels – i.e., no more or no fewer people than are needed to operate, maintain and fight its warships safely and achieve mission success – the USN discovered that traditional rates and ratings no longer made sense for advanced ships like *Freedom*. Indeed, top-down functional analyses determined that the officers and sailors of these new warships must be cross-functional and highly skilled in several areas of shipboard operations, not just experts in electronics or propulsion systems or food service. Hence the concept of a 'hybrid sailor' – comprising a mixture of different skill-sets for the men and women serving in these next-generation ships – that is already generating 'ripples' far beyond the waterfront.

For example, the forty-person core crew for the LCS is more like a SEAL/Naval Special Warfare team rather than the typical pyramidal, hierarchical structure of a traditionally-crewed ship. Every member of a SEAL squad has to have principal skill areas and responsibilities but each must also be able to carry out other critical tasks should another member of the team be wounded or killed. The same considerations shaped navy thinking for LCS core crews. In the LCS, when the sailor reports to the ship he or she must be a 'full-up round', completely trained and needing no 'spin-up' to do all his or her assigned jobs – and potentially more.

This thinking also affects the USN acquisition community's approach to training. It requires onboard systems to have data collection mechanisms designed in 'up-front' to ensure commanding officers can quickly evaluate and track the readiness of their people. It also has to make certain that refresher training can be provided onboard, that scenario simulations can be quickly tailored to exercise individual and team needs as mission requirements change and that these systems ensure the ability to 'train as you fight', so as to provide sailors the ability to operate effectively in changing environments under stressful situations.

To help meet those needs, in spring 2007 Lockheed Martin delivered the USN's first fully integrated, shore-based trainer for LCS sailors, the Future Surface Combatant-Scalable Shore Based Trainer (FSC-SSBT). The FSC-SSBT enables the crew of *Freedom* and follow-on Lockheed Martin-designed LCSs to undertake high-fidelity, realistic shipboard bridge, combat system and engineering duties – in an integrated training environment – well before they actually board the ship. The first *Freedom* crewmembers began training at the facility in early May 2007.

There is significant interest in the LCS-1 *Freedom* design from other navies. This is an evolved LCS design with the Aegis SPY-1F radar and vertical launch missile systems. *(Lockheed Martin)*

Corporate materials note that the FSC-SSBT supports the navy's LCS concept of operations through the re-use of shipboard software, integrated simulations, virtual environments and commercially available hardware. The facility's bridge simulator allows the crew to 'virtually' drive the LCS and perform specialised scenarios and manoeuvres. The mission control centre component of the training facility – which is the actual size of the centre on the ship – will allow sailors to use operational software from COMBATSS-21, the ship's combat management system. The FSC-SSBT also supports the navy's Blue and Gold crew manning concept, allowing for one crew to be trained while the other is deployed and operational. Already familiar with the training facility's realistic LCS environment, *Freedom*'s 'hybrid' crews can allocate more time focused on operational needs as opposed to on-the-job training.

FUTURE DEVELOPMENTS

The USN has put in place an aggressive and potentially far-reaching plan and programme to acquire perhaps as many as fifty-five littoral combatants, many based on the USS *Freedom* design. To do so, however, costs must be reined in, particularly in the anticipated 'squeaky-tight' fiscal environment forecast for the next four-to-eight years.

In addition to the USN, there has been some USCG interest in LCS as a component of the 'Deepwater' fleet, as well as from foreign navies, e.g., Saudi Arabia and Israel. In April 2006, for example, the navy awarded Lockheed Martin a foreign military sales contract to conduct a LCS feasibility study for the Israeli navy. The company examined possible modifications to its LCS design to meet specific Israeli naval requirements, primarily in the HM&E system compatibility with the Israeli Navy's combat systems and other requirements. A follow-on contract awarded in November 2007 focused on developing a technical specification and acquisition cost package for the LCS-I ('I' for 'Israel') combat system that assessed multiple Israeli and US sensor and weapon systems, for example, the Mk-41 vertical launch system, the lightweight Aegis SPY-1F radar, Typhoon gun and Barak missile. In late June 2009, however, reports began to circulate that the Israeli navy was no longer interested in the LCS, largely because of increasing costs. 'At the end of the day,' an Israeli source remarked, 'we had no choice but to face the fact that, for us, it was unaffordable.' Still conversations with several navies continue, potentially making the LCS something of a 'world ship'.

Notes

1. The following list of selected sources, arranged chronologically, provide useful additional information on the LCS concept:

– Vice Admiral A K Cebrowski, USN, and Captain Wayne P Hughes, Jr., USN (Ret.), 'Rebalancing the Fleet' *Proceedings – November 1999* (Annapolis, MD, US Naval Institute, 1999).

– 'Littoral Combat Ship Concept of Operations' (Newport, RI, Navy Warfare Development Command, February 2003).

– Brien Alkire, John Birkler, Lisa Dolan, James Dryden, Bryce Mason, Gordon T Lee, John F Schank and Michael Hayes, *Littoral Combat Ships: Relating Performance to Mission Package Inventories, Homeports, and Installation Sites* (Santa Monica, CA, RAND Corporation, 2007).

– Duncan Long and Stuart Johnson, *The Littoral Combat Ship: From Concept to Program – Case Studies in National Security Transformation Number 7* (Washington, DC, Department of Defense Center for Technology and National Security Policy, 2007).

– Christopher P Cavas, 'LCS-1 and 2; Much Progress, Much to Do', *Defense News* – 12 January 2009 (Springfield VA, Army Times Publishing, 2009).

– Ronald O'Rourke, *Navy Littoral Combat Ship (LCS) Program: Background, Oversight Issues, and Options for Congress* (Washington, DC, Congressional Research Service, 2009).

– Statement of Rear Adm. Victor Guillory, USN, Director of Surface Warfare; Rear Adm. William E. Landay, Program Executive Officer Ships; and Ms. E. Anne Sandel, Program Executive Officer Littoral and Mine Warfare; before the Subcommittee on Seapower and Expeditionary forces, House Armed Services Committee, US Congress, on the Current Status of the Littoral Combat Ship Program, 10 March 2009. (Washington DC, United States House of Representatives, 2009).

– Neal Rauhauser, 'Somali Piracy of Maersk Alabama Places Littoral Combat Ships in Perspective', *The Cutting Edge* – 13 April 2009: www.thecuttingedgenews.com

4.1 TECHNOLOGICAL REVIEWS

NAVAL SENSORS AND WEAPONS The Picture's the Thing

What is happening to naval sensors and to the weapons they control affects, and is affected by, two great developments in larger naval policy.[1] One is the shrinkage of navies. Naval handbooks such as *Combat Fleets* or *Jane's* keep growing, but the number of combatants in the major navies continues to fall. However, naval missions, particularly in a post-Cold War world, seem to demand more, not fewer, hulls – or at least more distinct naval groups – to handle more separate contingencies. For example, the piracy problem off Somalia is only very loosely connected to the need for a naval blocking force in the Arabian Sea, and that in turn has nothing to do with ships operating off North Korea to enforce, if that is possible, a UN mandate which prohibits that country from exporting nuclear material and long-range ballistic missiles. Yet the same navies must try to cover all three, plus many other missions in distant places. At one time it could be argued that US forces, for example, could concentrate in the North Atlantic to deal with the single likely enemy, the Soviet Union. Since the Cold War, however, the problem has become amorphous. The other development is the continuing dramatic rise of computers and their relatives, usually expressed in Moore's Law. Although the original statement was that the cost of a unit of computing power would halve every eighteen months – which we certainly see in the personal computer market – the more typical formulation is that computing power doubles every eighteen months, or even more rapidly. Among many other things, Moore's Law has made robotic naval vehicles, such as unmanned underwater vehicles, an increasingly important reality. The two trends have come together, for example, in the US Navy's Littoral Combat Ship programme, which may indicate where navies will have to go.

Author: Norman Friedman

Norman Friedman is one of the best-known naval analysts and historians in the US and the author of over thirty books. He has written on broad issues of modern military interest, including an award-winning history of the Cold War, whilst in the field of warship development his greatest sustained achievement is probably an eight-volume series on the design of different US warship types. A specialist in the intersection of technology and national strategy, his acclaimed *Network Centric-Warfare* has recently been published by the US Naval Institute Press. The holder of a PhD in theoretical physics from Columbia, Dr Friedman is a regular guest commentator on television and lectures widely on professional defence issues. He is a resident of New York.

THE COST OF SOPHISTICATION

It seems fair to say that the first reality, the shrinkage, can be blamed on the exploding cost and sophistication of the weapons and sensors warships carry. In every category, ships are larger than their predecessors, but their increasing cost is due much more to what they carry. The proportion of ship cost due not only to buying but also to maintaining and modernising weapons and sensors exploded because the pace of weapon and sensor development rose dramatically after about 1939 and then again after about 1950. There is a reason the modern US Navy

Left: The problem is always numbers. How many air-defence ships does it take, e.g., to beat off an attack of a given size? *York*, shown here in 2009, was designed to handle two targets at a time, one for each of her dome-enclosed Type 909 radars. This limitation was typical of air defence ships built prior to Aegis. The tactical picture the ship used to assign targets to the two radars was relatively imprecise, so that once a target was assigned the tracking/illuminating radar had to be dedicated to that target. The problem is usually expressed as saturation: one ship could be defeated by a mass attack. However, it could also be expressed in terms of the unacceptable cost of providing enough ships to hold off a massive attack. Even a large ship could only accommodate two to four such radar directors; whatever improvement was made had to come from the nature of the defensive system. *(Conrad Waters)*

Below: A Standard SM-2 missile at the point of launch. Such missiles depend not on illumination but instead on up-links which periodically reset their autopilots. As a consequence, they can fly more energy-efficient paths, and reach greater ranges. The combination of range plus the much greater capacity associated with a precision tactical picture greatly increases the number of targets each ship can handle. The step beyond is for ships to add external data to their internal pictures, so that they can engage targets they cannot see, at least initially. *(US Navy)*

If the ship's internal picture was precise enough, there was no need to dedicate a tracking radar to each target, because the picture would be good enough for missile guidance via a commandable autopilot using an up-link from the ship. That is the core of the USN's Aegis system. The Japanese Aegis ship *Ashigara* (DDG-178) is seen passing *Chaffee* (DDG-90) at Pearl Harbor in this 2008 view. They may appear to have tracking dishes atop their superstructures, but these are slaved illuminators, pointed at the target by the ship's combat system on the basis of the picture it contains, and switched on as needed for terminal missile homing. *(US Navy)*

The picture inside the combat system is the key, not the radar or the illuminators. The German missile destroyer *Sachsen*, pictured in July 2005, uses the Dutch APAR X-band active-array radar and the Anglo-Dutch SMART-L long-range search radar. The core anti-aircraft system is that used in Aegis ships, as is the SM-2 missile. *(Josef Straczek)*

considers it a dramatic improvement to achieve a 313-ship fleet, whereas in 1945 it had about 5,000 ships in commission, in 1960 about 1,200, and in 1980 the goal was the 600-ship navy. An important reason why the US Navy is less than half its 1990 size is that a conscious decision was taken to trade numbers for increasing sophistication, on the theory that a single more effective warship was well worth two or more less effective ones. In addition, the naval mission changed: Cold War anti-submarine warfare, and with it many frigates, became obsolete, at least temporarily. In addition, existing ships required too many sailors: naval manpower was and is increasingly expensive. The irony of the *Zumwalt* (DDG-1000) class, which has become the most expensive surface combatant in history, is that it was conceived as a limited-cost ship with a drastically limited crew, the hope being that cutting operating costs would balance increased purchase cost. The factors affecting the US Navy affect all the others, too. Many in Britain, for example, see 'sea blindness' as the reason that the destroyer/frigate force has shrunk so horribly, but the reality of increased unit cost – due to increased sophistication – cannot be neglected. Nor can the fact that the Cold War Royal Navy was focussed on a kind of anti-submarine warfare which is unlikely to return soon (the US Navy was far less focussed, hence has suffered less).

The increased sophistication, moreover, is not gold-plating by fools, or systematic surrender to a bloated defence industry. Ships really are being required to do more against increasingly difficult threats. Navies have always had a combination of offensive and defensive roles. During the Cold War, NATO navies were expected to beat off a Soviet attempt to block free use of the North Atlantic sea lanes. The US Navy solution, as expressed in its Maritime Strategy, was to force the Soviets to fight for their own maritime assets (mainly for the security of the bastions in which their strategic missile submarines operated), the idea being that winning such a battle or battles would destroy the Soviet anti-shipping force. In either case, the level of sophistication was set by the quality and quantity of Soviet anti-ship missiles and other weapons, such as submarine torpedoes and mines.

With the end of the Cold War, the offensive or expeditionary side of naval operations took over. The unpleasant reality was that the Third World countries Western navies now confronted had the sorts of anti-ship weapons the Soviets had planned to deploy, albeit in much smaller numbers, and usually in earlier and less capable versions.

Much of the collapse of Western naval numbers at the end of the Cold War came because large numbers of less sophisticated ships had to be discarded, leaving the smaller numbers of more expensive ships built at the end of the Cold War. For example, the US Navy discarded numerous cruisers armed with New Threat Upgrade versions of the Standard Missile. These ships had been modernised to handle greater numbers of air targets, and so to help beat off Soviet saturation attacks. Unfortunately modernisation did not improve their ability to deal with pop-up threats such as those from land-based missiles. Only the new Aegis technology could do that. The US cruiser force was thus halved at a stroke.

REPLACING LOST NUMBERS

Unfortunately sea power is not always exercised by small compact forces of overwhelming strength. Often it is essential to apply sea power in many places more or less at the same time, so a fleet needs numbers, too. After 9/11, the US Navy proposed a new way of looking at naval power. The centrepiece of an elaborate set of briefing slides was titled 'A Bad Day in 2003'. In the past, US doctrine had focussed on two simultaneous crises, which was really because the United States operates in two oceans. By 2001, declining resources had led to the idea that the United States should be able to fight one war while deterring an aggressor elsewhere. To avoid spending money, the assumption was made that the ships which fought the first war could shift to the second (a friend walked out of a briefing after hearing that this could be done because defensive weapons were so good that all the ships from the first war would be available for the second). The point of the slide – the lesson the US Navy took from 9/11 – was that the United States would likely have to deal with far more than two simultaneous crises, because the crises would have disparate causes. Instead of two deployed fleets, the country needed more numerous self-contained naval forces. The US Navy proposed to build separate strike forces (Expeditionary Strike Forces) around large amphibious ships, and also to form surface action groups. These are classic ways in which a navy tries to handle more threats at once. Big ships like carriers and large-deck amphibious ships take a long time to build, so there is no way to multiply them (alas, the days of a large reserve fleet are long gone). The only way out is to build numerous (hopefully) inexpensive surface combatants, which will fill out the more numerous naval strike forces.

These combatants became the current Littoral Combat Ship, because in 2002 the only new surface combatant under discussion below the size of the *Zumwalt* class was called that. In 2002–3 LCS was a rubber ship; all that was set was that about sixty-eight or even seventy-five were wanted, which meant a unit cost of about a quarter-billion dollars – a quarter as much as a *Burke* class destroyer. It is perfectly possible to build a hull of roughly destroyer or frigate size and speed for that kind of money, but that leaves

out the reason navies have shrunk – the hull and machinery are not the problem. Weapons and sensors are.

At the outset, it seemed that the answer was already obvious. The Royal Danish Navy had demonstrated that a single hull could be designed so that different functions could be provided by modules. The Danes saved money on their fleet by building only a limited number of such StanFlex corvettes to replace more numerous fast attack boats, mine countermeasures craft, etc., the theory being that their fleet would cycle through various roles (as in the discussion mentioned above, apparently losses while the ships were performing one role were not contemplated, as then the modularity would be pointless).

By this time it seemed to many in the US Navy that, at least in the near term, the main fleet role would be expeditionary warfare in littoral areas, which implied the need for numerous shallow-water

ASW craft, craft to deal with fast attack craft, and mine countermeasures craft. The Danish model did not quite fit, because these different roles would have to be performed more or less simultaneously.

SENSOR IMPROVEMENTS ENTER THE EQUATION

Then the US Navy came up with something new, which may have profound implications for future naval sensors and weapons. It was well aware that past littoral operations had generally involved very large numbers of ships and craft – which were affordable, in the Second World War, because the individual units were inexpensive. So many craft had been needed – and littorals were so dangerous – because lines of sight or sensing (e.g. underwater sound) were so short. Short lines of sensing made surprise relatively easy, and that gave a less sophisticated enemy considerable advantages.

Ships with short-range missiles can benefit from an over-the-horizon picture, because they can launch their weapons to maximum range, rather than to the maximum range consistent with the horizon. The Royal Navy has decided to adopt the US Cooperative Engagement Capability, which offers ships exactly such a picture, for Type 23 frigates armed with short-range Seawolf defensive missiles – *Westminster* is pictured here in September 2005. The US Navy did much the same with ships armed with Sea Sparrow. In each case, there is a vast difference between firing a missile which needs guidance at the ship's horizon, and waiting to fire until the target crosses the horizon. That might be particularly important near a coast, where terrain would block lines of sight from the sea. *(Conrad Waters)*

In the Second World War, a ship and personnel were attached to each sensor, e.g. to each short-range sonar, and that sensor directed the ship's weapons. The question about 2005 was whether anything had changed. Could the presence of one ship somehow be magnified, so that numbers could be reduced? In blue water, a single ship with long-range sonar and radar can, in theory, detect and combat threats over a wide area. This belief justifies reducing numbers in favour of unit sophistication.

Modern anti-aircraft systems like Aegis do more, however. Prior systems assigned a single radar director to each target and to the missiles attacking it. For example, a British Type 42 destroyer has two Type 909 radars. When the ship detects a target, her combat system assigns a Type 909 to a target. The Sea Dart missiles the ship fires home on energy (from the Type 909) reflected by the target. Thus the Type 42 can handle only two targets at a time. When the ship was conceived, that seemed reasonable, particularly since she could detect targets at a considerable distance and, in theory, destroy one and switch to another.

Aegis is different. The combat system creates a precise picture of targets and keeps track of the missiles it fires. Each SM-2 missile has a commandable autopilot. It is sent towards the target by a series of commands, homing on illumination only at the last possible moment. The system was conceived because the radar associated with Aegis, the phased-array SPY-1, combined long range with the sort of precision previously reserved for fire-control radars. The European PAAMS system (Aster missile), of which the Sea Viper system onboard the new British Type 45 is an example, operates similarly, but provides each missile with its own active radar seeker, again to be used late in the missile's flight. Aegis now has a missile with an active seeker (SM-6), which is described as a means of dealing with targets beyond the ship's horizon, hence beyond her ability to illuminate, such as low-flying cruise missiles hiding behind coastal hills. In both cases, one ship can handle as many targets as several of the earlier ones using homing-all-the-way missile guidance.

The focus of these systems has shifted in a subtle but very important way. The ship's own search radar normally feeds the computer which creates the key tactical picture. However, there is nothing in the concept that limits the ship to her own radar. About a quarter-century ago the Applied Physics Laboratory of Johns Hopkins University, the US

The current European PAAMS system (Sea Viper in the Royal Navy version) is also based on a tactical picture created by a precision radar, in the case of the French *Forbin* (shown in the Arabian Sea in May 2009), the EMPAR rotating electronically-scanned radar in the radome atop the foremast. There are no illuminators because the Aster missile has an active seeker. One advantage of a command system like that in Aegis or PAAMS is that missiles can be launched vertically and commanded to turn in any direction; there is no delay while an illuminator is trained and locked onto a target. *(US Navy)*

Navy's anti-aircraft think-tank, pointed out that a group of Aegis ships could combine their radar data to create a better overall picture – which could then be used by each ship. It took about a decade to turn this vision into the current Cooperative Engagement Capability (CEC), which uses a high-capacity data link. CEC also provides non-Aegis ships, such as Type 23 frigates, with a picture extending beyond their horizon, and that greatly improves their own performance. The new Franco-Italian FREMM frigates are to have a combat system incorporating an analogous link. In each case, the point is that the tactical picture is central. It can be co-operatively created, and it is the preferred basis for action. CEC showed, moreover, that creating a picture co-operatively made it possible for a group of ships to get around obstacles like islands which might hide an incoming attacker. As long as individual ships saw the attacker part of the time, the overall picture could combine their glimpses to give a reasonable idea of the attacker's course and speed, so that its position could be projected – and so that it could be dealt with.

CEC is about large missile cruisers sharing their information. However, Moore's Law is also about what can be extracted from unmanned sensors. Just as the cruisers can share what they know, the sensors can share. The rub, both in CEC and in any sensor-sharing arrangement, is that each contributor must know exactly where it is in relation to the others. Otherwise the picture the sensors create becomes distorted to the point of being useless. However, if the picture is good enough, weapons can be commanded into place, homing (if at all) only at the last moment.

A NEW APPROACH TO LITTORAL WARFARE

Imagine, then, a new approach to littoral – which generally means fairly shallow-water – anti-submarine warfare. The problem is that the tricks usually used to get long sonar ranges, such as working at lower frequencies and higher power, often fail. Sound bounces off the surface and the bottom. Submarines can be hidden by underwater hills, and diesel (though not nuclear) ones can hide on the bottom.[2] In addition, the submarines can generally hear surface ship sonars before they are detected. What to do?

Like other electronic components, the Tx/Rx (transmitter-receiver) modules of active-array radars are becoming smaller and less expensive. Singapore's frigate *Intrepid*, which is equipped with Aster, uses the French Herakles active-array radar, housed in the angular box atop her foremast. It is a hybrid. A matrix of Tx/Rx elements creates one or more beams, but they are manipulated by an electronic lens through which they pass. Presumably when the radar was designed these elements were not yet small enough to suffice both to create and to manipulate the radar beams. Now it is possible to build active arrays small enough to fit aboard fighters, but possibly not with the longer wavelength desirable in a surface-ship air-defence set. The ship is shown in July 2009. *(US Navy)*

At the other end of the scale, littoral warfare has always demanded large numbers of ships, because lines of sight/sensing are so short. To be affordable, ships have to be small, so they are generally single-purpose. In the 1980s Denmark needed to replace a numerous fleet of diverse, small craft. Moore's Law suggested a solution. An affordable, compact combat system could accommodate software for all these roles. Thus a single hull could be designed so that containers used for any particular role could be placed aboard, the ship's combat system picking out the software associated with the container. This StanFlex solution was widely admired; the Danish corvette *Viben* is shown. The StanFlex idea was later applied to frigates and to the current *Absalon* class of multi-purpose ships. It seems to have convinced the USN that its LCS was affordable. *(US Navy)*

Some forms of sonar will still work. For example, a short line of upward-looking sensors on the bottom will pick up the disturbance in the water due to a submarine passing overhead. The fence of sensors then knows that at such and such a time a submarine passed above the gap between two of its individual sensors (it may even be able to estimate the submarine's speed from the disturbance). If the bottom is strewn with such fences, and their reports collated, the submarine which passed one fence and then another has in effect given its course and speed. It is no great step from there to projecting ahead its position, i.e., creating a relevant tactical picture based on a combination of numerous sensors. It is unlikely, moreover, that the submarine commander will be aware that a system aboard a distant ship has worked out where he is and where he is going, so he is unlikely to take evasive action – which would greatly delay him. Given a precise estimate of future submarine position, a command system can direct a helicopter to drop a homing torpedo in the right place to deal with the submarine. The US Navy calls this precision ASW, and it is developing an ultra-light torpedo (6.75in [171mm] diameter, rather than the 12.75in [232mm] of conventional lightweight torpedoes) to exploit the tactical picture it hopes to create. The ultra-light torpedo makes sense if the torpedo needs very little time to find a submarine whose location is known fairly precisely. The helicopter making the attack is not connected directly to any particular sensor, but rather to the picture created by all the sensors, just as the SM-2 missile which an Aegis ship fires is not connected to any particular fire control illuminator as it rises into the sky. As it evolved, LCS came to be associated with unmanned vehicles which would strew sensors to create various tactical pictures. It may or may not be the base for the other vehicles which attack based on the picture. As the base from which sensors covering an area come, LCS is also to be the processor of their data – although that may not ultimately be the case.

Will this vision work? It is probably the only way in which an affordable number of ships can dominate a littoral area. The picture, not the particular sensors or the particular vehicles strewing them, is the key. The US Navy is betting that it can apply the same methods to other littoral roles, such as mine countermeasures (which was actually the first LCS module) and dealing with swarms of small attacking boats. Given the limited number of LCS in any one area, ideally each would support a variety of sensors.

Unfortunately LCS was conceived before the current modular approach was mature. At the outset the navy argued that LCS would be affordable because, unlike a destroyer, it would be focussed on a single mission. Mission components could be changed as needed, so that instead of buying minehunters and patrol craft, only a limited number of LCS would be bought. In fact the new concept makes the LCS something more like an aircraft carrier, and experience with those ships shows that flexible mixed air wings are an enormous advantage. The basic idea, that the hull itself should be simple and inexpensive and capacious, is the same. It is not at all clear that the LCS as reflected in the two current prototypes will fill this bill, but the idea seems to be the most radical that any navy has developed over the past several decades. Moreover, an LCS without its unmanned vehicles and sensors is well suited to fulfil basic naval missions, such as interdiction at sea, and this kind of ship has the best chance of restoring the numbers Western navies need for the sort of distributed challenges they now face.

The US Navy is not alone in applying this kind of thinking. The Royal Norwegian Navy is experimenting with an unmanned underwater vehicle called Hugin, which carries a small mine-hunting sonar. The hope is that one or more Hugins can in effect map a minefield, after which anti-mine torpedoes can be sent to destroy whatever it has seen. This and other types of remote mine-hunting are often described as ways of keeping humans out of minefields. Their real point is that conventional minehunting, like everything that happens in a littoral, is cursed by short sensing range. That is why a minehunter has to come so close to each mine, and why it takes that minehunter so long to clear a lane (or, alternatively, why it takes so many such craft working in parallel to achieve much progress). The remote option collects the sort of data the minehunters collect, but because Hugin is unlikely to set off a mine, they can do it in parallel, and they can do it rapidly. The human part of the system is needed to evaluate what the sonars see. In the past, the humans had to be at the sonar because they had to be sure that the anti-mine charge was placed at the mine. If Hugin knows where it is, hence where whatever it sees is, the anti-mine charge need not be placed at the same time that the mine is seen and identified – and seeing and identification need not be simultaneous. Hugin and its ilk may or may not work; it may turn out that the human is still needed to adjust the sonar

to answer questions which arise from the initial picture. However, Hugin or a similar vehicle is probably the only way to clear a minefield rapidly, without vast numbers of minecraft. Speed matters a lot more now that operations will probably be expeditionary. Landings usually succeed because the victim is not sure where the Marines will turn up. Spending three weeks clearing mines off a beach may just give the victim an idea of what is coming.

DEVELOPMENTS IN ANTI-AIR WARFARE
At the other end of the scale, the tactical picture type of operation has greatly extended the reach of anti-air capability. Threats to ships are still becoming more sophisticated. The most prominent example is the

Chinese DF-21E ballistic missile, with a manoeuvring re-entry vehicle. Compared to the fastest current anti-ship missiles, this vehicle is probably about twice as fast and, moreover, it approaches from overhead, where radar coverage is usually weak. DF-21E has apparently been tested against land targets, but hitting a manoeuvring ship would be a very different proposition, as it involves considerable co-ordination between an ocean surveillance system and the launcher.

From the US Navy point of view, fortunately this new anti-ship threat is blossoming just as the navy has put into service the SM-3 (Aegis) missile designed specifically to deal with land-based ballistic missiles fired at distant land targets, as part of wider anti-missile defence systems. The European PAAMS

The USN became interested in an alternative kind of modularity, illustrated by the prototype LCS-1 *Freedom*, shown at Old Town Alexandria in the spring of 2009. She has a massive superstructure to provide the sort of internal volume needed by her unmanned vehicles (and their support systems).The many radomes provide the communications capacity needed to send the pieces of tactical picture she assembles to other ships in a force. By herself, *Freedom* is a fast, under-armed and rather large coastal ship with little to recommend her. But given her unmanned systems and her ability to assemble a usable tactical picture, *Freedom* becomes something very different. The pier shows two prototype unmanned vehicles, a surface boat on the left and an unmanned semi-submersible minehunting device on the right. The boat can, for example, accommodate dipping sonar. Again, neither is very valuable in its own right, yet each has the potential to provide a battle group with the sort of picture which, in the past, would have been created (implicitly) by the sort of massed small manned ships and boats unaffordable since the end of the Second World War. (US Navy)

consortium envisages a somewhat similar development of its Aster missile, again primarily to deal with threats against land targets (but a threat against a sea-based force is not too different).

Aegis is suited to the anti-ballistic missile role not because it has a wonderful radar in its SPY-1, but because its central tactical picture can accept information from external sources, such as satellites, so that it sees objects well beyond radar range. The concept of intermittent command guidance via autopilot is extended to place the SM-3 missile within homing range of an incoming re-entry vehicle. SM-3 itself uses an infra-red seeker to distinguish its target against the blackness of space. In 2009 *Lake Erie* (CG-70) used her Aegis system to shoot down a US satellite tumbling into the atmosphere out of control. Much of the data involved came from space-based sensors. Again, much

depended on precise navigation, because the externally-supplied data would have been useless if it had not provided the ship with a good idea of where the target really was. SM-3 is a very effective missile, but it cannot be expected to search a wide volume of space as it tries to attack its target.

Moore's Law makes the picture-based kind of air defence much more widespread than may be imagined. For example, the South African Umkhonto, which has been adopted by Finland and by Sweden for relatively small ships, creates a tactical picture, and commands its infra-red guided missiles by uplink. Modern track-while-scan fighter radars embody a kind of tactical picture, and efforts have been underway for years to embed these aircraft in a precise picture carried by data link.

Meanwhile the sensors are changing, again in response to Moore's Law. The SPY-1 Aegis radar was

practicable because computers had become both much more powerful and much more reliable – and because the phase shifters in the antenna had become affordable (because solid-state devices in general were becoming cheaper). In its passive array, all elements are fed the same radar signal. Each element is commanded to modify that signal in such a way that the broad beams from all the elements add up into a single steerable beam. That beam is remarkably agile, but it is still only one beam, and whatever time it takes searching one part of the sky it cannot spend searching elsewhere. The single beam also cannot easily cancel out jamming signals.

The next step seems to be an active array: each element is in effect a separate radar. Groups of elements can be commanded to work together, so that each group can generate a separate radar beam – the radar is, in effect, several radars stacked together. Alternatively, the elements can all work together to create a single beam. This type of radar can also null out jamming beams. Thanks to Moore's Law, Active Electronically-Scanned Arrays are now becoming prominent aboard fighters such as the later versions of the F/A-18 Hornet. They are also appearing at sea, one example being the APAR radar onboard the Dutch *de Zeven Provincien* and the German *Sachsen* class. The Sampson radar aboard the new British *Daring* class is a revolving active array radar with two faces back to back, whilst the Japanese have been deploying single-face active arrays for some years (and have a multi-face array in their large new helicopter destroyer/carrier).

Perhaps most interestingly, the two Chinese *Lanzhou* class destroyers have a four-faced apparently active array radar, reportedly using Ukrainian technology. It is not clear what the Chinese system is. The *Lanzhou* class uses revolver launchers like those of Russian ships carrying the long-range SA-N-6, a naval version of the land-based S-300 (SA-10). The Chinese are thought to have attempted production of SA-10 as HQ-9, and the missile involved may be its naval version. However, SA-10 is a large missile, and a ship with fine lines does not have enormous volume near its bow. The other candidate for the *Lanzhou* class is HQ-16, which is generally described as Buk (SA-N-7) with Aspide electronics modified for intermittent illumination, hence able to handle multiple targets (the missile presumably coasts between bursts of illumination, and the phased array is needed to provide multiple missiles with such bursts as needed). That the Chinese separately

Missiles like Exocet Block III seem to have little to do with tactical pictures. In anti-ship mode, they are simply fired off, to hit the targets their seekers find. However, they are not so numerous that they can be fired at random – something indicates that a target is in a limited area, and the missile is sent there. The better the initial location, the less effort the missile has to make to find the target, and the better the chance that it can overcome countermeasures. The extreme case is a land target with a very limited radar signature. In that case it is much clearer that the reconnaissance systems which locate the target are as much part of the missile system as the missile itself. Exocet and similar weapons were originally attractive because it did not take a large ship to support them (in this they were much like the torpedoes of the turn of the twentieth century). However, if the future lies with operations against shore targets, it is reasonable to ask how much a few such weapons can do. In that case the need is for large numbers, or for missiles which are somehow reusable – aircraft. Perhaps, if most land targets are struck on the basis of reconnaissance by other systems, it is time to see the lines of missile and aircraft evolution come together. This full-scale model of Block III, which has a turbojet for longer range and a GPS receiver to hit land targets, was shown at Euronaval 2006. *(Norman Friedman)*

bought S-300 for another class of destroyer of about the same size, with only two (rather than six) launchers forward (and on the centreline) and four more in the wider space aft, suggests that the more or less standard Chinese destroyer hull could not accommodate the larger missile forward in the numbers seen in the *Lanzhou* class. The reference to Aspide, which the Chinese adapted as the LY-60 missile, recalls that during the 1980s NATO countries sold modern technology to China to build that country up as a threat to the Soviets, a way of relieving pressure on NATO in Europe.

OTHER DEVELOPMENTS

If the current naval theme, at least in the West, is expeditionary warfare, that will at some point mean attacking land targets. Moore's Law made it possible to modify many existing anti-ship missiles, such as Harpoon and RBS 15 and Exocet, with GPS guidance to bring them to targets which would probably not show up very well on their radars. However, Western surface combatants generally carry no more than eight such missiles, which seems less than impressive alongside the massed gunfire of past generations of heavy warships. The irony is that eight missiles with (say) a 75 per cent chance of hitting really were comparable to a gun battery which might make few or even no hits on a rapidly-manoeuvring ship target. They would be a lot less impressive if their task were, say, to deal with enemy armour attacking some lightly-armed Marines who had just come ashore. Moreover, there is no way of replacing such missiles at sea. Even the US Navy, which is far better placed with about a hundred launchers onboard its missile cruisers and destroyers, cannot replenish them at sea. Aircraft carriers are a different proposition, because their flight decks and elevators make it easy to transfer delicate missiles horizontally. It would seem to follow that the role of carriers should be expanding, despite their high cost.

Can anything be done to reduce the cost of naval airpower? Can Moore's Law do any good? Experience in Iraq and in Afghanistan already suggests that precision weapons – weapons directed to coordinates rather than to something seen at the moment on the ground – can typically be fired from well outside the range of enemy air defences, so that aircraft are far more effective than in the past. The use of coordinates suggests that the idea of the tactical picture matters in this kind of warfare as in the others. Some combination of sensors, some of which may be on satellites, locates the targets (humans make sense of what the sensors show, of course). Once the coordinates are known, an aircraft can be sent to drop a bomb or missile which will know how to fly to that place.

In such a system, what is the pilot's role? How different is his aircraft from a missile like Tactical Tomahawk, which uses GPS to find its target, and which has a human in the loop to insure that it is hitting the right one? One formulation would be that attack aircraft are increasingly difficult to distinguish from reusable missiles. If that is true – a big if – then perhaps the future of naval aviation lies largely with unmanned carrier aircraft. If they work as advertised, which means if they can be recovered safely onboard a carrier, and if they can operate conventionally on a flight deck, then they can replace existing attack aircraft (pilots would still be needed in fighters, because on-the-spot judgement would be essential). That might make a tremendous economic difference. Pilots have to fly constantly to maintain their proficiency. Training them requires a massive system and numerous aircraft. Aircraft which flew only when needed for combat would consume far less fuel, and would suffer far less wear and tear. It might even be possible to refuel unmanned aircraft in flight, dramatically extending their endurance, because their pilots would not suffer from fatigue. If nearly all targets are now located by intelligence or reconnaissance systems, then the pilot's eye for the target comes to mean less and less, and perhaps it is time to look at unmanned systems. In December 2008 Northrop-Grumman rolled out the X-47B, the air vehicle of the US Navy's Unmanned Combat Air System – Demonstrator. It might be envisaged as yet another attempt to extend the power of a single expensive ship, using unmanned vehicles working with a co-operatively-formed tactical picture.

The aircraft involved is about the size of a strike fighter, and it is unlikely to be much less expensive (it may need less in the way of complex sensors). It will need just as many maintainers onboard ship, perhaps a few more. Its impact, if it works, will be in the overall system of which a carrier is the visible part. A carrier operating an unmanned air wing would have to be as large as a current one, and about as expensive – but aircraft account for about two-thirds of the total cost of the carrier *system*, and that omits the cost of supporting ships such as tankers and their wartime escorts.

Finally, there are submarines. Once inexpensive and numerous, now at least the nuclear ones are both capable and relatively rare. In the post-Cold War world they seem to be most useful for reconnaissance, their main virtue being their invisibility. As with surface ships, the question is how a single very powerful submarine can spread its presence. It seems pointless to keep it in a foreign harbour to listen to the radio traffic there, both because it is vulnerable and because there are probably many places worthy of surveillance. As with the LCS, the future seems to lie with unmanned vehicles the submarine can launch, recover and support. One key is the rise of effective underwater data links, which allow the mother submarine to control these craft, and to receive what they obtain. The great barrier right now is the absence of a suitable power source. Even so, the US Navy, and probably others, is experimenting with unmanned vehicles which could explore possible minefields, and with other more exotic roles such as tagging enemy submarines. A few years ago a large unmanned vehicle was used both to supply a Special Forces unit and to bring back material it found for analysis. Work is also ongoing on air vehicles a submarine could launch – and recover.

Notes

1. Given constraints on space, this account concentrates on a very few salient developments.

2. Nuclear submarines generally do not lie on the bottom for fear of silting up their condenser inlets. The technique described here would not be useful against a bottomed submarine. It turns out that combining the sounds heard by multiple sonobuoys or towed arrays when a charge is exploded or a 'pinger' set off will give the position of a bottomed submarine. The key is the sort of intensive signal processing now possible, and the fact that the processor is combining multiple views (from different sensors) of the same thing. This concept was developed by the US DARPA agency under a project called Distant Thunder, and it has been operational for some years.

3. The author's latest book, Norman Friedman, *Network Centric-Warfare – How Navies Learned to Fight Smarter Through Three World Wars* (Annapolis, MD, Naval Institute Press, 2009), describes the history of how navies – particularly the US Navy – have steadily moved towards a concept of warfare that uses an almost real-time, shared picture of the military situation as the basis for operations.

WORLD NAVAL

AVIATION
A Global Overview of Current Developments

Naval aviation remains a key element in the exercise of maritime power. In addition to carriers and their air groups, most other major warships now carry at least one helicopter. Amphibious platforms, able to operate both STOVL (short take-off and vertical landing) fighters and helicopters have assumed a position of strategic significance in the US Navy's expeditionary strike groups and other nations are building similar ships. The US Navy is procuring a new generation of aircraft based on proven airframes with new 'cutting-edge' avionics. In contrast the Royal Navy has virtually lost the ability to embark fast jets in the short term from its squadrons deployed to Afghanistan as constituents of joint forces but has staked everything on the future with orders for two large carriers and the STOVL variant of the Joint Strike Fighter. The rapid expansion of Unmanned Combat Air Vehicle (UCAV) operations marks the beginning of a new and fascinating era for naval aviation.

Author: David Hobbs

David Hobbs is a well-known author and naval historian. He has written eight books and co-authored eight more. He writes for several journals and magazines and in 2005 won the Aerospace Journalist of the Year, Best Defence Submission. He lectures on naval subjects world-wide and has been on radio and TV in several countries. He served in the Royal Navy from 1964 until 1997 and retired with the rank of Commander. He qualified as both a fixed and rotary wing pilot and his log book contains 2,300 hours with over 800 carrier landings, 150 of which were at night.

CARRIER AVIATION – UNITED STATES NAVY

The United States Navy (USN) deploys the largest and most capable aircraft carrier force and these ships form the core of its ability to project power. Following the withdrawal of the conventionally-powered *Kitty Hawk* (CV-63) from service the USN has eleven aircraft carriers, all of them nuclear-powered. The oldest, *Enterprise* (CVN-65), was completed in 1961 and is due to decommission by 2013, reducing the fleet to ten. The remainder comprise the *Nimitz* class, of which the name-ship commissioned in 1975 and the last, *George H W Bush* (CVN-77), entered operational service from 2009. They were delivered at intervals of between two and five years with gradual improvements, although the internal layout of the hull is similar to that of the *Forrestal* (CV-59), completed in 1955.

Work has begun on the first of the next-generation carriers under a project designated CVN-21. The first ship, the *Gerald R Ford* (CVN-78), is due for completion in 2015. Like their predecessors the new ships are to be built in sequence at Northrop Grumman's Newport News yard and a second ship is expected to be ordered for eventual completion in 2019/20. The hull will be similar in size to *Nimitz* but redesigned internally to improve weapons supply and to allow more efficient systems that require 30 per cent less manpower to run. CVN-21 is designed around a new, more efficient nuclear powerplant and improvements in aircraft operation will include Electro-Magnetic Aircraft Launch Systems (EMALS) to replace steam catapults and a system of Advanced Arrester Gear (AAG); it will have an electrical generation capacity three times greater than any previous carrier.

The most obvious feature of CVN-78 is the smaller island, sited further aft than in *Nimitz*, with its distinctive phased-array radar faces for Raytheon's X and S-band Dual Band Radar (DBR). Decreasing the size of the island has allowed a more efficient flight deck layout with space designed for 'pit-stop' style aircraft turnaround and rearmament between flights that will increase sortie generation rates. Air group size will vary through long projected hull lives but is expected to be about eighty for the first ships. The new design reflects the USN's contemporary view of aircraft operation, which is no longer centred on the deck-load or 'Alpha' strike by a large number of aircraft. Today, carriers sustain a small number of aircraft airborne around the clock for days on end in support of littoral operations. Whereas a dozen aircraft might once have been needed to guarantee hitting a single target, improved sensors, 'smart' weapons and information awareness systems within cockpits mean that a single aircraft can strike several targets successfully in a single sortie. The need to

An impression of the first of the USN's next-generation carriers, *Gerald R Ford* (CVN-78), which is due for completion in 2015. *(Northrop Grumman)*

reduce the possibility of collateral damage in a counter-terrorist action has led to the extensive use of smaller weapons such as AGM-65 'Maverick' and 500lb-class bombs like the Joint Direct Attack Munition (JDAM) fitted with both GPS and laser guidance. Lighter weapons mean, in turn, that more or a greater variety of munitions can be carried to support the specific requirements of forward air controllers.

Present USN carrier air groups comprise squadrons of F/A-18 B/C 'legacy' Hornets, F/A-18 E/F Super Hornets, EA-6B Prowlers, E-2C Hawkeyes and MH-60 Seahawk helicopters. The last S-3 Viking squadron, VS-22, decommissioned early in 2009 ending the type's 35-year career during which it served with eighteen USN squadrons and accumulated 1.7 million flying hours. As another sign of the changing priorities faced by US Naval aviation units, VS-22 was most recently employed on shore-based intelligence gathering operations in Iraq. The EA-6B is also coming to the end of its long career and its replacement, the EA-18G Growler carried out operational environment tests in the *John C Stennis* (CVN-74) in early 2009, preparing the way for squadron service with the fleet. The EA-18G has the same airframe as the F/A-18F and improved computer systems allow the crew of two to fly the same mission as the four-man crew of the EA-6B. The economy of scale created by using a common airframe and engines will drive down the cost of air group operation and simplify both air and ground crew training. It will also allow the EA-18G to expand the electronic attack role envelope with the carriage of air-to-air missiles for self defence as well as anti-radiation missiles. Tests in 2008 proved the type's ability to interface with and launch AGM-88 High-Speed Anti-Radiation Missiles (HARM) which can detect, attack and destroy target emitters with minimal aircrew input. Under present production plans the USN intends to procure eighty-eight Growlers by 2013.

The F/A-18E/F Super Hornet is a key element of the USN tactical fighter force, the 'E' being a single-seat variant intended primarily for the strike mission and the 'F' a two-seat version that replaced the F-14 Tomcat in service as an interceptor. However, both

The F-35 Lightning II JSF prototype AA-1. STOVL 'B' and carrier-based 'C' variants will form an important part of USN and USMC maritime air power within the next decade. *(US Air Force)*

are perfectly capable of flying either mission and can carry the same weapon load. From Block II production the cockpit systems in the F/A-18F can be worked independently if necessary to engage two separate targets on land, sea or in the air using onboard and off-board sensor information that is fused and displayed on large colour screens that give excellent situational awareness. Onboard sensors include the APG-79 Active Electronically Scanned Array (AESA) Radar which may not need workshop maintenance in the entire life of the aircraft and an aircrew helmet-mounted cueing system that keeps critical sensor and weapons data in their field of view and enables air and ground targets to be engaged well wide of the aircraft centreline. A camera and both electro-optical and infrared images from the SHARP reconnaissance pod can be transmitted through the Joint Tactical Information Distribution System (JTIDS)/Link 16 to third parties for attack or target confirmation and similar information can be received and acted upon. There are also advanced secure communications, a defensive aids suite and an integrated GPS/inertial navigation system. Over 500 Super Hornets have been contracted, with 388 delivered as of 1 April 2009 – most of them early.

Some 'legacy' C/D model Hornets will remain and the USN is studying ways to extend their individual fatigue lives from 6,000 to 10,000 flying hours, although no definitive scheme has been costed or approved. The US Marine Corps (USMC) has not participated in the Super Hornet programme and plans to replace all its AV-8B Harriers and F/A-18C/D Hornets with F-35B Lightning II STOVL Joint Strike Fighters (JSF). The USN plans to buy the F-35C 'tail-hook' version of the JSF to replace its own 'legacy' Hornets but has not yet made clear what the split between 'B' and 'C' variants will be in the overall production run of c.650 intended for the Navy and Marine Corps. The Navy expects the Super Hornet to be the principal aircraft within its carrier air groups until 2030. From 2018 F-35Cs will begin to deploy operationally and by 2030 the USN expects to deploy forty-eight fast-jets in each carrier air wing, of which half will be Super Hornets and half Lightning IIs.

The USN has made practical use of an Automated Carrier Landing System (ACLS) for several years and reliability has advanced to the point where taking the pilot input out of deck landing can be considered a viable everyday possibility. First flight of the Northrop Grumman X-47

The first Northrop Grumman X-47B naval unmanned combat air vehicle is unveiled at a ceremony at Palmdale CA on 16 December 2008. *(Northrop Grumman)*

A MH-60R Seahawk assigned to Helicopter Maritime Strike Squadron (HSM) 71 prepares to land on the carrier *John C Stennis* (CVN-74) during a Pacific deployment on 24 February 2009. *(US Navy)*

Unmanned Combat Air Vehicle (UCAV) is planned for late 2009 and the USN plans to carry out deck-landing trials with the type in 2011, 100 years after Eugene Ely first landed on the *Pennsylvania* (ACR-4). The Service announced in 2008 that it anticipates that the eventual replacement for the F/A-18E/F will be a UCAV derived from the X-47 which will begin to enter fleet service in 2025 by which time carriers will be able to operate both manned and unmanned aircraft in the same launch and recovery cycle: a fascinating prospect.

The F/A-18 family illustrates how the USN has invested wisely in proven airframes and engines procured in significant numbers using lean production techniques that have driven down costs. 'Cutting-edge' development funding has been aimed at avionic systems such as the APG-79 AESA radar and communication systems that maintain the air wings' competitive edge over likely opposition. The E-2D Hawkeye is another example of incremental development, retaining the airframe of its predecessor, the E-2C, but incorporating a new fully-automated battle management system featuring the AN/APS-145 radar, new electronic support measures, JTIDS and a commercial off-the-shelf open architecture computer system that is capable of absorbing frequent upgrades. Satellite communications and a navigation system that combines Global Positioning System (GPS) information with inertial Carrier Aircraft Inertial Navigation System (CAINS) give the 'D' variant of the Hawkeye capabilities far beyond the type's original airborne early warning role and the USN now refers to them as battle management aircraft. They are key to the USN's co-operative engagement capability and the emerging theatre ballistic missile defence mission beside the more traditional roles of air and surface surveillance, strike and intercept control and combat search and rescue (SAR) support. The crew comprises two pilots and three naval flight officers, each of whom has a multi-mission advanced tactical screen so that in high-workload conditions, the non-flying pilot can act as a tactical co-ordinator.

Carrier-borne helicopters also reflect the USN's policy of utilising tried and trusted airframes with new avionic systems to hold down development costs. Two new versions of the Seahawk are in production and service, the MH-60R and MH-60S; the new 'M' designation reflects their increased roles across the spectrum of maritime warfare. Originally they were to utilise remanufactured old airframes but

A picture of the initial E-2D Advanced Hawkeye on its maiden flight in August 2007. It retains the airframe of the preceding E-2C but incorporates a new automated battle management system. *(Northrop Grumman)*

the USN decided that new-build represented a more cost-effective option with the potential for longer service and has ordered 298 'Romeos' and 237 'Sierras' in multi-year blocks.

The 'Romeo' has 'glass cockpit' display screens, AQS-22 low frequency dipping sonar, an improved acoustic system, ALQ-210 ESM, AN/APS-147 multi-mode imaging radar and an AAS-44C infrared imaging device. The helicopters they replaced operated both as carrier ASW units and in HS squadrons as light ASW units designated HSL, with individual flights attached to destroyers and frigates on a semi-permanent basis. These have been replaced by Helicopter Maritime Strike (HSM) squadrons with ten aircraft each, which form part of the carrier air wings. Individual aircraft from the squadron are detached to escorts and logistic ships within the carrier battle group. The 'Sierra' is based more closely on the Blackhawk airframe and equips Helicopter Sea Combat (HSC) squadrons which form a second helicopter unit within carrier air wings. These fulfil a utility role and detach to logistic ships from the parent squadron to perform tasks once carried out by permanently assigned CH-46 Sea Knight units in those ships. The new helicopter policy capitalises on using a single airframe to hold down training, maintenance and support costs, whilst giving carrier air wings a broader capability. The USN plans to develop the 'Sierra' to give HSC squadrons a mine clearance capability using a towed array, replacing the

CH-53E, and wiring to carry up to eight Hellfire missiles together with armour for the crew to operate in the light surface strike role.

CARRIER AVIATION – ROYAL NAVY

In stark contrast, Britain's Royal Navy has virtually lost its capability to embark fixed-wing aircraft in its two operational carriers, *Ark Royal* and *Illustrious*, since the ill-conceived withdrawal of the Sea Harrier from service in 2006. In 2000 the Navy's fighter force was linked with the RAF Harrier ground attack units to form Joint Force Harrier (JFH) under RAF administrative control, a political 'marriage' that resembled earlier unsuccessful attempts to produce a unified flying organisation. In 2006 JFH was reduced to four small squadrons, two RN and two RAF, equipped with Harrier GR7 ground-attack aircraft, all capable of embarking. The aircraft have been up-graded to GR9 standard with an open-architecture computer system and improved weapons capability. However, other government cuts deleted the RAF's Jaguar ground-attack force and reduced the number of Tornado squadrons with the result that operations in Iraq and Afghanistan since 2003 have absorbed virtually the whole of the UK's fast-jet capability. This has included 800 and 801 Naval Air Squadrons (NAS) operating as a Naval Strike Wing for rotational operations ashore in Afghanistan. No fast jets have been available for three years to embark in significant numbers and whole-ship training for flight deck crews, aircraft controllers, operations staff and others has had to be derived from the embarkation of AV-8 units from the USMC and both the Spanish and Italian navies. The 'blank decade' from 2006 to 2016 risks leaving a legacy of inexperience at the very time when the Royal Navy needs to expand its carrier operating skill bases to prepare its people for every aspect of introducing two new carriers.

These new ships, to be named *Queen Elizabeth* and *Prince of Wales*, ordered from BVT on 3 July 2008 were to have commissioned in 2014 and 2016. However, a review in late 2008 adjusted these dates to 2016 and 2018 to save money in the short-term, although the long-term cost will be higher. The ships are central to the Royal Navy's future as a viable force capable of independent action or even operations as a competent coalition ally. The design is both large and potentially flexible, allowing the ships to deploy about thirty-six STOVL fighters with a 'ski-jump' or, alternatively, be converted with wires and catapults for 'tail-hook' aircraft. At 65,000 tons they are the largest warships ever ordered for the Royal Navy. Since 2002 the UK Ministry of Defence has funded the F-35B STOVL variant of the JSF and is the only 'Level 1' partner in the project. Three prototypes were ordered in early 2009 allowing the UK to participate in the Initial Operational Test and Evaluation (IOT & E) phase of the type's development alongside the relevant US services. Production blocks have yet to be ordered but the UK requirement is expected to be reduced from an initial requirement of 150 to 136 – or fewer.

Assuming the UK orders production F-35Bs, the next step after IOT & E will be the formation of a Joint Trials Unit. This will be in the USA as the facilities needed to train pilots and maintenance personnel will not yet exist in the UK. Once operational British squadrons have been formed, the trials unit will become an Operational Evaluation Unit (OEU), remaining in the USA alongside its US equivalents. The US armed forces plan to have a sophisticated support package for the JSF known as the Global Sustainment System (GSS); the UK has not yet said whether it wishes to replicate this with an all-British system to give greater 'sovereignty' over the aircraft's use or buy into the US system. Lossiemouth in Scotland, a former RN air station and now a major RAF airfield has been chosen as the UK F-35 base but no work has been carried out to equip it for the new role. The UK might still change its mind during IOT & E, completing *Queen*

The Royal Navy carrier *Illustrious* depicted with USMC AV-8B Harriers embarked during 2007 North Atlantic exercises with the USN's *Harry S Truman* (CVN-75) and *Dwight D Eisenhower* (CVN-69). *(US Navy)*

The Royal Navy has staked its future maritime air capability on the CVF future carrier and F-35B Lightning II JSF STOVL variant combination. This impression shows an F-35B landing on *Queen Elizabeth*. (BVT Surface Fleet)

Elizabeth with EMALS and AAG like CVN-21 and buying the F-35C 'tail-hook' version of JSF. This would give full commonality with the USN's variant, which is more versatile and has greater radius of action. In such a case, the new carrier's low top speed might be an issue since the F-35C was designed to operate from the much faster *Nimitz* class. After the Joint Trials Unit, the first two UK squadrons will also have to form and work up in the USA, one of them being a naval squadron preparing for embarkation when it is declared operational in about 2018. By then *Queen Elizabeth* should have finished the sea trials that will follow her completion.

The Harrier GR9 is due to leave service in 2018 and may not embark in *Queen Elizabeth* but the initial air group will include Merlin HM2 and Sea King ASaC7 helicopters. Present plans call for the formation of Tailored Air Groups (TAG) made up of task-specific fast-jets and helicopters for individual operations rather than permanently assigned air wings. This lack of structure will make it difficult for task force commanders to keep their battle groups at peak efficiency. There may also be a gap between the

demise of the Harrier and the arrival in the UK of its successor, which will be made worse by the present shortage of fast-jet pilots for JFH. Once squadrons start to form up and train in the USA there will effectively be two joint forces, one old and one new. To supply both may limit the operational capability of the former. Whatever the eventual air group of the new RN carriers, their size gives them considerably more potential than their small, cramped and much-modified predecessors, providing the Royal Navy with the capability it needs once current short-term difficulties have been resolved and embarked air groups are available permanently. However, JFH has proved that the concept of having a single force that may need to concentrate on two or more operational capabilities does not work. The Navy deserves a more honest solution. Significantly, none of the navies operating or building carriers has followed the UK's system of joint forces with dual land/sea-based roles.

The RN operates a variety of different helicopter types. The Merlin HM1 is a large, three-engined ASW helicopter with sensors that include low frequency dipping sonar, sono-buoys and radar. It

lacks JTIDS and an optical/infrared sensor although an upgrade to HM2 standard is funded and is addressing these deficiencies. Surprisingly, in view of the fact that the Italian Navy carries air-to-surface weapons on its Merlins, the RN version can only carry ASW torpedoes or depth charges. If used in the surface surveillance role it has to call up another aircraft or ship to act as a 'shooter' and the current lack of JTIDS limits its value in a co-operative engagement context. The ASaC7 version of the Sea King combines an airframe that is over forty years old with the modern 'Cerberus' sensor suite which includes the Searchwater 2000 pulse/pulse-doppler radar and ESM with an open architecture commercially derived computer system and large, coloured 'touch-screen' display units. Like the E-2D it can track targets over both land and sea.

CARRIER AVIATION – OTHER NAVIES
There is growing international interest in aircraft carrier procurement. Russia has only one carrier, the *Admiral Kuznetsov*, which embarks an air group of Sukhoi Su-33 'Flanker' and Su-25 'Frogfoot' fast jets, and Kamov Ka-27 'Helix' helicopters. The fixed-wing aircraft use a unique STOBAR launch and recovery that combines a short take-off from a ski-jump with an arrested recovery using a tail-hook. She was built during the Soviet era at the Nikolaev Shipyard in what is now the Ukraine and Russia has started talks to see if it would be possible to re-open the yard to build new ships.

A former Russian carrier, the *Admiral Gorshkov*, was sold to India in 2004 and is being refurbished and modernised at the Sevmash Shipyard in Northern Russia renamed *Vikramaditya*. Work was to have been completed in 2008 but was under-estimated and Russia's state arms exporter Rosoboronexport wants at least an extra US$1bn for completion. The latest estimate is that reconstruction will be complete in 2010, sea trials will commence in 2011 and the ship will be handed over in 2012. She will embark an air group of Mig-29K 'Fulcrum' strike fighters and Ka-27 'Helix' helicopters and will use a STOBAR operating technique. The Indian Navy plans to use her to replace *Viraat*, formerly HMS *Hermes*, which is now fifty years old and continues to operate a version of the Sea Harrier; *Vikramaditya* has a planned life of thirty years after delivery. The keel was laid for a second new Indian carrier on 28 February 2009 at Cochin Shipyard Ltd. Known as the 'Indigenous Aircraft Carrier Project', it

An Indian Navy Sea Harrier FRS51 on the deck of the vintage carrier *Viraat* (ex-*Hermes*). Delays to replacement Russian equipment will mean that they have to serve a little while longer. *(US Navy)*

is the most complex ever undertaken by the Indian Navy and is designed to operate an air group of about thirty, comprising Mig-29Ks, Indian light-weight fighters and Ka-31 helicopters.

France operates the only nuclear-powered carrier to have been built outside the USA, the *Charles de Gaulle*, which is small at c. 36,000 tons standard (42,000 tons full load) displacement but capable of operating an air group of twenty Super Etendard strike fighters, twelve Rafale fighters, two E-2C Hawkeye and two SAR helicopters. In spite of its small size, the French carrier air group is probably closest in capability to that of the USN and is carrying out frequent cross-decking exercises, even embarking Rafales for a period in US carriers. With its modern avionics and progressive development to take on the strike role, the Rafale is an impressive aircraft and the concept of designing a common airframe for use by both the navy and air force was a wise one. The French navy requires a second carrier and is considering a version of the new British carrier equipped with catapults and arrester wires. China is expanding its navy and shows interest in building carriers using the Russian STOBAR principle. A discarded Russian carrier hull has been acquired and is being studied by Chinese naval architects; there is doubt whether it will ever be completed for operational use but it might well form the basis of an indigenous design.

Brazil operates A-4 Skyhawks from its single carrier *São Paulo*, formerly the French *Foch*, and has close ties with the USN. A number of other nations, including Italy, Spain and Thailand operate STOVL carriers capable of operating versions of the AV-8 Harrier family. The first two intend to buy the F-35B as a replacement. The Italian Government has announced plans to set up a JSF production and maintenance line in Italy, making it a potential centre for European operators. The newly commissioned 27,000-ton *Cavour* is a well designed 'medium' carrier and offers the Italian fleet a

A French Rafale fighter on the deck of the US carrier *John C Stennis* (CVN-74) during cross-deck operations in the Arabian Sea. French carrier air groups are closest in capability to those fielded by the USN. *(US Navy)*

significant capability with an initial air group of eight Harriers and twelve Merlin helicopters, numbers that can be varied as circumstances require.

AMPHIBIOUS 'CARRIERS'

There is growing fusion between STOVL aircraft carriers and amphibious helicopter carriers of the LPH, LHA and LHD types. The USN is by far the largest operator of such vessels, with 40,000-ton ships of the *Tarawa* (LHA-1) and *Wasp* (LHD-1) classes in commission that combine a dock space for landing craft with a full-length flight deck and hangar for a flexible mix of USMC helicopters and AV-8B Harriers. MV-22 Osprey tilt-rotor aircraft are beginning to replace the CH-46 Sea Knight assault helicopter in these ships, which have an overall capability to land tactical marine forces with armour, artillery and 'gunship' helicopters. They also have extensive medical facilities including a 600-bed hospital and six operating theatres. Significantly many of the *Wasp* class have been given names formerly associated with aircraft carriers. These impressive ships now deploy as the core units of Expeditionary Strike Groups (ESGs) that also typically comprise other landing ships, surface escorts armed with Tomahawk missiles and a nuclear-powered attack submarine. ESGs are major factors in the growing areas of low-intensity conflict around the world and the ability to land marines at specific points from the sea and support them for a prolonged period gives strike warfare a new edge. The MV-22 is capable of carrying a section of marines a long way at high speed and landing them with pinpoint accuracy in rough terrain, a dynamic new capability that is being viewed with interest by other nations.

The Royal Navy has operated LPHs since 1960 and has recently invested in a new generation of amphibious warships. The present fleet comprises the LPH *Ocean*, the two landing platform docks (LPDs) – *Albion* and *Bulwark* – and four auxiliary dock landing ships LSD(A)s of the 'Bay' class. The latter RFA-manned ships lack command and control facilities but are capable of carrying and landing troops, heavy vehicles and stores. The CVS *Ark Royal* has also been used in the LPH role when *Ocean* has been unavailable due to refit. Whilst modern, the RN fleet has arguably not been designed as an integrated force and therefore lacks cohesion. *Ocean* can carry a range of helicopters including RN Sea King HC4s, Army AH1 Apaches and RAF Chinooks, all of them

An NFH-90 sea control variant of the NH-90 helicopter pictured during trials with the Italian Navy. (*Augusta Westland*)

administered by the Joint Helicopter Force (JHF). She can embark a Royal Marines Commando and light vehicles but has no dock and cannot embark or land heavy vehicles or bulk stores. *Albion* and *Bulwark* have command and control facilities and can both carry and land heavy vehicles and bulk stores in landing craft operating from their docks. However, they have a small flight deck and no hangar or aircraft maintenance facilities and cannot, therefore, deploy with helicopters embarked. To be effective the RN needs to operate an LPH and LPD together and it would have seemed more logical to have built two LHDs similar to the USS *Wasp* capable of operating independently if necessary. Indeed, this option is being considered when the current ships fall due for replacement. Meanwhile, the assault helicopter force is ageing but no replacements are in sight. The Sea King HC4 has been in service for thirty years and is undergoing an upgrade; the Chinook has no blade-fold system and therefore cannot be struck down into the hangar of the present small LPH.

Internationally, LHDs are seen as important fleet units and new ships are being built for a number of navies including Spain, France, Australia and the Republic of Korea. The two Australian ships, to be known as the *Canberra* class, are based on the

Spanish ship *Juan Carlos I* built by Navantia at Ferrol and their hulls are being built in the same yard for eventual completion in Australia. The Korean *Dokdo* is another impressive design, around 200m long and nearly 19,000 tons, based loosely on the USN *Wasp*. It is capable of acting as a fleet flagship and carrying 720 troops, ten battle tanks and thirty-five other vehicles, which can be taken ashore by landing craft from the dock at the stern. Up to ten helicopters can be embarked. A second ship, *Marada*, is under construction and a third, *Baeknyendo*, is planned.[1] The latter is to be enlarged to over 20,000 tons and is intended to operate VSTOL strike fighters, a further example of the LHD's 'crossover' potential. The RAN's *Canberra*s will be built with ski-jumps like their Spanish half-sister. The Australian Government has announced an intention to procure the JSF but whether some of these will be the F-35B STOVL capable of deploying in the LHDs remains to be seen.

SEA CONTROL HELICOPTERS

Helicopters are regarded now as a primary weapons system on most warship types. Third-generation designs such as the NFH90 and MH-60R Seahawk are, in many ways, more capable than their parent

The eighth and final *Wasp* class amphibous assault ship *Makin Island* (LHD-8) pictured shortly before delivery to the USN in 2009. She is a modified and improved version of a class that currently form the core of Expeditionary Strike Groups (ESGs). *(Northrop Grumman)*

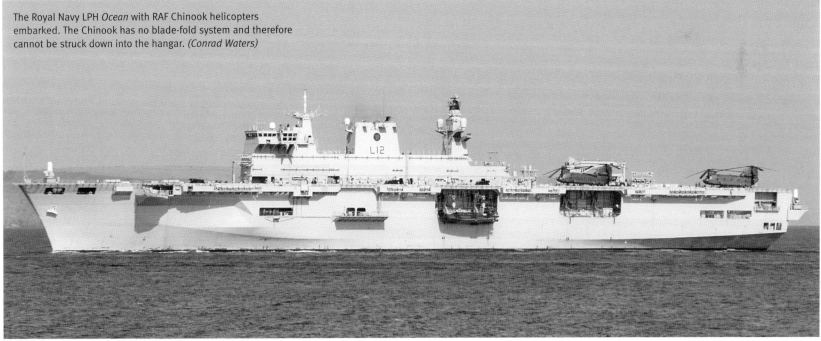

The Royal Navy LPH *Ocean* with RAF Chinook helicopters embarked. The Chinook has no blade-fold system and therefore cannot be struck down into the hangar. *(Conrad Waters)*

Left: A Royal Navy search and seizure team ropes down onto the deck of a US warship from an Augusta Westland Lynx helicopter during training exercises. *(US Navy)*

Above: The French LHD *Mistral*. LHDs are seen as important fleet units internationally and France has recently ordered a third class member. *(DCNS)*

Below: The Republic of Korea Navy's impressive new LHD *Dokdo*. Further members of the class are planned. *(Korean Navy)*

Above: A computer-generated graphic of the AW159 Lynx Wildcat. Twenty-eight of these helicopters have been ordered for the Royal Navy to enter service from 2015. *(Augusta Westland)*

Right: Russian cruisers, destroyers and frigates operate the Kamov Ka-27 Helix, the standard ship-borne helicopter which has been exported to China, India, the Ukraine and Vietnam. *(US Navy)*

ship and can be considered as 'flying frigates'. As we have seen, the USN now deploys helicopters from carriers to smaller ship decks within the battle group but other navies maintain specialised squadrons that embark flights to ships on a semi-permanent basis. The Royal Navy embarks the Merlin HM1 and two marks of Lynx, the HAS3 and HMA8 in its destroyers and frigates. The latter have the advantage that they can engage surface targets with Sea Skua missiles although the HAS3 is decidedly dated now and is used mainly in low-threat environments where it can rope down marines onto vessels to be searched and support them with a door-mounted machine gun. The HMA8 has an improved sensor suite with low light and infrared cameras in addition to the frequency-agile 'Sea Spray' radar. The Merlin is the same type that operates from carriers and rather than concentrate on it, the RN is somewhat surprisingly investing in a new version of the Lynx to be known as the Wildcat when it enters service in 2015. Unlike the USN, therefore, the RN plans to operate a dissimilar mix of helicopter types into the foreseeable future, each with its unique requirement for training and support. It seems an expensive option.

A new type, the NH90, will replace the Lynx in the French, German and Dutch navies and further orders have been placed for the navies of Italy, Norway, Sweden, Belgium and Australia, in addition to commitments for other branches of the armed

An artist's impression of the Poseidon P-8A multi-mission maritime aircraft that is being developed by Boeing from the B737 civil airliner. *(Boeing)*

services. Over 450 have been ordered in two versions, tactical transport (TTH) and sea control (NFH). Larger than the Lynx, it is smaller than the Merlin and, with only two engines, it is cheaper to operate. It has a glass cockpit, 'fly-by-wire' electric flight controls. Sensors in the NFH version include a forward-looking infrared sensor in the nose, FLASH dipping sonar and sonobuoys with a TMS 2000 acoustic processing system. Weapons include Marte Mk2S air-to-surface missiles, torpedoes, depth charges and even air-to-air missiles aimed using the pilot's helmet-mounted sight. With its range of capability options it is an ideal single helicopter type for medium navies. It is on order for the RAN as a Sea King replacement and would be a logical replacement for the failed Sea Sprite and, eventually, the SH-60 Seahawk in due course. Numbers are also on order for the Australian Army which will operate them from the LHDs as well as ashore and the two services will combine maintenance and training facilities for the new helicopter to drive down cost.

A number of other helicopters serve with the world's navies ranging from the AgustaWestland 109M ordered by Sweden for its *Visby* class corvettes to the Eurocopter AS 565MA Dauphin/Panther series with their distinctive fenestron tail rotor. These are used by the US Coast Guard, France, Saudi Arabia and the United Arab Emirates and manufactured under licence in China as the Harbin Zhi-9C for operation by the People's Liberation Army Naval Air Force from destroyers and frigates. Russian cruisers, destroyers and frigates operate the Kamov Ka-27 'Helix', the standard shipborne helicopter which has been exported to China, India, the Ukraine and Vietnam. Canada is having a difficult time replacing its ageing Sea King helicopters which first entered service in 1961. Earlier attempts to replace them with Merlins were cancelled, incurring considerable compensation costs, despite the fact that the type was procured for the SAR role. In 2004, however, the Canadian Government announced the purchase of twenty-eight ASW helicopters based on the Sikorsky S-92. Originally the first was due to be delivered in 2008 but flying trials have barely started and the cost of developing the type's unique weapons system has yet to be finalised.

SHORE-BASED NAVAL AVIATION

The P-3C Orion is the most widely-used maritime aircraft with over 200 in USN service and another 200 in service with air arms in Argentina, Australia, Brazil, Canada, Chile, Germany, Greece, Iran, New Zealand, Norway, Pakistan, Portugal, South Korea, Spain and Thailand. The USN versions are approaching the end of their fatigue lives and considerable urgency has been placed on the development of the Boeing P-8A Poseidon chosen as their replacement. Again the USN has focused on an affordable package based on the commercially successful Boeing 737 airliner modified with an internal weapons bay, underwing stores pylons and sensors equivalent to the current P-3C. The first prototype is undergoing testing following a first flight on 25 April 2009, with service entry planned for 2013. The Navy plans to buy 108 and, since the P-3 was such an export success, Boeing hopes to sell at least as many to export customers. India has already elected to buy eight of a P-8I version with Indian avionics and Australia has selected the type as the eventual replacement for its AP-3C fleet.

The USN has chosen an unmanned aircraft to act as a partner for the P-8 in the Broad Area Maritime Surveillance (BAMS) system. The Northrop Grumman RQ-4N – derived from the RQ-4B Block 30 Global Hawk ordered by the US Air Force – will be acquired with multi-function active and passive sensors coupled with JTIDS to send information to other platforms. Individual RQ-4Ns will detect

A picture of the first Boeing Poseidon P-8A maritime patrol aircraft on its initial test flight in April 2009. *(Boeing)*

The Northrop Grumman RQ-4N derivative of the Global Hawk UAV has been selected by the USN for the Broad Area maritime Surveillance (BAMS) system. *(Northrop Grumman)*

surface targets in patrol 'boxes' each 2,000 nautical miles square. The aircraft will search initially at heights up to 60,000 feet but will be programmed to descend to low level to identify specific targets if necessary to provide data for other aircraft and warships. Both Poseidon and BAMS are designed to play a key role in the USN co-operative engagement concept and provide elements of a fleet-wide network. Australia is interested in acquiring RQ-4Ns but has delayed a final decision until after the P-8 is in service.

In this specialist area, as in others, the UK has elected to follow a lonely and expensive national policy and is developing an upgraded version of the Nimrod designated the MRA4. Development and conversion costs are about £4bn, close to the cost of the two new aircraft carriers, and contracts have only been signed to convert three prototypes and nine operational airframes from the original MR2 standard. There is, as yet, no contract to bring the prototypes up to operational standard. The project contrasts starkly with the cost-conscious USN approach but is expected to offer a similar capability, albeit with higher running costs. Ilyushin IL-38 'May' patrol aircraft, broadly similar to the P-3, remain in service with the Russian and Indian Navies, the latter to be replaced by the P-8I.[2]

Notes

1. Editor's Note: Sources vary widely on the status of the Korean LHD programme. In addition, acquisition of the F-35B variant of the JSF is reportedly under consideration to equip all ships of the class.

2. This chapter has been compiled from a wide range of periodicals, of which *Air International*, *Flight*, *Jane's Defence Weekly* and *Warship World* provide particularly good sources of further reading. Reference should also be made to the following publications, as well as to the websites of relevant aircraft manufacturers and navies:

– Gunter Endres and Michael J Gething, *Janes's Aircraft Recognition Guide*- Fifth Edition (London, Collins-Jane's, 2007).

– Norman Friedman, *The Naval Institute Guide to World Naval Weapon Systems* – Fifth Edition (Annapolis, MD, Naval Institute Press, 2006).

– David Hobbs, *A Century of Carrier Aviation* (Barnsley, Seaforth Publishing, 2009).

– *Jane's Fighting Ships* – Various Editions (Couldson, Surrey, Janes's Information Group).

The UK has elected to follow a lonely and expensive national policy in maritime reconnaissance and is developing an upgraded version of the Nimrod designated the MRA4. *(BAE Systems)*

A prototype Nimrod MRA4 overflies the Type 45 destroyer *Daring* during the latter's sea trials in August 2007. *(BAE Systems)*

INDEX

Numbers in *italics* refer to illustrations.